book, Heracleous, Wirtz and Pangarkar doc… pillars of Singapore's service delivery system which offers unique … to its customers. It is my prediction that managers capable of developing a core competence of cost-effective service excellence and the cultural values to support it will be the winners in the new decade. While the recipe is simple its execution is hard. This book will provide you with a jumpstart in the race.

Tor W. Andreassen, Professor of Marketing, Norwegian School of Management

This book delivers an independent and detailed assessment of one of the world's best service organisations. Using a blend of theory and practice the authors provide a deep insight into the reasons for the success of SIA.

Professor Robert Johnston, Warwick Business School

This is a thoughtful book describing and analysing the success story of a corporate icon in Singapore. It reveals a spectrum of hidden business practices that cause travellers to feel so good that they have chosen to fly with SIA. And it is also a treasure chest of trade secrets of how to build a great company. What an exciting read! I recommend it to all high-flying executives.

Dr Tan Tay Keong, Former Executive Director, Singapore International Foundation

In their lucid and insightful account of what makes Singapore Airlines such a distinctive company, Heracleous, Wirtz and Pangarkar offer a salutary reminder that there are no such things as industries that are 'good' or 'bad' or economic sectors that are 'old' or 'new'. At best such characterisations are oversimplifications of the basic economic structures of an industry. In contrast, the story of Singapore Airlines adds further proof to the thesis that what ultimately matters is whether companies can marshall their resources effectively and efficiently to create value for their shareholders, their customers and their employees. The 'non-secret' of success: A clear strategy realised through seamless execution. As a former management consultant and management practitioner in a 'very old economy' sector, I commend this practical, no-nonsense book.

Stavros Yiannouka, Vice Dean, Lee Kuan Yew School of Public Policy and former senior consultant with McKinsey & Company

In the rough and tumble world of cut-throat airline competition, one company stands out as the undisputed global leader in almost every measurable category of performance year after year. That company is Singapore Airlines and this exceptional book tells you the story of exactly how they do it. The last chapter, summarising strategic insights and lessons learned, is both an invaluable guide to managers seeking to benchmark the 'best of the best', as well as a major contribution to thinking about business strategy, execution and performance excellence.

Robert J. Marshak, Ph.D., Adjunct Professor-in-Residence, American University, Washington, DC, USA; and Former Associate Editor of the *Journal of Applied Behavioral Science*

Flying High in a Competitive Industry

(Revised Edition)

Secrets of the World's Leading Airline

Loizos Heracleous
Jochen Wirtz
Nitin Pangarkar

Mc Graw Hill

Singapore • Boston • Burr Ridge, IL • Dubuque, IA • Madison, WI
New York • San Francisco • St. Louis • Bangkok • Kuala Lumpur
Lisbon • London • Madrid • Mexico City • Milan • Montreal
New Delhi • Seoul • Sydney • Taipei • Toronto

Flying High in a Competitive Industry (Revised Edition)
Secrets of the World's Leading Airline

Mc Graw Hill Education

Photos on pages xxii, 36, 62, 86, 114, 138, 168, 190 and 214 are used with
permission from Singapore Airlines.

1 2 3 4 5 6 7 8 9 10 CTP BJE 20 10 09

**When ordering this title, use ISBN 978-007-128196-6 or
MHID 007-128196-7**

Printed in Singapore

To Fiona, the light of my life

Loizos Heracleous

*To my mum, Hannelore, thank you for your love
and support that made everything possible*

Jochen Wirtz

*To Ashwini and our children, Natasha and Anish,
with love*

Nitin Pangarkar

CONTENTS

CONTENTS

PREFACE

This book aims to answer a simple but intriguing question: How has Singapore Airlines (SIA) managed to make healthy profits year in year out, in an industry whose financial performance over the years has been dismal? SIA's profitability on the other hand has been exceptional, superior in the long term to any competitor in its peer group. Our purpose in writing this book is to answer this question, based on our in-depth research on the airline industry and SIA, and derive some general lessons for managers in other industries.

We begin the book with an analysis of the airline industry and its key trends (Chapters 1 and 2), moving on to a broad outline of SIA's strategic drivers of success (Chapter 3). We then focus on specific elements of SIA's strategy and organisation, such as its core competency of cost-effective service excellence (Chapter 4), its innovation capabilities (Chapter 5), and its human resource management practices (Chapter 6). We end with some strategic lessons that we believe apply to any organisation that aims to achieve sustainable success in hyper-competitive markets (Chapters 7 and 8).

Chapter 1 analyses the airline industry as a whole, reviewing its historical development, important trends over time and key aspects of the industry economics. Issues discussed include the impact of government intervention; uncontrollable factors such as oil prices or political events; factors such as the perishability of seats, seasonality of demand and long time horizons in infrastructural decisions, injecting additional levels of complexity; airlines' fixed and variable direct operating costs, and indirect operating costs; and lastly the chronically poor and volatile performance of the whole industry. Key trends in the industry such as the formation of alliances, the emergence of budget carriers and regional growth are addressed.

Chapter 2 outlines macro-environmental trends affecting the airline industry such as political, economic, social and technological elements, and then engages with the industry's underlying structural dynamics such as the rivalry among competitors, threat of new entrants, power of suppliers and buyers and threat of substitutes. Lastly, strategic imperatives for airlines to succeed in this difficult environment are discussed, such as the need to utilise cutting-edge technology, the importance of cost-control, alliance management, avoiding the herd instinct and strategies to address commoditisation.

Chapter 3 proceeds to focus on SIA itself, addressing important strategic choices and resource deployment decisions at SIA, in order to get a broad understanding of the company's superior performance. Factors discussed include SIA's young fleet, low staff costs, global revenue base, push for efficiency, brand reputation, strategic consistency, response to crises, and alliance and acquisition strategies. In addition to having a significant stand-alone impact on SIA's performance, these factors also interact with other factors, thus enhancing the magnitude of their impact. A key conclusion drawn from this analysis is that SIA's superior performance is attributable to a complex array of strategic decisions which have been highly consistent over time. As we further discuss in Chapter 4, imitators would have to copy many of SIA's strategic and organisational aspects to achieve similar levels of performance; this is always a more difficult task than copying single aspects.

Chapter 4 addresses what we believe is SIA's core competence, cost-effective service excellence. It is relatively easy to deliver excellent service if one pours money into doing so. It is also relatively easy to achieve low costs if one does not aim to deliver excellent service. What is much harder to do is to deliver service excellence in an efficient manner, in other words implementing a strategy that integrates elements of differentiation and cost leadership. SIA is known for its service excellence, but what is less often appreciated is that its costs (seen as cents per available seat kilometre) are among the lowest in its peer group. How has SIA managed to achieve this? In common with other organisations with a reputation for excellent service, SIA displays characteristics such as top management commitment, customer-focused staff and systems, and a customer-oriented culture. However, our research has uncovered further insights into the development and maintenance of a reputation for service excellence while controlling cost – what we call the 'five pillars' of SIA's activity system. These pillars are rigorous service design and development; total innovation (integrating continuous incremental improvements with discontinuous innovations); profit and cost consciousness ingrained in all employees; holistic staff development; and reaping of strategic synergies through related diversification and world-class infrastructure. These five pillars of SIA's cost-effective service excellence are supported, operationalised and made real in everyday decisions and actions through a self-reinforcing activity system of virtuous circles, presented in the chapter. The core competence of cost-effective service excellence and the cultural values supporting it are thus more than just abstract ideas. They are ingrained into both the hearts and minds of employees as well as organisational processes. This may help to explain why SIA's competitive advantage has been sustained for decades. While it is easy to copy single elements, it is much harder to reproduce an entire self-reinforcing activity system.

Chapter 5 continues the theme of service excellence with a focus on innovation. This chapter sheds light on SIA's ability to be a serial innovator, introducing many firsts in the airline industry, and sustaining this innovative orientation over decades in the face of intense cost pressures, industry crises and the push towards commoditisation. We first present senior management's perspective of the key challenges they face in delivering sustained and cost-effective service excellence. These challenges include, firstly, how to consistently satisfy the sky-high and rising expectations of SIA's demanding customer base; secondly, how to balance standardisation and customisation of its services, and deal effectively with the tension between offering uniform service that is at the same time personalised; and thirdly, how to approach a large number of services and their support sub-processes in a holistic manner to attain consistent excellence in all related processes and sub-processes.

The chapter proceeds to address SIA's innovation process, characterised by the ability to seamlessly combine the hard and soft aspects of innovation. SIA's unique approach to new service development involves the seamless combination of both hard, structured, rigorous, centralised innovation, led mainly by the Product Innovation Department, with the soft, emergent, distributed, but equally significant innovation led by different functional departments. This competence is further enhanced by SIA's integrated customer and frontline staff feedback systems that provide valuable insights for both the Product Innovation Department and other functional departments.

Chapter 6 then addresses SIA's human resource management processes, a crucial aspect of any service business where people, especially frontline staff, are a core part of the offering and the most visible element of the service. Frontline staff from a customer's point of view can be seen as an integral element of the service firm itself, delivering the service and ideally acting as a conduit for understanding the customer's needs and wants; an understanding that can then be used as an important input in the innovation process. Frontline staff are also a core part of the brand, determining whether the brand promise gets delivered. After addressing these issues with examples from SIA, the chapter turns to a discussion of the five elements forming SIA's human resource management, and how each of these elements reinforces SIA's service excellence strategy. The five elements are stringent selection and hiring of people, followed by extensive training and re-training, formation of successful service delivery teams, empowerment of the frontline staff, and motivation.

Even though these service elements are simple to state, very few firms have been able to implement systems that deliver these to a high level.

In this chapter, drawing from further insights from SIA's strategic human resource management practices, we also outline how SIA manages to address the three key service-related challenges introduced in the earlier chapter; namely how to deal with sky-high customer expectations, how to achieve balance between service standardisation as well as personalisation, and how to approach a large number of services and support sub-processes in totality to attain service excellence.

The reason we undertook this study was to gain a deeper understanding of the factors that can help a company achieve sustainable success in extremely tough industries, so we based our study on the analysis of the strategy and organisational features of a company that has achieved just that. Chapters 7 and 8 present some lessons from our research in SIA, which we believe apply to any company in search of sustainable competitive advantage, the holy grail of strategy. We do not aim to provide silver bullets (which are not possible in such situations anyway given the context specificity of business challenges and solutions) but rather to suggest useful strategic principles, and to help executives ask the right questions.

Chapter 7 begins by reminding us why it is so hard to be successful in the airline industry. We then address one of the most important findings and also a key principle for success: the importance of achieving strategic alignment, and of recognising and dealing with misalignments before they become destructive. We discuss the nature of strategic alignment, as well as the main misalignments that companies should be vigilant of. We offer frameworks to help managers diagnose the levels of strategic alignment in their organisations and to take corrective actions where needed. We note that achieving strategic alignment is a pre-condition for achieving sustainable competitive advantage.

Chapter 8 then proceeds with further strategic lessons, which relate to the need to be clear about the company's generic strategy (or a combination of elements of generic strategies), the importance of identifying, nurturing and investing in capabilities and core competencies that support the strategy, and the need to understand and foster strategic innovation. We then examine SIA's institutional context and culture, and suggest that even though SIA has definitely gained from being located in a supportive institutional context, this is far from a comprehensive explanation of its success; its success can ultimately be traced to robust strategies, seamless execution and continuous vigilance and realignment.

In addition to the eight chapters, we also provide a self-contained case study of SIA, which presents key information from our research on the main elements of the company's success. This case study can be employed by instructors, organisation development practitioners and consultants as a launching pad for debate on the strategic and organisational issues involved. The case study has been successfully used at different levels of instruction (undergraduate, MBA, EMBA and executive levels) in courses relating to strategy and services marketing. Instructors who wish to use this case study can contact the publisher or one of the authors for further information.

We are grateful to all the people at SIA who kindly allowed us to interview them to gain a deeper understanding of what makes SIA tick. These include, in alphabetical order, Mr Choo Poh Leong, Mr Timothy Chua, Dr Goh Ban Eng, Mrs Lam Seet Mui, Mr Lee Lik Hsin, Ms Lim Suet Kwee, Ms Lim Suu Kuan, Mr Patrick Seow, Mr Sim Kay Wee, Mr Sim Kim Chui, Mr Toh Giam Ming, Ms Betty Wong, Mr Yap Kim Wah and Dr Yeo Teng Kwong. We would also like to thank Ms How Hwee Yin, Ms Karen Liaw and Ms Roshini Prakash of SIA's public affairs office, who were instrumental in helping us arrange the interviews at SIA. We are also grateful to the people at CAAS who gave us insights into the development of their joint biometrics project with SIA, in particular Mr Poh Young Peng and Mr Wang Pei Chong. Furthermore, we are indebted to Professor Robert Johnston at Warwick Business School, who has collaborated with us on a number of research projects involving SIA. We also thank our publishers, McGraw-Hill, and in particular Ms Pauline Chua. Lastly, we would like to thank our families who did not mind the countless hours we spent in front of the computer working on this book.

ABOUT THE AUTHORS

As a team, Loizos Heracleous, Jochen Wirtz and Nitin Pangarkar possess a unique blend of skills and experience that is ideally suited to writing this definitive, illustrative and engaging book on achieving sustainable competitive advantage in a highly competitive industry.

 **Loizos Heracleous** holds a Chair in Strategy at Warwick Business School. He is also an associate fellow of Green Templeton College and the Saïd Business School at Oxford University. He has lived and worked in Asia for eight years in his previous post as associate professor of business policy at the National University of Singapore (NUS). Dr Heracleous earned his Ph.D. at the Judge Institute of Management Studies, University of Cambridge. He is the author of *Strategy and Organization: Realizing Strategic Management*, (2003, Cambridge University Press) and *Discourse, Interpretation, Organization* (2006, Cambridge University Press) as well as the co-author of *Business Strategy in Asia: A Casebook* (2004, Thomson Learning).

Currently serving as associate editor of the *Journal of Applied Behavioral Science*, Dr Heracleous was senior editor of *Organization Studies*, and now on the Journal's editorial board. He is also on the editorial boards of the *Journal of Management Studies* and the *Asia Pacific Journal of Management.* He has published over 45 research papers in international journals, including the *Academy of Management Journal, Harvard Business Review, MIT Sloan Management Review, Journal of Management Studies, Human Relations, Journal of Applied Behavioral Science* and *Long Range Planning.* His research received three Best Paper Awards from the US Academy of Management in 1999, 2004 and 2006, and a Highly Commended Paper Award from Emerald in 2007.

Born in Cyprus, Dr Heracleous has lived and worked in the UK, Ireland, Hong Kong and Singapore, and has travelled extensively around the world. He has developed and conducted several executive development programmes in areas such as strategic thinking and planning, corporate governance, corporate social responsibility, diagnosing and managing organisational culture, managing transformational change, and organising for the future. He has trained company directors in Singapore on corporate governance on behalf of the Singapore Institute of Directors from 1999 to 2004. He has also trained executives and advised several organisations in areas related to strategy, organisation and leadership. Dr Heracleous has been listed in the Marquis Who's Who in the World since 2003.

Jochen Wirtz is an associate professor of marketing at NUS, the founding director of the UCLA–NUS Executive MBA Program, and an associate fellow of the Saïd Business School, University of Oxford.

Dr Wirtz is a leading authority in the field of services marketing. *Services Marketing – People, Technology, Strategy* (2007, 6th edition, Prentice Hall), which he co-authored with Professor Christopher Lovelock, is the best-selling services marketing text book worldwide, and *Essentials of Services Marketing* (2009, Prentice Hall), which he co-wrote with Lovelock and Professor Patricia Chew, is the world's first full-colour services marketing text.

Dr Wirtz's research focuses on service management. He has published some 70 academic articles in, among others, *Harvard Business Review, Journal of Consumer Psychology, Journal of Retailing* and *Journal of the Academy of Marketing Science.* He serves on the editorial boards of 11 academic journals, including the *Cornell Hospitality Quarterly, Journal of Service Management, Journal of Service Research, Managing Service Quality* and the *Service Industries Journal.* His excellence in research and teaching has been recognised with 16 awards, including the prestigious Emerald Literati Club Award for Excellence and the university-wide Outstanding Educator Award at NUS. Dr Wirtz is also active as a management consultant, working with both international consulting firms including Accenture, Arthur D. Little and KPMG, and major service companies in the areas of service management, business development and strategy.

Dr Wirtz received his Ph.D. in services marketing from the London Business School, holds a BA (Hons) in marketing and accounting, and a professional certification in banking. Originally from Germany, Dr Wirtz moved to Asia in 1992 after studying and working in London for seven years.

Nitin Pangarkar is an associate professor of business policy at the NUS Business School. Previously, he held academic positions at the University of Minnesota (USA) and the Helsinki School of Economics (Finland). His research interests lie in the areas of strategic management and international business – specifically cross-border strategic alliances and global strategy.

Dr Pangarkar's research has been presented in several international conferences around the world and published in more than 30 international journal articles, conference proceedings, cases and books. He is a member of several professional organisations and serves as the vice president of the Asia Academy of Management, the leading regional association for management scholars in Asia. He also serves on the editorial boards of two international journals.

Dr Pangarkar is a co-author of *Business Strategy in Asia: A Casebook* (Thomson Learning, 2001 and 2004). The book has been translated into Mandarin. His teaching and case materials have been used in many universities around the world including MIT, the Chinese University of Hong Kong, Macquarie University, the University of Western Australia, Copenhagen Business School and the Nanyang Technological University. He has taught several executive development programmes at NUS and has also been an invited speaker for several managerial conferences such as the Latin Asia Business Forum (2008). He has been quoted in reputable newspapers and publications including the *Asian Wall Street Journal, Economic Times* (India), *Forbes, International Herald Tribune, The Edge* (Malaysia), *Today* (Singapore) and interviewed on Channel NewsAsia (Singapore). He is a recipient of several awards including the Outstanding Educator Award and the Outstanding Service Award from the NUS Business School, the Favorite Business School Professor Award from the NUS MBA Alumni and the Excellent Teacher Award from NUS.

1

THE AIRLINE INDUSTRY: ECONOMICS AND STRATEGIC TRENDS

'I made the comment that if a capitalist had been present at Kittyhawk back in the early 1900s, he should have shot Orville Wright. He would have saved his progeny money. But seriously, the airline business has been extraordinary. It has eaten up capital over the past century like almost no other business because people seem to keep coming back to it and putting fresh money in. You've got huge fixed costs, you've got strong labor unions and you've got commodity pricing. That is not a great recipe for success. I have an 800 number now that I call if I get the urge to buy an airline stock. I call at two in the morning and I say: "My name is Warren and I'm an aeroholic." And then they talk me down.'[1]

Legendary investor Warren Buffett

Despite its enormous economic, policy and societal importance, the airline industry has been a disaster for investors. As we will see in Chapters 1 and 2, the industry is structurally unattractive, weighed down by regulations, and influenced by several uncontrollable factors. The combined effect of these factors is that the industry has never earned a rate of return above its investors' capital over its period of existence;[2] in fact it has destroyed more value for its investors than it has created. Despite this less than conducive environment, some airlines consistently manage to navigate the treacherous waters effectively and to perform at a high standard. Singapore Airlines (SIA) stands tall among this select group of airlines. The most awarded airline in the

1

world, recognised innovation and service leader, and the only airline to be listed in *Fortune* magazine's global 50 most admired companies,[3] it not only regularly outperforms competitors in terms of financial performance, but it has never shown an annual loss since its inception as an independent airline in 1972. In this book, we explore how SIA has achieved this feat, and what lessons can be learned and implemented by other organisations in hyper-competitive environments.

Industry Evolution and Economic Importance

The ubiquitous airline industry is of immense economic importance to national economies and global commerce, having developed swiftly since 1912, when the first scheduled airline flight took off. During its first 30 years of development, the technology underlying the aircraft (piston engines) placed severe constraints on the growth of the industry due to the slow speed of travel, lower level of comfort available to customers, limited range of flights and poor cost-effectiveness. During the 1950s, however, Turbo-prop engine powered aircraft were introduced, which dramatically improved the productivity, reach and capacity of the industry (see Table 1.1). An even bigger technological advance, in the form of the introduction of jet engines, took place in the 1960s, which significantly fostered the fast-paced development of the industry.

In 2006, the world's 900 scheduled airlines carried 2.1 billion passengers, flew over 3.9 billion passenger-kilometres,[5] and carried 38.9 million tones of freight. The aviation industry also carried almost 40% (by value) of the world's manufactured exports and around half of the world's international tourists.[6] The industry is expected to assume even greater importance over the coming years, especially in terms of freight transport, accounting for as much as 80% of the world's freight (by value) by 2014. It also has a multiplier effect, which goes well beyond its direct contribution, spanning interdependent industries such as travel agencies and the range of businesses associated with the shipment of freight. The direct, indirect induced and catalytic contribution of the civil aviation industry to the global economy has been estimated to be

Table 1.1

Evolution of aircraft technology

Period	Most productive model (technology)	Year of introduction	Number of seats	Hourly productivity (tonne-km/hour)[4]	Annual production capacity ('000 tonne-km)
1930s–1940s	DC-3 (Piston)	1936	21	527	1,571
1950s	Britannia 310 (Turbo-prop)	1956	139	6,048	18,144
1960s	Boeing 720B	1960	149 (single class)	11,256	33,770
	Boeing 747 (Turbo-jet)	1969	550	31,935	95,805
1980s	Boeing 747-400	1989	568	44,350	133,050

Source: Compiled by the authors based on data provided by Doganis (1991).

US$3,560 billion,[7] or 7.5% of world gross domestic product, generating 32 million jobs.[8]

Despite the industry's impressive scale and healthy growth in passenger traffic of 5.1% and in freight-tonne kilometres of 6.6% from 1985–2005,[9] a lot of passenger and cargo capacity remains unused. The passenger load factor during this period was 75% and the weight load factor 63%, indicating that the industry has been experiencing significant over-capacity, which has contributed to lower yields and lower profitability relative to most other industries.[10,11] As we will see below, in addition to over-capacity, there are various other factors leading to low levels of industry financial performance. These factors have long-term relevance and influence, indicating that conditions will continue to be highly challenging for the industry.

Industry Characteristics

Government Intervention

The airline industry is characterised by an unusually high degree of government intervention, particularly for international air routes. Government intervention has several motivations, which include patriotism, strategic importance of the sector (from economic and national security angles) and safety of passengers. As a starting basis of intervention, many governments historically believed that having their own 'flag carrier' was a matter of national pride. Many governments also consider air transport to be essential for the functioning of the country and its economy, or even a matter of national security. Finally, since a single aircraft can carry several hundred passengers whose safety may be jeopardised by inappropriate airline policies or practices, such as poor maintenance and safety standards, government agencies, such as the Federal Aviation Administration in the US, stipulate safety standards and policies for the industry and oversee compliance by airlines.

Government intervention in the airline sector can take several different forms. With the notable exception of countries that have signed 'open skies' agreements with each other, and actually practise the provisions of these agreements, the servicing of particular international routes and flight frequencies need to be approved by the home and host governments. In fact, an elaborate categorisation of freedoms determines what a particular airline can or cannot do in a foreign market (see Table 1.2).

Table 1.2
Regulation of air traffic

Freedom	Implication
1st Freedom	The right of an airline of one country to fly over the territory of another country without landing.
2nd Freedom	The right of an airline of one country to land in another country for non-traffic reasons, such as maintenance or refueling, while en route to another country.
3rd Freedom	The right of an airline of one country to carry traffic from its country of registry to another country.
4th Freedom	The right of an airline of one country to carry traffic from another country to its own country of registry.
5th Freedom	The right of an airline of one country to carry traffic between two countries outside of its own country of registry as long as the flight originates or terminates in its own country of registry.
6th Freedom	The right of an airline of one country to carry traffic between foreign countries via its own country of registry. This is a combination of the third and fourth freedoms.
7th Freedom	The right of an airline of one country to operate stand-alone services entirely outside the territory of its home country, to carry traffic between two foreign countries.
8th Freedom	The right of an airline of one country to carry traffic between two points within the territory of a foreign country (Cabotage).

Source: Kenneth Button, Kingsley Haynes and Roger Stough (1998) Flying into the Future. Cheltenham, England: Edward Elgar, p. 31.

There are several examples of such regulations constraining airlines from selecting routes and frequencies. Before 1990, SIA was prevented for many years from flying from Singapore to Kota Kinabalu and Kuching in East Malaysia.[12] Only three airlines are permitted to operate flights on the busy Hong Kong–London Heathrow route: Cathay Pacific, British Airways and Virgin Atlantic.[13] While SIA flies as many as 80 times a week from Singapore to Australia, all its flights have to terminate in Australia and cannot proceed to the US, despite several efforts to convince the Australian government to allow this freedom. Qantas, which has a 75% market share on Australia–US routes and derives over 40% of its international profits from these routes, is strongly opposed to SIA obtaining these flying rights.[14]

Leaving aside full ownership, local governments often place restrictions even on the purchase of equity stakes in airlines by foreign investors. For instance, non-US investors cannot own more than 25% of a US airline's voting stock, while the percentage in Canada is 31%, and in the European Union the cut-off point is 49%. AMR Corporation (the parent of American Airlines), for instance, was denied the opportunity to bail out the financially strapped Canadian Airlines by a Quebec judge, on the basis that it violated Canada's foreign ownership limit.[15]

Further, the landing and other rights of airlines are attached to the nationality of ownership of the airline rather than the airline itself, which places further severe constraints on cross-border mergers and acquisitions. If an airline from country A acquired an airline from country B, the latter airline would lose its landing rights since its nationality of ownership would change. This limits much-needed industry consolidation and rationalisation that could help to address industry over-capacity and sustain yields to more healthy levels. These restrictions also encourage higher dependence on various kinds of alliances as vehicles for market access and growth.

In the past, many governments intervened by providing subsidies to loss-making airlines. The approved state aid to eight European airlines, for example, during the 1990s amounted to an average of US$1.511 billion.[16] Such aid distorts market forces (such as aiding the persistence of excess capacity and delaying rationalisation), makes the playing field uneven, and places unfair pressure on healthy airlines with capable managements that take decisions based on economic criteria rather than political ones, for example. Fortunately, some governments have recently exhibited reluctance to shore up financially struggling airlines. Belgium, for instance, chose not to save the struggling Sabena through subsidies. The airline, instead, was bought by Swissair prior to the latter's bankruptcy. Further, after the September 11 terrorist attacks, no government in Latin America gave support to its national carrier.[17]

Over the last two decades, the degree of government intervention in civil aviation has been on a downward trend. As a first sign, governments are becoming more open to divesting their stakes in airlines. Between 1985 and 2003, about 130 countries announced privatisation plans or expressed their intention to privatise approximately 190 nationally owned airlines.[18] The plans were not always followed up with action, however, and, by the end of 2000, only 62 carriers had been privatised, 37 of them since 1995.[19] Some governments, for example, Malaysia and New Zealand, have even gone in the opposite direction, buying back airlines after privatising them.[20]

The trend of deregulation has spilled over into the choice of routes. The US pioneered deregulation of its internal airline market in 1978, and its lead was followed by Europe (starting in 1989 and implemented on a broader scale in 1997). Most Asian countries are lagging in this respect. Further, on a bilateral basis, many governments have signed 'open skies' agreements, which give complete freedom to their carriers to choose their routes and frequencies. In April 2007, an 'open skies' agreement was signed between the US and the European Union, allowing airlines to fly from any point in the US to any point in the 27 member countries of the European Union, and vice versa; this was implemented from 30 March 2008 onwards.[21]

Managing the Uncontrollables: A Key Challenge for Airline Executives

The airline industry is atypical in the sense that, to a greater extent than most other industries, it is impacted by several factors beyond its control. Further, these factors, such as the cost of oil and security concerns, are integral to their operations and therefore have high impact in terms of operational effectiveness and risk management. In addition to the significant government intervention discussed above, factors such as oil prices, airport and other charges, quality of infrastructure, political and socio-cultural events, natural disasters or health emergencies, which affect the financial health of the industry, lie outside the control of airline executives (see Figure 1.1).

Oil, which forms one of the most important inputs for an airline, is a globally traded commodity, whose price is determined by market forces

Figure 1.1
Determinants of airline profitability

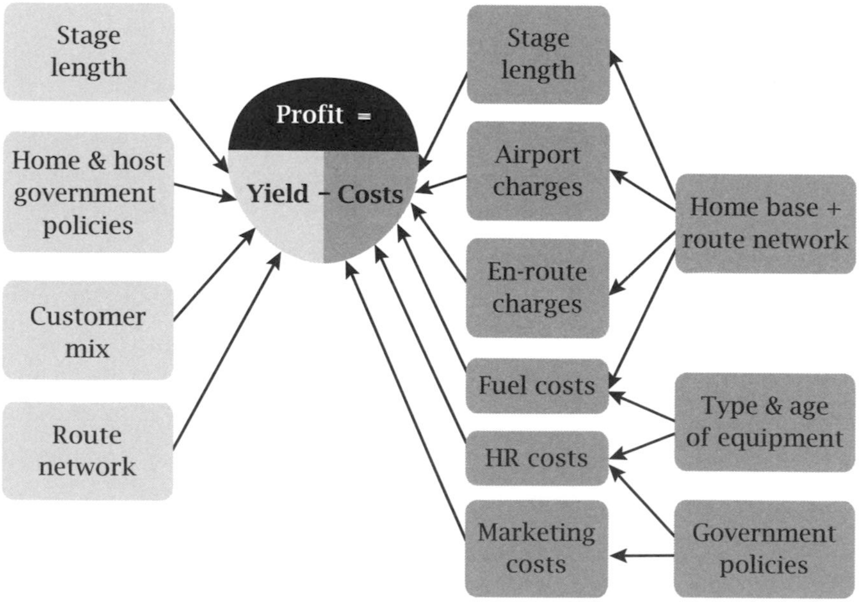

of demand and supply (see Figure 1.2), which are themselves influenced by not just geological but also socio-political factors. Oil price is also denominated in US dollars, while many of the international airlines earn a substantial percentage of their revenues in local currencies. Consequently, many international airlines incur a significant element of foreign exchange risk.[22] Fuel accounted for 30% of airlines' operating costs in 2007,[23] and the figure is rising (see Figure 1.3). This figure was higher for operationally efficient airlines and airlines with older fleets. The unpredictability and fast rise in fuel prices since 2003 significantly affects airline performance.[24] United Airlines, for instance, incurred a $75 million operating loss for April 2004 due to abnormally high fuel prices, which constituted its second largest category of expenses, behind labour. Even Southwest Airlines, an efficiently managed and well-performing airline, was forced in 2004 to offer buyout packages to its non-executive employees as a belt-tightening measure in partial response to high oil prices.[25]

Figure 1.2
Crude oil prices over time (1918–2008)
adjusted for inflation

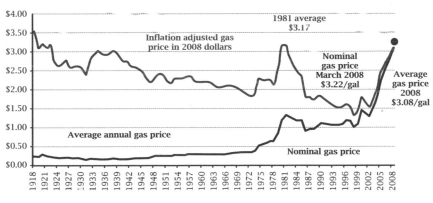

Note: Prices are average annual prices, not peak prices, so peaks are smoothed out considerably.

Source of data: US Energy Information Administration CPI-U Inflation index, http://www.bls.gov

Source: © 2008 Financial Trend Forecaster, http://inflationdata.com/.

Figure 1.3
Fuel bill in billions of US dollars and as percentage of operating costs (1997–2007)

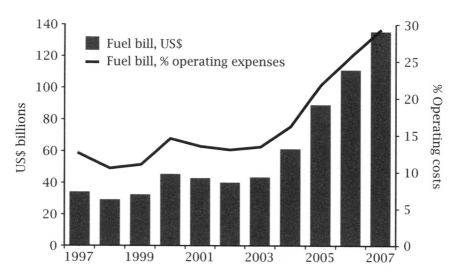

Source: *IATA Annual Report 2008.*

In addition to oil prices, governments and local airports impose charges such as landing and aircraft parking fees, which sometimes diverge from market-based prices. Airlines must take these imposed fees and prices as 'given', with little possibility of negotiation, if they want to fly to and from a specific airport. Further, issues such as the quality of the local infrastructure, which is the responsibility of the local government, also critically impact the growth and profitability of airlines. The US government readily accepts that the traffic system in the country is based on 1960s technology and operating concepts, and is close to gridlock due to the rapid increase in traffic.[26] In countries such as Scandinavia and India, inappropriate government policies have held back the development of airlines. Because of the lack of infrastructure, air travel in India, for instance, is only available to the residents of large and medium-sized cities, is expensive (regulatory barriers prop up inefficient firms) and offers generally low convenience (especially in terms of flight frequency, on-time arrivals and departures, and airport efficiency).

Airlines are also impacted by political, terrorist and other events that might influence travel and tourism. Due to the Gulf War in 1991, air traffic declined from the previous year for the first time in aviation history. By 1992, a combination of lower traffic, excess capacity and high oil prices led to huge earnings losses for airlines that exceeded the cumulative profits earned by the industry since its founding.[27] Such factors have assumed greater importance over the last decade as a series of events including the terrorist attacks of September 11, the wars in Afghanistan and Iraq and the outbreak of SARS unfolded. While the impact of the crises themselves is quite visible in terms of reduced demand for travel, there are also second-order consequences that impact the airline industry after the crises. For instance, post-September 11, the added security procedures put in place have increased the time and inconvenience of pre-flight activities, made air travel more challenging and expensive for passengers and also increased costs for governments, airports and airlines. Many airports and governments have imposed taxes to cover the costs of additional security procedures, which can increase the cost to passengers (especially those travelling on short-haul routes or by budget airlines) by as much as 20%.[28] Higher inconvenience and costs have impacted the demand for air travel especially at the margin where air travel is discretionary, for example, for leisure, or may be substituted by alternatives, for example, cars or trains for price-sensitive customers going to nearby destinations and private or corporate jet travel for high-end business travellers.

Operational and Strategic Complexity

A number of factors on the demand side, such as the perishable nature of seats on a particular flight, high levels of seasonality as well as cyclicality and exceptionally long time horizons for important decisions such as aircraft acquisition, increase the complexity of managing airlines. Airline seats are perishable commodities and cannot be inventorised. While airlines have devised a variety of price-discrimination strategies for yield management, reflected in the wide array of fares charged to different passengers on any one flight, they have often shown a tendency to engage in destructive price competition while trying to fill seats.

Further, demand for air travel is cyclical as well as seasonal. While seasonality is easy to anticipate (peak travel during holiday periods), it is still challenging to address since catering to peak demand by adding capacity can lead to excess capacity during other times, unless capacity is temporarily diverted from elsewhere, or leasing arrangements are employed (which give rise to their own particular challenges). On the other hand, not maintaining excess capacity will lead to lost revenues during the peak seasons. The difficulty in forecasting demand, the cyclicality of the industry and the barriers to consolidation encourage the maintenance of over-capacity; the industry passenger load factor in 2006, for example, was 76%, having risen from 69% in 1997.[29]

Cyclical demand poses significant challenges to airline executives. During the trough of the business cycle, the high fixed costs adversely impact financial performance. The peaks of the business cycle, on the other hand, often induce executives to over-extend themselves by ordering new planes, hiring employees or promising generous pay packages during union negotiations, all of which might prove unsustainable in the later stages of the cycle. Airline executives also face the difficult task of planning for exceptionally long time horizons, for example, in aircraft procurement. A large jet aircraft costs in excess of US$200 million,[30] and its procurement typically involves significant lead time. Since an aircraft has an operating life span of 25 to 30 years and, depending on the average age of the company's fleet, airline executives may be committing themselves to a time frame of decades, creating huge strategic commitments,[31] when placing a new aircraft order.[32] Existing assumptions regarding the regulatory, economic or operating environments easily go awry over such a long period of time, increasing the strategic risk for airlines.

Cost Structure of Airlines

Broadly, airline operating costs fall into three categories:[33] *variable direct operating costs, fixed direct operating costs* and *indirect operating costs.* Variable direct operating costs are activity- (flight) related and are escapable in the short term if the airline reduces its flights. These include fuel costs, variable flight crew costs such as allowances, direct engineering costs (which are related to the number of flying cycles or hours), airport and en-route charges and passenger service costs such as meals. Fixed direct operating costs are fleet-size-related and are escapable in the medium term if the airline reduces its overall capacity. They include aircraft depreciation or rental, annual flight and cabin crew costs (fixed salaries), and engineering overheads (such as fixed engineering costs unrelated to aircraft utilisation). Indirect operating costs are route- (product) related and are escapable in the medium or long term if the airline aims to enhance efficiency. These include station and ground expenses, passenger services (such as passenger service staff and passenger insurance), ticketing sales, promotion costs and general and administrative costs.

While the cost structure (percentage of total costs accounted by each of these categories) varies across airlines, all airlines are impacted by several common issues. Operating costs vary by the route structure due to significant variation in the local charges (landing, parking, en-route charges) and costs such as jet fuel. Operating costs decline with longer stage length, providing a cost advantage to airlines that focus on long-haul routes. The four largest categories of costs include labour, fuel, aircraft acquisition, and maintenance and repair. In developed countries, labour costs constitute the biggest proportion of costs, often amounting to as much as 35%. Airlines from developing countries enjoy an advantage in this respect since their wages and social costs are lower. Further, a significant portion (75% by some estimates) of an airline's costs are 'fixed', that is, independent of whether a particular flight is operated or not on a given day or the number of passengers in a particular flight.[34] In other words, the marginal cost of carrying an additional passenger is very low, which has strong implications for the variability of net revenues of airlines; a small increase in load factor can lead to a disproportionate increase in profitability.

Industry Performance

While commercial aviation enjoys a prominent role in the world economy and has experienced healthy growth over the last few decades, industry participants have faced significant challenges in attaining consistent levels of profitability. An industry executive says, 'When we first started flying, we launched an airplane to a destination in the hope that it would get there. A few years later, we launched an airplane in the hope that it would get there on time. Today, we launch an airplane and hope that it will make a dollar.'[35] Further, according to Adam Thomson, the charismatic founder of British Caledonian Airlines, 'recession is when you tighten your belt. Depression is when you no longer have a belt to tighten. When you've lost your trousers, you're in the airline business.'[36] Despite the overall bleak industry performance,[37] over the years there have been a few bright periods, mostly coinciding with a combination of a significant technological advance (such as the introduction of jet engines in the 1960s), economic boom (such as the period between 1993 and 2000) or low fuel prices. Unfortunately for airline industry participants, prosperity has been followed by severe adversity attributable to broader economic conditions such as high fuel prices, the cyclicality of the industry, or other factors such as terrorist attacks (see Table 1.3).

Table 1.4 shows the operating and financial results of the airline industry during the period 1996–2005.

In 2006, the global airline industry generated a net loss of US$500 million, or 0.1% of revenues, accumulating net losses of US$42 billion between 2001 and 2006,[39] and in 2007, the airline industry made a modest net profit of US$5.6 billion on revenues of US$490 billion, equivalent to less than 2% margin.[40]

Falling passenger yields (the equivalent of prices for the industry) represent a key cause of the low industry profitability. Passenger yield

Table 1.3
Financial performance of the airline sector over time

Time period	Financial performance of airline sector	Factors
1960-1967	Good	Strong productivity gains due to new generation of aircraft (jet)
1967-1974	Poor, major losses	Excess capacity in late 1960s, first oil shock, poor political climate (e.g., Arab-Israel war) and threat of terrorism dried up demand
1975-1978	Good	Falling (on a real basis) fuel costs and other costs and buoyant demand lifted results
1979-1983	Poor	Second oil shock and intense competition among airlines to fill seats led to bankruptcies of carriers
1984-1990	Good	Despite a few untoward events (e.g., American bombing of Libya; Chernobyl disaster), world economy performed robustly, and falling costs for many airlines led to good results. However debt burdens were heavy for some carriers by the end of the period and were expected to get even heavier with almost 7,000 planes on order for delivery between 1990 and 2001
1990-1992	Poor, major losses	Recession in many parts of the world coupled with the Gulf War and high oil prices led to losses
1993-2000	Good, strong profits	Booming world economy, low oil prices and interest rates and political stability led to unprecedented profits

Table 1.3   (continued)

Time period	Financial performance of airline sector	Factors
2001–2008	Poor, major losses	The September 11 terrorist attacks and the subsequent political events impacted traffic in the short term and increased security costs in the long term. In the short term, reduced demand and overhang of excess capacity led to unprecedented losses with several major carriers in the US seeking bankruptcy protection. Net revenues of industry were negative throughout this period except in 2007. Despite the slight recovery in 2007, the price of oil rose to historic highs; by June 2008 it hit $135 per barrel, with expectations for rising even higher, precipitating further bankruptcies and continued losses for the airline industry. Airline business confidence weakened sharply in early 2008.[38]
Outlook	Uncertain	Despite consolidation of the airline industry being a possibility, at least where regulatory barriers allow, the underlying structure of the industry (see Chapter 2 for a detailed analysis) does not seem to be improving. The industry will continue to be a highly uncertain and challenging place to achieve financial returns.

Sources: For 1967–1990 data, Doganis (1991); for data after 1991, ICAO Journal *and IATA.*

Table 1.4
Airline industry performance (1996–2005)

Year	Operating revenues US$ (millions)	Operating expenses US$ (millions)	Operating result		Net result[3]		Income taxes US$ (millions)
			Amount US$ (millions)	Percentage of operating revenues	Amount US$ (millions)	Percentage of operating revenues	
1996	282,500	270,200	12,300	4.4	5,300	1.9	-2,500
1997	291,000	274,700	16,300	5.6	8,550	2.9	-4,200
1998	295,500	279,600	15,900	5.4	8,200	2.8	-4,800
1999	305,500	293,200	12,300	4.0	8,500	2.8	-4,300
2000	328,500	317,800	10,700	3.3	3,700	1.1	-2,750
2001	307,500	319,300	-11,800	-3.8	-13,000	-4.2	3,610
2002	306,000	310,900	-4,900	-1.6	-11,300	-3.7	2,300
2003	321,800	323,300	-1,500	-0.5	7,560	-2.3	-1,460
2004	378,800	375,500	3,300	0.9	-5,570	-1.5	-2,460
2005	413,300	409,000	4,300	1.0	-3,200	-0.8	n/a

Source: ICAO Journal (2006) Annual Review of Civil Aviation, Vol. 61, No. 5, p. 15.

fell at an annualised rate of 2.2% for the period 1985–1999 and at a rate of 3% for 1990–1999. Freight yield fell at an annualised rate of 3.2% for 1985–1999 and 2.8% for 1990–1999. According to one estimate, the real yield, that is, prices adjusted by inflation, fell from 12.5 US cents per revenue passenger-km in 1970 to just over 6 US cents in 2001.[41]

Though profitability has proven to be an elusive goal, the world's airlines have succeeded, without doubt, in providing high levels of safety to their passengers. In fact, due to industry diligence and effective oversight by governments, the industry has achieved a far superior safety record than most other alternative modes of transportation, especially cars. The odds of being killed on a single airline flight vary from 1 in 7.71 million for the 25 airlines with the best safety records to 1 in 558,000 for the 25 airlines with the worst safety records respectively. The odds of being on an airline flight which results in at least one fatality vary from 1 in 3.72 million for the 25 airlines with the best safety records to 1 in 419,000 for the 25 airlines with the worst safety records.[42]

The airline industry has also succeeded in other aspects, for example, providing improved accessibility through high frequency of flights and far-reaching networks. The frequency of flights available between high-density markets (for example, Boston–New York, Taipei–Hong Kong, Kuala Lumpur–Singapore) is especially remarkable. Further, the industry has attained high reliability in terms of completed flights and flights arriving on time despite uncontrollable factors such as weather, airport and air-traffic control capacities. In addition, the industry has provided affordable travel options through continuous improvements in technology (such as new generations of planes) and yield-management systems, and achieved substantial innovation, especially for the passengers travelling in higher classes who can now enjoy bed-like seats, a range of entertainment options and high service levels in the best carriers. According to Skytrax, in 2008 there were six airlines whose service levels achieved the top 5-star category, five international and one domestic. These airlines were SIA, Cathay Pacific Airways, Qatar

Airways, Malaysian Airlines, Asiana Airlines and Kingfisher Airways (domestic).[43]

Recent Strategic Trends

Airline Alliances

The concept of airline alliances is not new. The International Air Transport Association (IATA), for example, can be considered as a giant alliance set up by the world's leading airlines to coordinate international fares. Alliances were first observed in the US domestic markets between major jet and commuter operators for the purpose of jointly developing the market (for example, by providing feeder services). Alliance activity, however, witnessed a significant growth during the 1980s and 1990s due to the intensification of globalising forces. Faced with the twin requirements of building a global presence and achieving more efficient cost structures, and yet constrained from undertaking mergers or starting new airlines in foreign markets, airlines found alliances to be a logical strategic alternative.

'Alliances' is a broad umbrella term which includes a variety of inter-firm co-operation agreements ranging from equity ownership in a partner to the coordination of frequent flyer programmes. The estimates of alliance activity vary across studies due to several reasons. First, alliances are dynamic and airlines may be continuously forming new ones as well as disbanding old ones. Secondly, the definition of alliances varies across studies and sources. The *Airline Business* journal, for instance, excludes frequent flyer programme coordination unless it is part of a broader alliance agreement. Thirdly, the coverage of individual surveys might again vary.[44] With these caveats in mind, the *Economist* magazine estimated that in 1995, there were 401 alliances, which was double the number it estimated four years earlier. In contrast, for 1995 and 1994, *Airline Business* estimated a total of 324 and 280 alliances respectively.[45] *Airline Business* further estimated that 500 alliances among 120 participants were in force as of June 2004.

Despite the varying estimates of alliance activities, most of the studies on the topic find that the number of alliances has been growing with a significant acceleration as observed in the early 1990s; that an increasingly larger proportion of alliances are informal (non-equity) rather than formal (equity); and that a larger proportion of alliances are international rather than domestic.

The broad motivations behind alliances include:

- Getting around the bilateral restrictions relating to expansion in international markets
- Getting around the restrictions relating to mergers and acquisitions (especially relevant to equity alliances)
- Enhancing the value of route networks by increasing the number of destinations and frequencies, and improving the quality of connections
- Reducing costs through economies of scale, scope and specialisation
- Gaining additional market and pricing power[46]

Alliances can take different forms, which are mostly grouped under equity or marketing alliances. The purchase of equity stakes (short of the levels required for a full acquisition) represents a common alliance strategy, which was especially popular in the 1980s and early 1990s. Equity alliances have proven to be especially attractive for international partnerships since full mergers, especially by foreign airlines, are forbidden by many host governments. Further, since flying and landing rights are attached to an airline's nationality, if a merger or an acquisition changes the effective nationality of ownership, these rights would be lost and would have to be re-negotiated.

Equity alliances serve a variety of purposes, including shoring up a struggling partner (as in the case of KLM's cash infusion into Northwest in 1989), helping a partner fend off unfriendly acquirers (for instance, Delta sold 5% stake each to SIA and Swissair in 1989 to discourage potential acquirers), or cementing partner relationships through equity swaps.

While equity alliances have positive aspects – they ensure commitment and often earn a tangible return on the investments in the form of dividends – there are downsides also. First, the level of control afforded by equity alliances is often less than the percentage of shares owned. Second, the equity stake could also lose value and in some cases (for example, failure of the partner) become completely worthless (as in the case of SAS' stake in Continental or British Airways' stake in US Airways[47]).

Marketing alliances typically involve the coordination of schedules and the sharing of codes of international flights, and may be of a narrow scope (for example, a single-route) or a broad scope (for example, network-wide). Such code-sharing alliances, which mean that one single flight bears the codes for two or more airlines, can provide the appearance of a seamless single-carrier flight to the customer. British Airways, for instance, was able to extend its reach into dozens of US cities by code-sharing with US Airways. According to a United Airlines manager, 'the profits on offer through route-sharing are something most airlines could never hope to achieve by themselves.'[48] Block-space agreements involve one airline committing itself to buying a certain number of seats on its partner's flights. If the volume of demand for the airline buying the seats is insufficient for it to operate a flight, a block-space agreement is likely to lead to cost savings. The airline that sells the seats also benefits due to the higher load factor. Block-space agreements are also useful for airlines that do not have the freedoms to operate particular routes, for example, Delta Airlines' block-space agreements for Virgin flights between six and seven European cities and the US before the signing of the 'open skies' agreement between the US and the EU.

Coordinating frequent flyer programmes offers customers the additional benefit of earning points on a partner's flights. A typical airline might have several such agreements, and increasingly airlines are also allowing customers additional convenience in the form of redeeming miles on a partner's flights, and depositing miles to the frequent flyer programme of their choice if they fly on partners' flights.

A recent trend in the industry has included the formation of mega-alliances (Star, Oneworld and SkyTeam alliances; see Figure 1.4). These alliances provide customers with unprecedented global connectivity in addition to most of the benefits also available to smaller alliances, for example, economies of scale and customer conveniences such as access to lounges. Mega-alliances may also be in a better position to secure corporate accounts.

Figure 1.4
Mega-alliances in the airline industry and their market shares

Star Alliance
Air Canada, Air China, Air New Zealand, ANA, Asiana Airlines, Austrian, bmi, Lot Polish Airlines, Lufthansa, Scandinavian Airlines, Shanghai Airlines, SIA, South African Airways, Spanair, Swiss, TAP Portugal, Thai, United, US Airways

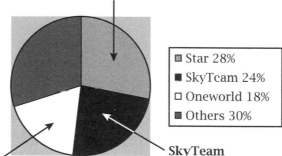

▣ Star 28%
■ SkyTeam 24%
□ Oneworld 18%
▨ Others 30%

Oneworld
American Airlines, British Airways, Cathay Pacific, Dragonair, Finnair, Iberia, JAL, LAN, Malev, Qantas, Royal Jordanian

SkyTeam
Aeroflot, Aeromexico, Air France-KLM, Alitalia, Delta Airlines, China Southern, Continental, CSA Czech Airlines, Delta Airlines, Korean Airlines, Northwest

Source: Puffer, M., December 2007, Star Alliance facts & figures presentation, http://www.staralliance.com/int/press/media_library/presentations/star_alliance_ network_facts_and_Figures_Dec_2007.pdf; Economist, Open Skies and Flights of Fancy, 2 October 2003. Market share figures based on number of passengers.

In spite of the uncertainty and risks inherent in strategic alliances, there are several examples where alliances resulted in substantial positive outcomes for the partners. In 2002, for example, Oneworld members expanded bilateral code-sharing, enhanced IT systems for improved customer service and predicted $1 billion in benefits 'through revenue generation, protection and feed, and savings from joint purchasing and shared airport and city facilities.'[49] In the same year, the consolidation of airport lounges and streamlined airport ground handling by Star Alliance members led to collective savings of US$70 million in addition to leveraged purchasing power with other suppliers.[50]

On the other hand, there is some scepticism regarding the benefits of alliances. Industry analysts, for example, believe that the proliferation of alliances could be attributed to herd behaviour. According to an article in *Airfinance Journal*, 'perhaps one of the drivers towards alliances is that making deals is simply good fun. Talking strategy is more exciting than examining the finer aspects of running an airline. Beating the other alliances to a deal is a buzz. There is also a feeling that, unless airlines act now, all the good partners will be lost. Like shoppers in January sales, airlines are looking for any bargains going, and not caring if they fit or not.'[51] An article in *Journal Records* adds, 'They're doing those things for many of the same reasons that kids join real gangs. The big airlines are seeking security and support so they can survive in one of the meanest 'hoods in the business world: the global airline industry, which is so tough that it still has a cumulative net loss for its entire history after three straight years of record profits. And the airlines are joining their high-flying, international gangs – which they call "alliances" – because, well, everybody else is doing it.'[52]

Employee scepticism of alliances is rooted in the fear of job losses or the reduction in pay or benefits. For instance, SPA (SkyTeam Pilots' Alliance) members feared that high-cost SkyTeam member airlines would transfer some activities to operators such as Korean Air to benefit from a substantially lower cost structure and more favourable labour pacts.[53] They believed that as a consequence the jobs and pay packets of employees based in developed countries such as France and the US may be at risk.

Many alliances suffer from instability since one or more partners view them as transitory arrangements while waiting for a better alternative. For instance, SAS and SIA, which used to be members of the Qualiflyer alliance and the Global Excellence Alliance respectively, abandoned those alliances to join the Star Alliance. The challenges in sustaining partnerships are so severe that in 2003, the alliance between Northwest/KLM, with its modest 14-year run, was considered the longest-lasting transatlantic airlines alliance.[54] The instability rates also vary across different types of alliances with non-equity alliances exhibiting a higher likelihood of termination.

The key problems in alliance management include the lack of preparation before forging the alliance, optimistic projections about potential benefits, incompatibility among partners, poor management of relationships, high costs of negotiating even minor decisions and variation in commitment and service levels across the partners. Regarding the lack of adequate preparation, one observer notes that 'alliances are a bit like marriage – companies often get together thinking that they've got a lot in common and then, for the least likely reasons, things start to go wrong.'[55] Swissair's CEO Philip Bruggiser comments, 'People say [alliances] are a waste of time. They spend half a day talking about peanuts. We're all fighting the same thing. It's the price you pay for a non-merger. When you're not independent, you're constantly negotiating.'[56]

Variation in service across alliance members is another area of concern, especially for code-sharing alliances. In the block-space agreement between Delta and Virgin, for instance, some Delta customers did not like the Virgin service concept while travelling on code-shared flights operated by Virgin. In this respect, one industry analyst notes that 'alliances are not the glue to create a seamless service product.'[57]

The Emergence of Budget Carriers

The airline industry has witnessed additional turbulence with the entry of airlines adopting new business models variously referred to as low cost carriers, no frills airlines and budget carriers. While budget carriers such as Southwest Airlines have been competing in the US market for more than 30 years, they have proliferated in Europe only over the last decade and are at a relatively early stage of development in the Asia Pacific and the rest of the world. Prominent examples of budget airlines include Ryanair and easyJet (Europe), VirginBlue (Australia), Westjet (Canada), Air Do and Skymark (Japan), Air Asia (Malaysia) and ValuAir, JetStar and Tiger Airways (Singapore). The proliferation of budget carriers has been rapid enough that four out of every five airline markets, that is, areas served by a pair of airports, now feature a budget carrier.[58]

The business model of budget carriers usually encompasses the following:

- Relatively narrow regional coverage (for example, Europe and Southeast Asia), thus eliminating the need to pay high overseas allowances to crew.

- 'Simple' (or standardised) fleet consisting of one type of aircraft (or at least variants of a family such as Boeing 737), which reduces crew training, maintenance and repair costs.

- Higher utilisation of aircraft. While British Midland (a conventional airline) uses a plane for 8.4 hours a day, easyJet pushes up the utilisation to 10.7 hours a day. Southwest Airlines' average utilisation rate for a Boeing 737 has been 11.3 hours per day versus only 9.8 hours per day for Delta.[59] The higher utilisation is possible due to the usage of less congested (and cheaper) secondary airports leading to faster turnaround, which can be as low as 20 minutes, and having point-to-point, rather than hub-and-spoke service, as well as no assignment of seats, facilitating rapid embarkation.

- Booking (for most budget carriers) through the Internet, therefore saving travel agent commissions, which could be as high as 9%; reducing handling costs due to the absence of paper tickets (the industry has been moving to e-tickets); and reducing wages paid to reservation agents – budget carriers have fewer or none of these agents and they are typically paid minimum wage.

- Higher seat density by around 15%, as typically found in a single class configuration.

- Continuous push to reduce costs. Almost all budget carriers have minimal cabin service (for example, no free meals), which reduces the number of flight attendants to the regulatory minimum. Budget carriers have also adopted a number of policies to reduce costs. Ryanair, for example, made its seats fixed since reclining seats are prone to breakdown, eliminated window blinds on new planes (at a saving of US$240,000 per plane) and did away with back-of-the-seat pockets which take time to clean.[60]

- Usage of secondary airports (which typically have much lower landing, parking and other charges) in cities with minimum catchment areas.

- Extensive use of outsourcing (such as maintenance, catering, IT, etc.) rather than owning subsidiaries, which makes the organisational design simpler and reduces bureaucratic costs.

- Having a lean management structure, flat organisation design and basic headquarters infrastructure.

Table 1.5 offers a comparison between a conventional carrier and a budget carrier.

The substantially different business model of the budget carriers leads to tremendous cost savings (see Figure 1.5) which enable them to undercut the fares of conventional rivals. It is observed, for example, that for a hypothetical booking from London to Glasgow in 2001, easyJet and Go could offer fares that were 40% lower than British Airways, 50% lower than British Midland and even lower than the train fare, though the train journey took four times as long.[61] Ryanair, for example, discounted its London to Dublin fares in 2004 down to as low as £9 (about US$13; versus the £209 charged by conventional airlines at the time of its entry), and £8 for a London to Venice (or Glasgow) roundtrip.[62]

While budget carriers are gaining increasing acceptance by serving price-sensitive customers, many of these carriers have found survival to be difficult. Some of the early, and storied, budget carriers such as

Table 1.5
Comparison between a conventional carrier versus a budget carrier

	Lufthansa	easyJet
Staff	47,230	5,674
Turnover	15,956 million Euros	2,289 million Euros (£1,797 million)
Profit before tax	826 million Euros	243 million Euros (£191 million)
Profit margin	6%	10.7%
Passenger load factor	77.4%	83.7%
Passengers	62.9 million	37.2 million
Fleet (Group)	513 planes 17 different types (396 owned and 117 on lease). Lufthansa & Swiss, 343 planes	137 planes (120 firm orders) 2 different types; 55 owned and 82 on lease
Destinations	206 destinations in 85 countries	289 destinations in 21 countries (Europe)
Departments	Logistics, maintenance, catering, travel, IT, passenger and other activities	Call centre, airport operations, cabin services and management

Source: Lufthansa and easyJet annual reports (2007). Lufthansa figures refer to the transportation sector within the Lufthansa Group (Lufthansa and Swiss airlines).

People Express and Laker Airways did not survive for long. Even among more recent start-ups, carriers such as Debonair (UK) and Color Air (Norway) have completely folded up within the first few years, while others such as Go (UK) have been absorbed by other budget carriers after continual losses.

Figure 1.5

Sources of cost advantage of budget airlines

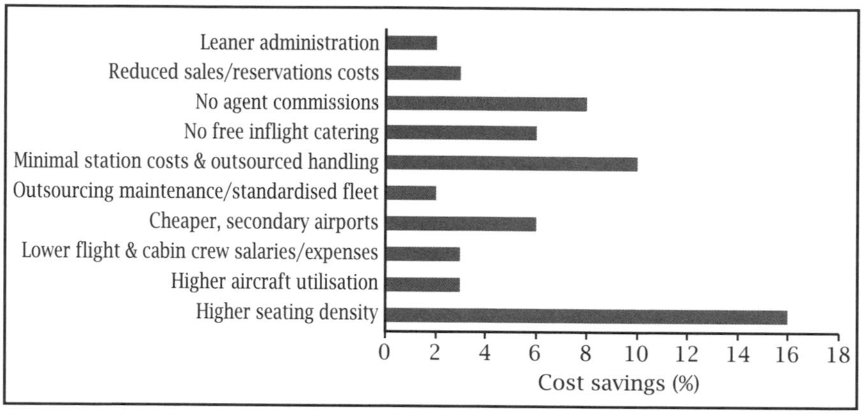

Category	Cost savings (%)
Leaner administration	~2
Reduced sales/reservations costs	~3
No agent commissions	~8
No free inflight catering	~6
Minimal station costs & outsourced handling	~10
Outsourcing maintenance/standardised fleet	~2
Cheaper, secondary airports	~6
Lower flight & cabin crew salaries/expenses	~3
Higher aircraft utilisation	~3
Higher seating density	~16

Source: Doganis (1991) Cost Advantages Based on Short-Haul Routes, *p. 150.*

Industry observers are also wondering whether many budget carriers can survive in the long run, especially if their cost advantage is diluted over time due to the following factors:

- Airports that grant the budget carriers favourable terms initially may not continue to do so at the time of renewal of contracts, especially if there are multiple budget carriers serving the same secondary airport.

- As employees gain seniority, budget carriers' labour costs might inch up.

- As new entrants flood the market (including budget carriers started by conventional airlines), price competition will increase further, eroding yields.

- With new entrants leading to higher excess capacity, load factors and capacity utilisation can drop, eroding budget carriers' cost advantages.

- Lured by steep discounts offered by Boeing and Airbus during the trough of the airline cycle, budget carriers such as Ryanair and

28

easyJet have a large number of aircraft on order, placing further pressures on capacity utilisation and yields.[63]

- Increasing overlap (and therefore competitive intensity) with the competitive space of charter airlines who sell packages to holiday tour operators and account for as much as a third of leisure traffic in Europe. Charter airlines have similar lean cost structures as budget carriers, yet more flexibility (for example, they can cancel flights that do not have a minimum load factor).

Regional Growth

Air travel used to be a luxury in many parts of the world in the past few decades and, as a result, domestic travel within developed countries such as the US formed by far the largest component of the industry. While the US domestic market continues to tower over other domestic markets in terms of size (for example, the domestic market in Japan is about one-seventh in terms of passengers compared to the US airline market),[64] over the last two decades, many developing countries (especially in the Asia Pacific) have prospered, hence their citizens have increasingly engaged in international air travel. Between 1980 and 1999, the growth in international revenue passenger-km and international passengers was more than twice the growth in world GDP (which was approximately 3%) and much faster than the growth in overall passengers.[65] Whereas in 1991 airlines in North America and Europe accounted for 71.1% of the worldwide traffic, this proportion had declined to 63% by 2002.[66] At the same time, countries such as China and India have been growing fast as Figure 1.6 shows.

These markets and, more generally, the Asia Pacific region are expected to sustain their growth trajectory in the next two decades as Figure 1.7 shows.

The increasing importance of international travel and Asia Pacific markets is expected to continue in the future due to three key

Figure 1.6

Comparison of growth in total passenger-kilometres between the world, India and China (2000–2006)

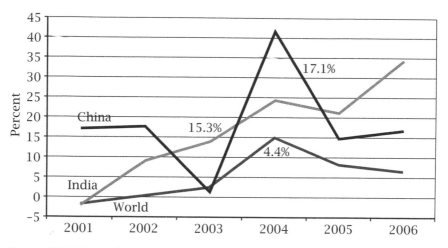

Source: ICAO Journal (2007) Performance Indicators, Vol. 62, No. 3, p. 5.

factors.[67] First, the continued strong performance of Asia Pacific economies will translate into a higher number of trips on a per capita basis for both business and leisure purposes. The low base makes this potential growth particularly salient and attractive. Second, demographics indicate that urbanisation, a key demographic predictor of the demand for air travel, is occurring rapidly in Asia Pacific economies.[68] Third, many Asia Pacific economies are exhibiting a robust growth in population in contrast to several developed countries (especially Europe and Japan) where population growth is slow or even flat.

Having offered an overview of the key characteristics and trends of the global aviation industry, we will conduct a more structured analysis of the industry in the next chapter in order to gain a deeper understanding of the industry's underlying structural dynamics as well as the critical success factors for individual competitors. This structural analysis not only helps to explain why the airline industry consistently under-performs relative to other industries in terms of returns, but also

Figure 1.7
Share of scheduled passenger traffic by region, 2005 vs 2025
(passenger-kilometres performed)

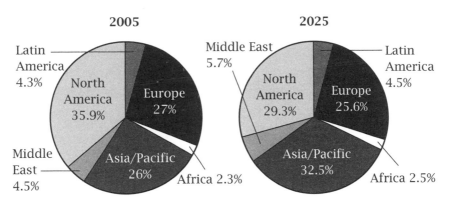

Source: ICAO Journal *(2007) Vol. 62, No. 2, p. 5.*

offers insights into how individual competitors can attempt to shield themselves from these dynamics, or take advantage of them, to deliver high performance in the context of such a structurally unattractive industry.

END NOTES

1. *The Age*, 24 September 2002, The Sage of Omaha's Trans Atlantic Game, http://www.theage.com.au/articles/2002/09/23/1032734111833.html

2. *Economist*, 2 October 2003, Open Skies and Flights of Fancy.

3. http://money.cnn.com/magazines/fortune/globalmostadmired/2007/top50/index.html, SIA was listed at number 17 in 2007.

4. Tonne-km/hr are arrived at by multiplying the capacity of the plane (in tonnes) by the speed of travel (km/hr).

5. *ICAO Journal* (2007) Performance Indicators, Vol. 62, No. 1.

6. *ICAO Journal*, September 2004.

7. Indirect impacts include suppliers to the industry and to airports, manufacturers of aircraft parts and related services such as call centres or IT. Induced impacts refer to the spending of those directly or indirectly

employed in airlines in other industries such as retail outlets and services. Catalytic impacts refer to the facilitating role of airlines in the world economy, tourism and other spin-off benefits.

8. The Economic and Social Benefits of Air Transport 2008, Air Transport Action Group, http://www.atag.org

9. *ICAO Journal* (2007) Performance Indicators, Vol. 62, No. 2.

10. *ICAO Journal* (2006) Annual Review of Aviation, Vol. 61, No. 5.

11. Fortune 500 industry performance figures consistently place the airline industry near the bottom in terms of various measures of performance.

12. Doganis (1991) see op. cit.

13. Taneja (2002) see op. cit.

14. *Straits Times*, 8 February 2005, Minister Seeks to Right S'pore–Aussie Air Links Imbalance, p. 3.

15. *The Investment Dealer's Digest: IDD*, 31 January 2000, Virtual Mergers: With Traditional Mergers Difficult to Pull Off, Airlines Are Finding Creative Ways to Consolidate, p. 1.

16. Doganis (2001).

17. Taneja (2003).

18. *ICAO Journal* (2003) no. 6.

19. *ICAO Journal* (2003) no. 6.

20. Nawal K. Taneja (2003) *Airline Survival Kit: Breaking Out of the Zero Profit Game*, Ashgate Publishing.

21. http://useu.usmission.gov/Dossiers/Open_Skies/Mar2808_Open_Skies_Accord_In_Force.asp

22. While some of the exchange rate risk can be hedged, hedging is neither costless, nor does it eliminate the exchange rate risk completely.

23. IATA Annual Report, 2008.

24. *ICAO Journal* (2006) Annual Review of Aviation, Vol. 61, No. 5.

25. High Fuel Prices Spark Southwest Buyouts, UAL Loss, 28 May 2004, http://www.smartmoney.com

26. Taneja (2003).

27. James Ott and Raymond E. Neidl (1995) *Airline Odyssey, The Airline Industry's Turbulent Flight into the Future.* New York: McGraw-Hill.

28. Taneja (2003) see op. cit.

29. *ICAO Journal* (2007) Performance Indicators, Vol. 62, No. 1.

30. For Boeing prices, for example, see http://www.boeing.com/commercial/prices/

31. Ghemawat, P. (1991) *Commitment: The Dynamic of Strategy*. Free Press.

32. While there is a secondary market for used aircraft, the prices for used aircraft vary significantly and tend to be quite low during recessionary periods for the industry.

33. Doganis (1991).

34. Taneja (2003) see op. cit.

35. An industry executive in Ott and Neidl (1995) see op. cit.

36. Cited in Stephen Holloway (2003) *Straight and Level: Practical Airline Economics*. Aldershot: Ashgate Publishing Company, p. 581.

37. For figures on industry performance and a discussion of underlying industry structure, see Chapter 2.

38. IATA Economic Briefing; Airline Business Confidence Index, April 2008.

39. IATA Annual Report, 2007.

40. IATA Annual Report, 2008.

41. Taneja (2002) p. 15, op. cit.

42. Risks based on data between 1987 and 1996. Source: http://www.planecrashinfo.com/cause.htm, accessed on 8 December 2004.

43. http://www.airlinequality.com

44. The *Airline Business* survey, for instance, focuses on the top 200 airlines.

45. Ott and Neidl (1995) see op. cit.

46. Taneja (2003) see op. cit.

47. Glisson et al., 1996.

48. Cyril Murphy, Vice President, International Affairs at United Airlines quoted in World Wide Webs, *Airfinance Journal*, 11 October 1997, p. 36.

49. *Business Travel News*, 8 April 2002, Star Alliance Membership Still Shines the Brightest, 19(6), pp. 16–17.

50. *Business Travel News*, 8 April 2002, Star Alliance Membership Still Shines the Brightest, 19(6), pp. 16–17.

51. *Airfinance Journal*, June 2000, Marry in Haste, Repent at Leisure, Issue 229, p. 7.

52. *Journal Record*, 12 November 1998, Alliances Changing the Airlines Industry, p. 1.

53. *Aviation Week and Space Technology*, 22 September 2003, Global Unionization SkyTeam member Airlines' Pilot Unions Tighten Cooperative Links as the Alliance Prepares to Expand, 159(2), p. 44.

54. *Memphis Business Journal*, 8 August 2003, Northwest Alliance with KLM Royal Dutch Airlines at Risk, 25(15), p. 12.

55. Fariba Allandari of Cranfield University quoted in World Wide Webs, *Airfinance Journal*, 11 October 1997, p. 36.

56. *Air Transport World*, June 2007, Swissair: Time to Deliver, Vol. 34, no. 6.

57. *The Investment Dealer's Digest: IDD*, 31 January 2000, Virtual Mergers: With Traditional Mergers Difficult to Pull Off, Airlines Are Finding Creative Ways to Consolidate, p. 1.

58. *Economist*, 27 March 2004.

59. Doganis (2001) p. 131.

60. *USA Today*, 16 February 2004, Ryanair Taking No-Frills Flying to New Heights: Report. http://www.usatoday.com.

61. Taneja (2002) op. cit. Reservation enquiry made on 27 December 2001 for travel on 28 December 2001.

62. Airline Zen: Less Is More, http://www.thetravelinsider.info, accessed on 30 December 2004.

63. *Economist*, 10 July 2004, Turbulent Skies – Low Cost Airlines, 372(8383), p. 68.

64. *ICAO Journal* (2004) no. 6.

65. Taneja (2002) p. 185, see op. cit.

66. Based on tonne-km; Rigas Doganis (1991) *Flying Off Course, The Economics of International Airlines*, 2nd Edition, Routledge.

67. Taneja (2002) see op. cit.

68. Residents of cities such as Singapore and Hong Kong undertake the highest number of trips on a per capita basis.

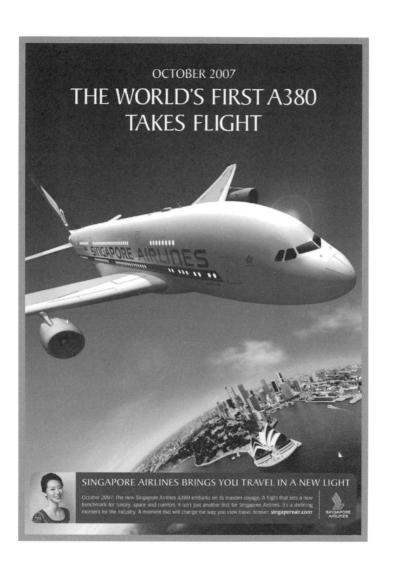

2

AIRLINE INDUSTRY STRUCTURE: DISASTROUS PERFORMANCE AND THE ROUTE TO SUCCESS

'Our industry is like Sisyphus – after a long uphill journey a giant boulder of bad news is driving us back down ... It's another perfect storm. The spreading impact of the US credit crunch is slowing traffic growth ... After enormous efficiency gains since 2001 there is no fat left and skyrocketing oil prices are changing everything ... The situation is desperate and potentially more destructive than our recent battles with all the Horsemen of the Apocalypse combined.'[1]

Giovanni Bisignani, Director General of IATA, June 2008

I n this chapter, we will explore macro-environmental trends affecting the airline industry, its underlying structural dynamics and the route to competitiveness for airlines that are able to exploit these success factors.

Disastrous Under-Performance in the Airline Industry

At first sight, the airline industry might seem relatively healthy. Air transportation has become ubiquitous and widely available, and has enjoyed a healthy growth in several markets. Over the last 20 years, airline revenue-passenger kilometres have been growing at over 5% per annum, passenger numbers at 4.2% and world gross domestic product at 3.5%. In some countries, growth has been exceptional; India, for example, enjoyed around 15% cumulative growth during 2001–2006, and China around 17% for the same period. Airline revenue growth has been lower, however, at around 2.8%, and industry net profits have been negative over half of the years.[2]

Fortunes have been lost in the airline industry, which *Fortune* magazine's Global 500 regularly features as one of the worst-performing industries.[3] Porter's study of return on invested capital in selected US industries between 1992 and 2006 found that the airline industry was the worst of the 31 industries studied, with 5.9% returns, as compared to the average return of 14.9%.[4] Such under-performance has prompted the *Economist* to comment that 'the airline business is an aberration. Distorted by decades of subsidies and international cartels, it has never earned a real rate of return on its investors' capital in its 60 years of existence'.[5]

IATA research has shown that the return on invested capital in the airline industry during 1996–2000 was 6.3%, and in 2001–2004 it was 3.3%, while the cost of capital was 7.2% (see Figure 2.1).

Figure 2.1
Return on invested capital in the airline industry vs cost of capital

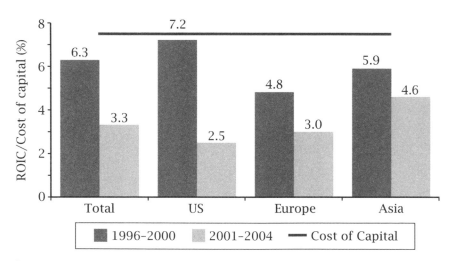

Source: IATA Economic Briefing no. 4, Value Chain Profitability.

The rather ironic part is that the airline industry, which is a key enabler of related sectors such as travel agents, ground handling, lessors and freight forwarders, achieved the lowest returns as compared with all these other sectors (see Figure 2.2).

If we carry out a conventional PEST analysis (political, economic, social and technological factors) affecting this and other industries, we can begin to see some of the issues that account for this disastrous under-performance. If we proceed further with a 5-forces analysis, our understanding of the industry's difficulties becomes more comprehensive.

Figure 2.2
Return on invested capital in the airline industry vs related sectors

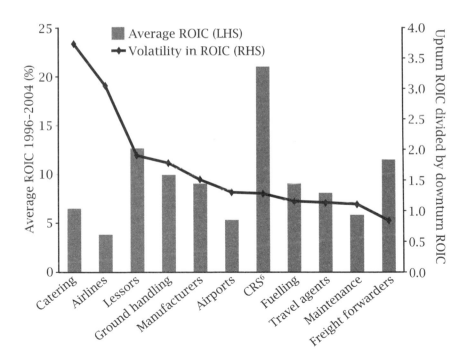

Source: IATA Economic Briefing no. 4, Value Chain Profitability.

Macro-Environmental Analysis

In terms of *political* factors, the impact of 'open skies' philosophy has prompted some deregulation in the industry in terms of entry, even though several constraints remain in terms of continued protectionism and red tape in several countries.[7] On many routes there is still a need to negotiate bilateral air services agreements, as well as significant infrastructure constraints, for example, in terms of availability of landing slots and airport passenger capacity. Higher levels of operational regulations have been introduced, partially as a result of terrorist threats.

Many industry executives regard the continued high levels of regulation in the airline industry as counter-productive. According to Chew Choon Seng, CEO of Singapore Airlines (SIA), 'Battered by forces and events, in part outside the airlines' control but also in part self-inflicted, the industry collectively and cumulatively has achieved the dubious feat of losing more money than it ever made ... The demand side is not in question. The irony is that with the multiplier effect of the airlines on the economies they serve, other businesses in the travel industry chain ... make profits but not the airlines themselves. What is needed on the supply side for the industry as a whole, to achieve sustainable economic viability, is freedom from many man-made shackles. Freedom from government intervention against free market forces, whether by subsidies or bailouts of failed carriers, or by allowing bankrupt carriers unfair advantages under court protection. Freedom from out-of-date air services agreements between states which exchange restrictions and which prohibit trans-national consolidation and rationalisation that have benefited almost every other industry. Freedom to compete in markets which are under-served or which have good potential demand. It is illogical to keep the airlines outside of free trade agreements and of the WTO framework.'[8]

In terms of *economic* factors, the world economy is mature, but there is high growth in emerging economies. Even in the areas of high growth, however, where air travel demand is also growing fast, the profitability of the airline industry is weak or negative; the reasons will become clearer when we conduct a 5-forces industry analysis. As noted in Chapter 1, the price of oil, a key input for airlines, has been very volatile and on a steep upward trend since 1999, placing severe pressure on profitability. A positive aspect of the industry is the rising real incomes and higher levels of disposable income that can be used for air travel; but a related negative aspect is income polarisation, which precipitates the exclusion of the poorer parts of the population from the industry.

In terms of *social* factors, there is a higher level of multi-culturalism and demand for learning about and understanding new cultures, which fuels demand for air travel. At the same time, though, environmental concerns lead to severe criticism of the industry and its effects on CO_2 emissions. Even though the airline industry is estimated to account for around 2–4% of CO_2 emissions compared to power stations which account for about 20%, it receives a disproportionate amount of criticism and attention from activists. Another key negative influence has been the effect of terrorist activities, leading to a tightening up of aviation security procedures, making air travel more arduous and time-consuming than it should be.

Finally, in terms of *technological* factors, the impact of the Internet has been tremendous. One of its greatest effects is to offer transparency of options to passengers and to reduce search costs. Given that price is a key attribute of the purchase decision, combined with the transparency of information, these two factors lead to pricing pressure for airlines with a consequent reduction in yields. At the same time, however, effective use of the Internet for individual airlines is also an opportunity to improve the quality of their service and at the same time reduce costs (for example, in online ticket sales and Internet check-in). Other techno-logical advances include new plane designs which enable longer range travel, as well as higher capacity in terms of passenger numbers and efficiency in terms of fuel consumption, for example. In addition, bio-metric check-in, customer relationship management (CRM) software and traffic management technologies for airports enable activities to be under-taken more efficiently as well as allow airlines to relate with their cus-tomer base more effectively. Table 2.1 gives an outline of the PEST factors.

Table 2.1
Macro-environmental factors: PEST analysis

Political	Economic	Social	Technological
'Open skies' philosophy, entry deregulation	Mature world economy/ high growth in emerging economies	Higher multi-culturalism & air travel demand	Internet provides transparency/ enables higher efficiency & quality
Operational regulation (e.g., safety)	Oil price growth and volatility	Environmental concerns	New plane designs (longer range, higher capacity, higher efficiency)
Continued protectionism/ red tape in some markets	Rising real incomes/income polarisation	Terrorist/ security concerns	Biometric/ CRM/traffic management technologies

Analysing the Underlying Structure of the Airline Industry

If we proceed with a 5-forces analysis, we can get a clearer idea of the reasons leading to the weak performance of the airline industry. This framework was proposed by Michael Porter as a way to understand the underlying structural elements of industries that influence profitability,[9] and can also provide a way for individual companies to explore how they can mitigate the impact of these forces on their own businesses. The framework suggests that the higher the intensity of each force, the lower the potential for industry profitability. Figure 2.3 portrays the 5-forces framework.

The level of competitive *rivalry* in the airline industry is intense in most markets. It may be lower in markets that are protected because of entry regulations, or on routes where the level of demand is unattractive, but given the deregulation trends and the increasing demand, this situation is harder to find. Several factors inherent in the industry contribute to

Figure 2.3
The five forces that shape industry competition

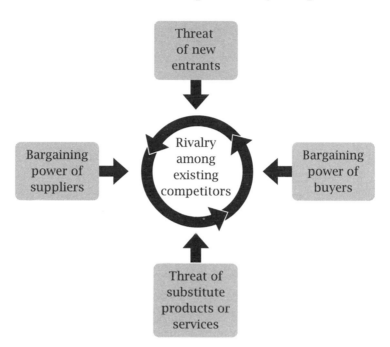

Source: Porter, M. (2008) The Five Competitive Forces that Shape Strategy, Harvard
Business Review, *January, pp. 2–17.*

the high intensity of rivalry. Firstly, it is a fragmented industry (in 2007
there were 984 airlines[10]), suffering from over-capacity, where around
a quarter of the seats on average are empty (see Figure 2.4). Given the
perishability of the product, over-capacity places severe pressure on
yields.

Secondly, this is an industry with high fixed costs and specialised
assets, especially where planes are owned rather than leased. This means
high sunk costs for airlines, which increase the costs of industry exit.
With high barriers to exit, firms tend to fight it out and over-capacity
persists, rather than leave the industry and return capacity to more
sustainable levels. Thirdly, it is difficult to differentiate the offering in
airlines, and in most cases, the offering is commoditised. When offerings

Figure 2.4
Passenger load factors in the airline industry

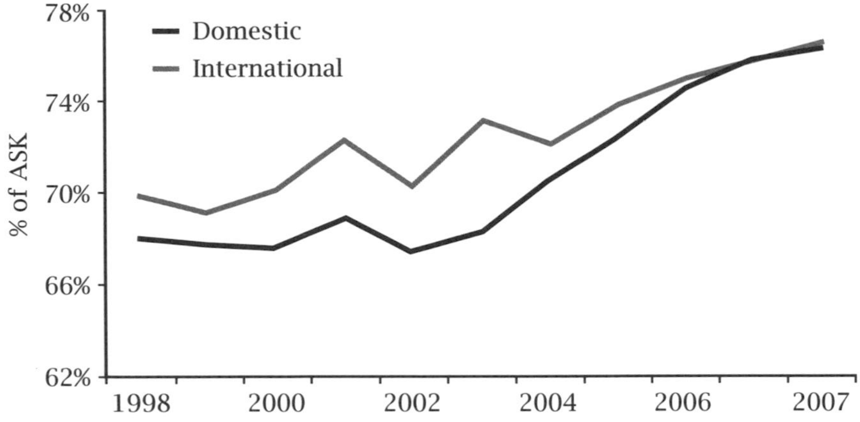

Source: IATA Annual Report 2008.

are commoditised, price becomes an important determinant of buying behaviour, encouraging airlines to compete on price rather than on an added value basis such as innovation. Budget carriers, which were first introduced in the US, then in Europe and more recently in Asia, exacerbate this trend.

Fourthly, there are low switching costs for customers. As long as a flight goes to the destination one wants to go, and offers the cheapest price, customers are usually happy to switch (unless they are business travellers, whose demand is less price-elastic, and the frequency of schedule is more important). Alliances such as the Star Alliance or Oneworld alliance introduce a low level of switching costs within the alliance for customers who care about collecting miles, but this is still not sufficient to create real and influential switching costs for most customers. Finally, the transparency of information afforded by the Internet, as discussed above, levels the playing field for customers in terms of information availability and the low cost of access to this information (in terms of both time and money), and shifts power to customers in terms of encouraging airlines to lower their prices to match competitors' prices. This raises the need for airlines to monitor competitive offerings and respond accordingly. All of these factors add up to an intense level of rivalry that does not bode well for industry profitability.

The *threat of new entrants* is moderate on a global level, but differs significantly depending on the specific market one is examining. For example, markets with high levels of growth incur a higher threat of new entrants, and mature markets such as the US and Europe incur a lower level of threat. Having said that, even a single new entrant can have significant impact on price and profitability levels in specific markets. Broadly speaking, however, deregulation trends, relatively easy access to most inputs (again depending on the specific inputs and specific markets one is examining), high growth in emerging markets and relatively low switching costs of customers from one airline to another means that it is possible for new entrants to come into the industry. Another way to express this is to say that there are no high barriers to entry in most markets, if the cash and regulatory licences are in place. The effect is that capacity closely matches demand, as Figure 2.5 shows.

Figure 2.5
Available seat kilometres vs revenue-passenger kilometres (capacity vs demand)

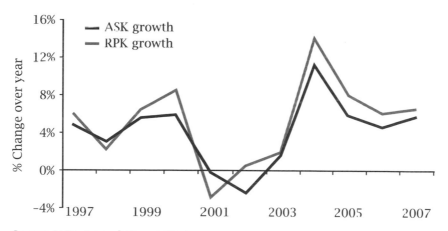

Source: IATA Annual Report 2008.

45

Buyer power is high, squeezing airlines for lower prices and higher quality. As outlined above, the Internet has afforded buyers high levels of transparency and the availability of information on competing choices. Even though customers have not formed formal groups to pressure airlines to reduce prices, the collective effect of individuals acting on similar decision making criteria is to place pressure on airlines to do just that. The fact that the airline product is commoditised and difficult to differentiate means that competition for most airlines tends to be on price and route availability rather than added value and innovation. The low switching costs for customers increase their power, since they are not tied to a single supplier but can shop around. Finally, the availability of substitutes (for example, train, ship and car) for most routes is limited, which reduces the power of buyers, but it is not enough to mitigate the impact of the other factors that increase buyer power.

The threat of substitutes is probably the only bright spot for the industry, out of the five forces. There is low propensity to substitute, given that for most routes the substitutes' cost/benefit ratio is weak compared with air travel. There is high switching cost to the alternatives, for example, the travel time involved. Information and communication technologies can substitute for some business travel, but they are an imperfect substitute since trust between parties is harder to develop unless there is direct interaction. Further, the desire to get to know other cultures and to be in other places reduces the plausibility of substitutes such as information and communication technologies (it is not the same to watch a jungle on television as to actually go to a safari). Therefore, the threat of substitutes is low, which is beneficial for the industry.

Finally, *the threat of suppliers* in terms of their ability to squeeze airlines for higher prices or a lower quality of supplied goods is medium to high, depending on which suppliers we examine. The main airports are a key supplier, which, given the level of excess demand and limited supply, have a high level of bargaining power to set prices for the services they provide. Pilot and crew unions have medium to high power for most airlines, because they are not easy to replace; if they go on strike, the effect on airlines' bottom line will be dramatic. Airplane makers (Boeing and Airbus) during this period have medium power. In addition to the fact that they are a duopoly, their order books are currently full so there is a waiting period of a few years for an airline before an order is fulfilled. An airline has high bargaining power against plane suppliers only if it is a launch customer for a new model, makes a relatively large order and has a positive reputation as a carrier. Other suppliers such as engineering or catering firms have low power if the services are outsourced, but if they are integrated within the airline, are unionised, or if there are no other immediate options for an airline, their bargaining power is higher. Finally, suppliers of oil, a key input, have high power, since the price is uncontrollable by airlines, and the input is essential to airline operations. Despite fuel efficiency of over 20% being achieved during the decade to 2006,[11] due to investment in new aircraft designs, the price of oil was responsible for the downward revision of the forecast of airline industry profitability by IATA. Whereas in March 2008 a profit of US$4.5 billion was forecasted, in June 2008 this was revised downwards to a loss of US$2.3 billion due to oil price increases. For every US$1 increase in the price of oil, the costs of the industry go up by $US1.6 billion.[12] On average, therefore, the bargaining power of suppliers is medium to high, reducing the potential for industry profitability.

The role of governments is not explicitly part of the 5 forces analysis, even though its effects can be seen through these forces. For example, governments have important regulatory roles in the industry that affect the bargaining power of suppliers such as airports, or the threat of new entrants through entry regulations. The bilateral system of negotiating new routes, however, is now seen as outdated by industry players. The Director General of IATA says, 'IATA is challenging governments around the world to deliver on their responsibilities – to ensure the highest levels of safety and security, to set a level playing field that encourages efficiency across the value chain and to deliver effective global policy on the global issue of climate change. After that, we are sending a message

– loud and clear – that governments must get out of the way and let us get on with business.'[13]

In summary, the only bright spot for the industry is the low threat of substitutes, which is not enough to mitigate the intensity of the other forces. The airline industry experiences intense rivalry and the high power of buyers. Several suppliers can squeeze airlines, and even though broadly speaking the threat of new entrants is medium, wherever there is potential, there will be new entrants, creating over-capacity and reducing yields (as has been the case in China and India). If we consider the 5-forces analysis and the PEST analysis conducted above, we get a clearer idea of why the industry has never covered its real cost of capital, and performs so poorly relative to other industries.

Even the legendary investor Warren Buffett lost money investing in airlines. When asked whether he still regarded USAir as his worst investment, he replied that 'the airline business ... has eaten up capital over the past century like almost no other business because people seem to keep coming back to it and putting fresh money in. You've got huge fixed costs, you've got strong labor unions and you've got commodity pricing. That is not a great recipe for success.'[14] Table 2.2 summarises the factors relevant to the five forces.

Table 2.2
Assessment of strength of the five forces and key elements relevant to each force

Competitive rivalry – High	Threat of new entrants – Medium	Buyer power – High	Threat of substitutes – Low	Supplier power – Medium/ High
Industry over-capacity	Deregulation trends	Information availability	Low propensity to substitute	Main airports: High power

Table 2.2 (continued)

Competitive rivalry – High	Threat of new entrants – Medium	Buyer power – High	Threat of substitutes – Low	Supplier power – Medium/ High
High fixed costs restrict exit	Relatively easy access to most inputs	Indirect buyer concentration	Substitutes' cost/benefit ratio weak	Pilots' and crew unions: Medium/High power
Commoditised offering (budget carriers)	High growth in emerging markets	Commoditised offering	High switching costs to most alternatives (e.g., travel time)	Airplane makers: Medium power
Low switching costs within industry	Low switching costs within industry	Low switching costs within industry	ICTs can substitute for some business travel	Oil suppliers: High power
Information availability	Low absolute cost advantages	Substitutes limited	Multi-culturalism reduces attractiveness of substitutes	Engineering, catering: Low unless integrated

The main challenges of the industry, identified in the analysis above and in Chapter 1, are reflected in the resolution passed at IATA's June 2008 annual meeting.[15]

Istanbul Resolution

The leaders of the world's airlines met in Istanbul on 2–3 June 2008.

They were pleased to report a new record level of safety performance.

They were proud to announce the full roll-out of electronic ticketing.

Airlines achieved modest profits for the first time since September 11.

Yet this was no time for celebration.

Record oil prices are now driving airlines into uncharted territory. At the fuel prices currently predicted by the forward price curve, IATA airlines could face an additional financial burden of USD99 billion over the next 12 months compared to 2007. A total of 24 airlines have ceased operations or entered into bankruptcy protection in the last five months. Many more will not survive.

Over the last six years, airlines have cut non-fuel unit costs by 18% and distribution costs by 25%; they have also improved fuel efficiency by 19% and there has also been a notable increase in labour productivity.

All these efforts are meaningless in the face of a tripling of oil prices since 2006, with a two-fold increase in the last year alone.

There is limited scope for airlines to lower their costs further. A concerted effort is now required.

This is not simply an airline crisis. Airlines are an engine for global prosperity and failure among them would send shockwaves throughout the world economy.

Extraordinary times call for extraordinary measures.

The CEOs of the world's airlines therefore call on governments and the entire industry value chain to show leadership and responsibility in this time of crisis.

- Governments must eliminate archaic rules that prevent airlines from restructuring across borders.

- In view of existing fees and charges, governments must refrain from imposing multiple and additional punitive taxes and other measures that will only deepen the crisis.

- State service providers must invest to modernise air transport infrastructure urgently, eliminating wasteful fuel consumption and emissions.

- Business partners, in particular monopoly service providers, must become as efficient as airlines are now. If not, regulators must restrain their appetite with tougher regulation.

- Labour unions must refrain from making irresponsible claims and join the effort to secure jobs in aviation and indeed in other industries.

- In the interest of the global economy and the flying public, we urge authorities to enforce the integrity of markets so that the cost of energy reflects its true value.

Given the structural unattractiveness of the airline industry and its dismal financial performance, it is an interesting question why fresh capital keeps flowing into it. One reason could be that traditionally, before deregulation and privatisation trends, most carriers were supported by the state, by taxpayers' money, and taxpayers have no immediate control over how the government spends their money. Inefficient carriers were propped up and shielded from market discipline. A related reason would be the cognitive bias of hubris, or over-confidence in one's abilities as an investor or manager. Hubris says 'where most others have failed, I will succeed', encouraging investments in questionable ventures and debatable strategic actions. A further reason could be due to emotional factors; the airline industry is an exciting, glamorous industry to be involved in, and this can mar rational evaluation of investment returns, or their likelihood. Further, demand in some emerging markets is growing so fast that investors find it hard to believe that their investments can perform badly in light of this fast growth, which is perfectly possible given that capacity expansion more than meets demand in those markets. Finally, the fact is that some airlines, such as SIA, Southwest or Ryanair, have been consistently profitable, which means that an investment in the airline industry does not have to be dismal if the right choices are made. All the above factors taken together can go some way towards explaining why fresh capital keeps flowing into an industry with dismal financial performance.

Strategic Imperatives

To flourish in an extremely difficult environment, airlines need clearly articulated and efficiently executed strategies. There are many variants of strategies that might lead to good performance, and we identify some key considerations and dimensions underlying successful strategies in the industry in the following section.

Dealing with the Five Forces: The Role of the Strategist

The role of the strategist, in any analysis, is to ask the 'so what' question. They have to ask: 'what are the implications of the analysis for my own company?' Specifically, an airline strategist would need to consider what the company should do to mitigate the impact of the forces on the company. Taking the 5-forces analysis above as an example, there is a real need to occupy a competitive position that mitigates the high levels of rivalry prompted by over-capacity, commoditisation and price competition. There is a need to discourage new entrants (often this is done by drowning the industry in over-capacity, leading to the incumbents suffering from this as well as any new entrants), to control the power of buyers and to reduce supplier power (often this is done by vertical integration, creating inflexibility in the corporate structure and strategic options of the buyer).

Creating differentiation through continuous innovation and service excellence is probably one of the best ways to address the forces of intense rivalry and high buyer power. It also helps to discourage new entrants (even though it probably would not stop them) and grants higher negotiating power to the differentiated company when dealing with most suppliers. With regard to rivalry, achieving a truly differentiated position allows the company to pull out of the commoditisation hole, and the option to not have to match every price reduction that the competitors offer. A truly differentiated company commands a price premium, which allows it to remain profitable in difficult conditions, and to have enough funds to invest in further innovation and service excellence initiatives. Further, with regard to buyer power, the most effective way to escape commoditisation is to be positioned in the mind of the buyer as a high quality option that deserves paying a bit extra for. While buyer power will not go away, it can be somewhat mitigated or controlled in this manner.

Five-star airlines, including SIA, have followed this route to success. Key considerations in such a strategy include people development in a way that aligns their competencies and mindset with the strategy of service excellence, as well as innovation that continually creates a gap between the differentiated company and would-be imitators. We will expand on these elements with regard to SIA in subsequent chapters. What is extraordinary, however, is that SIA has managed to offer a truly differentiated product at a level of cost (in terms of cents per available seat kilometre) that borders on that of the budget sector, something that conventional strategy theory as proposed by Michael Porter does not deem possible. We will expand on this in subsequent chapters.

The other route is to be a truly low cost airline, so that even when low yields hurt most of the competitors, you can still survive. Most low cost airlines make losses, just as traditional airlines do. Being the lowest cost (or near the lowest cost) competitor requires high levels of alignment and discipline, and only a handful of airlines such as Ryanair or Southwest have achieved this. Low cost airlines, instead of trying to mitigate intense rivalry by adopting a differentiated position, do so by being able to withstand the yield pressures of this rivalry. Instead of attempting to mitigate buyer power by convincing the buyer that their service is worth paying a bit more for, they entice the buyer by offering a deal that cannot be refused by price-sensitive customers. They mitigate supplier power by outsourcing as much as possible, and simplifying their corporate structure to be as lean as possible. They attempt to discourage new entrants by honing their efficiency capabilities and by adopting highly aggressive pricing (and perhaps increasing route frequency) whenever a threat of entry materialises.

These routes to success are not easy; both require high levels of discipline, management capability and strategic alignment. Below we expand on the strategic imperatives for success in the airline industry. The discussion will go into more depth in the subsequent chapters, with specific reference to SIA's competitive success.

In addition to clarity on the business strategies of airlines, some other factors are also essential, as outlined below.

Cutting-Edge Technology

Deployment of cutting-edge technology remains one of the key imperatives for airlines – especially since new technology, such as new plane designs, offers the potential to improve productivity and reduce costs, thus mitigating the negative impact of falling yields. Successive generations of aircraft have brought about a dramatic increase in the number of seats and the flying range (for example, the A380 offers 35% more seats than the Boeing 747-400). The latest aircraft also helps airlines to overcome infrastructural constraints such as overloaded air traffic control systems (for example, by using long-range aircraft to eliminate stopovers) and airport congestion (by using aircraft with higher capacity for destinations where landing slots cannot be increased), and can increase differentiation by offering a higher level of inflight facilities.

Though it often leads to improved productivity, the purchase of new planes also implies significantly greater capital expenditures, with the price of a single large aircraft being between US$150 and US$250 million. When these expenditures are financed with debt, they increase the company's risk levels given the cyclical nature of the industry and the numerous uncontrollable factors impacting its fortunes. Having a strong balance sheet is a key advantage in adopting cutting-edge technology since it reduces the need for taking on debt in a cyclical and unpredictable industry. Even for airlines that mostly lease rather than buy planes, a strong balance sheet is useful for tiding over the troughs of the business cycle.

The employment of technology can go well beyond acquiring new planes and can help airlines reduce costs as well as improve service quality. For example, the deployment of e-business technology can reduce maintenance costs by providing better information to technicians and lowering material costs such as inventories.[16] Air Canada Technical Service, for instance, achieved a 22% reduction in turnaround times and a 28% increase in labour productivity by using an enterprise resource planning software.[17] Further, selling tickets through the Internet can help save on travel agent commissions and lead to better yield management. In some parts of the world, where agent-based distribution is still prevalent, encouraging Internet sales can lead to substantial improvement in yields. According to one estimate, online sales can reduce distribution costs, which used to amount to 15–25% of total costs in the pre-Internet days, by as much as 50%.[18] Further, technology such as radio frequency identification (RFID) luggage tags and biometric scanning could improve the efficiency and accuracy of several aspects of airline operations such as check-in, boarding and baggage tracking. Finally, technology deployment can also improve service levels (for example, state-of-the-art inflight entertainment), resulting in improved metrics such as customer loyalty, improved load factors and enhanced revenue potential.

Cost Control

Given the difficult economics of the airline industry, cost control is one of the key strategic priorities for airlines. As noted in Chapter 1, however, many elements of airline costs such as fuel prices and airport charges are uncontrollable. Hence, airlines have often focused on labour cost savings to improve results, especially in lean times. Many airline managers, however, have erroneously emphasised wage levels as the sole determinants of labour costs, while forgetting that productivity is the other important element in the equation. Poor productivity can translate even low wages into high labour costs. For instance, many state-owned airlines from developing countries, despite having low wage costs, have high labour costs (as a proportion of total costs) due to the issues of over-staffing, which itself may be attributed to unions and government intervention.[19]

Within the developed country context, adversarial labour management relations have undermined the competitive position of the once-dominant American Airlines. According to an American judge, 'if you would look up bad labor relations in the dictionary, you would have an American Airlines logo beside it.'[20] In May 1994, conflicts between the unions and management meant that American Airlines had to stop selling tickets on 20% of its flights and cancel another 40% on the system. Losses came to $10 million per day for five days and President Clinton intervened to resolve the issue.[21]

On the other hand, high labour productivity can lead to significant benefits for an airline. There can be large variations in productivity across airlines even if they are based in the same country. Productivity and overall performance of the airline are positively correlated. Striving to improve productivity, rather than wage levels, makes sense because wage levels are significantly influenced by the context in which the airline is operating including local laws relating to employee benefits or unions, the level of unionisation and the cost of living, and are hence less controllable.

In the US, Southwest Airlines, famous for treating its employees well, outperforms its rivals in terms of a variety of productivity metrics. Southwest needs only 80 workers to fly and support each aircraft, compared with 115 or more on a conventional network carrier. For operating an identical aircraft model (Boeing 737-3000), Southwest's direct operating costs per seat mile are 36–44% lower than network carriers such as Delta and United. The average number of hours flown by a Southwest pilot is 62 versus 36 for United; and output per employee is 20% higher at Southwest than United though Southwest operates smaller capacity aircraft and flies shorter distances.[22]

Managing Alliances

Alliances generate varied reactions from industry executives partly due to the different degrees of success enjoyed, and because relative to acquisitions, they afford less management control. SIA, for example, would have preferred the barriers to consolidation in the industry to be relaxed, so that it could pursue a strategy of growth via taking strategic stakes in other companies.[23] CEO Chew Choon Seng notes, 'Our domestic base in Singapore is confined by geographical limits ... to continue growing at a rate that exceeds what would be organic growth ... we do have to venture, to take positions in companies elsewhere. We do see that as the way to continue forward.'[24] In this light, he regards alliances as 'a substitute – a surrogate for true business combinations'. He adds, 'So if you accept that Star is a halfway house, it's as good as it gets and you just want it to get better and see where else we can do more together.'

In the context of a highly constrained industry, in terms of acquisitions and developing new routes organically, alliances can serve useful purposes. Alliances can offer global connectivity to passengers who increasingly demand it. Further, in an industry where lean cost structures are essential to survival, airlines can ill afford to keep performing activities where they lack economies of scale, or do not have the best-in-class skills, and must cede these activities to alliance partners. Alliances may be particularly useful in lean times when schedule coordination, providing reciprocal services (such as maintenance or check-in services) and economies of scale through pooled purchasing is vital.

An advantage of alliances is that they have fewer hidden costs than mergers and hence would be important even in a world where there are no regulatory barriers. Mergers, for instance, lead to fleet diversity, which can raise a variety of costs such as maintenance, repair and crew salaries. If mergers are financed through debt, they lead to increased risk. Even if further dismantling of regulatory barriers makes mergers and acquisitions possible, alliances will remain an important strategic option for airlines. Airline managers might do well to take alliance instability as a given (after all, low entry and exit costs are two key benefits of alliances) and work towards developing their 'alliance competence'. Alliances that have obtained the best results have typically brought together partners with complementary capabilities and compatible cultures as well as service levels.

Avoiding the Herd Instinct

The cyclical nature of the airline industry renders executives vulnerable to making decisions regarding such issues as aircraft acquisitions and wages, which even though seemingly appropriate at the time might come back to haunt them later. In the second half of the 1980s, for example, based on optimistic projections regarding traffic growth, airline executives went on an aircraft acquisition spree which led to 7,000 aircraft being on order for delivery between 1990 and 2001, representing a financial commitment of US$400 billion.[25] When the traffic growth did not materialise as expected due to recession and the Gulf War, many planes were put up for sale.[26] Interestingly, many of these were acquired at bargain prices by new entrants (budget carriers) who would later on compete vigorously with the traditional carriers. The excess capacity in the industry also led to some destructive price wars (such as those in the US in 1992).

Several industry executives also have similar opinions about the decision-making process in the airlines. Michael Levine, executive vice president of Northwest Airlines, said in 1996, 'I think historically, the airline business has not been run as a real business. That is, a business designed to achieve a return on capital that is then passed on to shareholders. It has historically been run as an extremely elaborate version of a model railroad, that is, one in which you try to make enough money to buy more equipment.' According to Sir Freddie Laker, founder of the now-defunct Laker Airways, 'none of them (the traditional airlines) seem to have the idea that perhaps they had too many aeroplanes, perhaps they were spending too much money on aeroplanes and not enough getting the aeroplanes in the air for the right number of hours.'[27]

As noted earlier, aircraft acquisition decisions need to be based on exceptionally long time horizons. They cannot simply be based on the current state of the economy (or a projection that it will continue, uninterrupted into the future) and the industry. The decisions must make economic sense not only under rosy scenarios, but also in a less favourable political and economic environment.

Avoiding Commoditisation

To overcome the commoditisation of its service and gain customer loyalty, American Airlines launched the first frequent flyer programme (FFP) in 1981, with the other airlines following suit. Many airlines, however, were overly generous in granting FFP points and built up massive contingent liabilities (FFP points that may be exchanged for free travel) in the process. To do damage control, they implemented complex restrictions on the FFP award travel, alienating customers in the process. It may be an opportune time for such airlines to re-examine their FFPs and adopt a sensible strategy where they reward customer loyalty, yet do it in a fashion that does not undermine profitability or alienate customers. Interestingly, a survey found that FFPs were the least important driver of customer satisfaction, behind factors such as airport check-in, flight availability and scheduling and flight attendants.[28] The FFP policies of many successful carriers are noteworthy in this respect. SIA and Qantas do not award FFP points for deeply discounted fares and thus eliminate one of the key sources of inequity (same mileage credit without regard to the fare paid) in many FFPs. Southwest has made its FFP valuable by placing no limits on available seats to the FFP members – if a seat is available on a particular flight, it can be obtained in exchange for FFP points.

Budget carriers, such as Ryanair, have introduced innovative strategies to entice the price-sensitive customers by unbundling the various aspects of airline service. Its ticket price, for instance, does not include the conveniences taken for granted in a conventional airline, such as checked-in baggage. The extra money charged for ancillary services can be an important source of revenue; in Ryanair's case, 16% of revenues in 2007 were from ancillary services, and the percentage is still growing. The highest category of ancillary service revenues was the 'non-flight scheduled' category, relating to the sale of tickets such as checked-in baggage, bus and rail tickets, and hotel reservations; followed by the 'inflight' category of sales of food, drink and merchandise.

END NOTES

1. Speech by the Director General of IATA, Giovanni Bisignani, at the IATA Annual Meeting on 2 June 2008.
2. See the ICAO figures cited in Chapter 1.
3. For the 2007 figures, see http://money.cnn.com/magazines/fortune/global500/2007/
4. Porter, M. E. (2008) The Five Competitive Forces that Shape Strategy. *Harvard Business Review*, January, pp. 2–17.
5. *Economist*, 2 October 2003, Open Skies and Flights of Fancy.
6. CRS stands for Central Reservation Systems.
7. See Doganis, R. (2006) *The Airline Business*, Chapters 2–3.

8. Chew Choon Seng, letter to *Airline Business*, dated 13 October 2005, in November 2005 issue.

9. Porter, M. E. (2008) The Five Competitive Forces that Shape Strategy. *Harvard Business Review*, January, pp. 2–17.

10. IATA Economic Briefing; World Air Transport Statistics 51st edition, June 2007.

11. IATA Economic Briefing; World Air Transport Statistics 51st edition, June 2007.

12. IATA press release, Crisis Again: Deep Losses Projected, 2 June 2008, http://www.iata.org/pressroom/pr/2008-06-02-01.htm

13. IATA Annual Report, 2008, Director General's message, p. 9.

14. *The Age*, 24 September 2002, The Sage of Omaha's Trans-Atlantic Game, http://www.theage.com.au/articles/2002/09/23/1032734111833.html

15. http://www.iata.org/events/agm/2008/istanbul_resolution.htm

16. Taneja (2002) op. cit.

17. *Air Transport World*, January 2004, Airlines Are Adopting Complex Software Solutions to Streamline Their Maintenance Departments, 41(1), p. 54.

18. Taneja (2003) see op. cit.

19. Job preservation may be a condition imposed by the government for shoring up the airline.

20. US district judge Joe Kendall issuing a restraining order against an American Airlines APA pilots' union sickout, 10 February 1999.

21. Ott and Neidl (1995) p. 37, see op. cit.

22. Taneja (2003) see op. cit.

23. If barriers to consolidation were lifted, the effects on industry structure would be positive, since the less efficient competitors would be acquired and capacity would be rationalised.

24. *Airline Business*, February 2004, Chew Choon Seng: Into the Spotlight.

25. Doganis 1991, see op. cit.

26. The number of aircraft available for sale or lease peaked at 854 in mid-1991 and remained at approximately 700 through 1993 (Ott and Neidl, 1995, p. 17).

27. That Was Then and This Is Now: Sir Freddie Laker, http://news.bbc.co.uk/1/hi/uk/2283244.stm, accessed on 27 December 2004.

28. Taneja (2002) op. cit.

3

KEY DRIVERS OF SIA'S PERFORMANCE: A STRATEGIC CHOICE AND RESOURCE DEPLOYMENT PERSPECTIVE

'For those of us who had started our careers in the then Malaysia-SIA, our initial forays into markets like Hong Kong, Japan, Australia, Europe and the UK had proved that there was strong demand for an international airline that operated to the highest standards of safety and reliability, with aircraft of the latest design and technology, and a clear focus on meeting the customers' wants and needs with our special fusion of Asian hospitality and multinational sophistication. These became the cornerstones for SIA ... these principles and the attainment of a consistently high level of delivery, which led to powerful word-of-mouth propagation, created and established the brand which positioned SIA as a, if not the, leading premium service airline in the world.'

Chew Choon Seng, CEO of Singapore Airlines[1]

This chapter focuses on the contribution of key strategic choices and resource deployment decisions towards explaining Singapore Airlines' (SIA's) superior performance. We focus on eight broad factors, which we believe to be the most salient. These include brand reputation and effective differentiation; a young aircraft fleet offering efficiency and quality advantages; low staff costs and high productivity; early exposure to competition fostering the development of core competencies; a global revenue base helping to reduce risk;

forward-looking response to crises; alliance and acquisition strategies; and service excellence through innovation and strategic human resource management. Besides having a significant stand-alone impact on SIA's performance, some of these factors also interact with other factors, thus enhancing the magnitude of their impact (see Figure 3.1). In the following sections, we identify how each of the above factors enhances SIA's performance. Given the importance of the factors of strategic human resource management, innovation and core competencies of cost-effective service excellence, we have devoted full chapters to each of these themes (Chapters 4 to 6).

Figure 3.1
Factors leading to SIA's superior performance

Brand Reputation

SIA is among the few airlines that have a strong positive brand reputation. According to Skytrax, only six airlines achieve a five-star rating in terms of customer service and product quality: SIA, Cathay Pacific Airways, Malaysian Airlines, Qatar Airways, Asiana Airlines and Kingfisher Airlines.[2] SIA was ranked 17th in *Fortune* magazine's list of most admired companies in 2007,[3] the only airline to make it in the top 50. The company also consistently receives prestigious industry awards. It has been voted the world's best international airline by *Travel + Leisure* magazine for the last 11 years; the world's best international route airline by *Conde Nast* magazine for the 18th time in the last 19 years; the best airline by *Business Traveller* Asia Pacific for the last 15 years and received the Readers' Digest Trusted Brands Platinum Award (Airline Category) for the seventh consecutive year.[4] A recent study placed the value of the SIA brand at S$354.7 million, the eighth highest among Singapore companies.[5]

The effectively differentiated SIA brand is a result of conscious decisions and strategies implemented over a long period of time. According to Dr Cheong Choong Kong, former CEO of SIA, 'the Singapore Girl was conceived, a personification of oriental charm and friendliness, which the airline made real through careful recruitment and painstaking training. Effective and original advertising, together with word of mouth praises from satisfied passengers, would create an aura of superior service and style. The aura, once established, had to be sustained through constant training, clever advertising and ingenuity in the cabin.'[6]

Several other aspects of SIA's branding strategy are remarkable. SIA adopts a global approach to advertising by using the same advertisements (containing the same message, except for language changes) in international media, as well as in overseas markets. Further, the broad themes of SIA's brand positioning (the Singapore Girl, a great way to fly and latest fleet) have also been consistently emphasised since its inception. Many other airlines, on the other hand, have changed their advertising theme every few years, thus creating an inconsistency of message and potentially confusing the customer.[7]

Finally, SIA's advertising investments are relatively heavy, and are maintained during industry downturns. During the first 21 years of its existence, SIA invested as much as S$750 million in advertising (at an average of S$35 million per year).[8] Currently the SIA advertising account is said to be worth around S$50 million annually.[9] Finally, SIA's product-related partnerships are with well-known brands; for example, on-board furnishings, chinaware and glassware are designed by Givenchy, and toiletries by Salvatore Ferragamo and L'Occitane.[10]

SIA's brand building efforts witnessed tremendous success in the first few years after it launched its advertising campaign, leading to a first mover advantage. In 1973, the year the campaign was launched, the recall rate of the advertisement was 21%; by 1997, it had jumped to 50%.[11] Since SIA was a pioneer in the industry in terms of brand building, later adopters of even a similar strategy would have found it difficult to overcome SIA's established reputation. SIA's success in branding was acknowledged by Madame Tussaud's wax museum when the Singapore Girl became the only commercial figure in the world-famous museum in June 1993. The museum described the Singapore Girl as 'one of the world's most instantly recognizable faces',[12] a 'global icon'.[13] According to the *New York Times*, 'seductively prim in her snug *sarong* and sandaled feet, she has been the epitome of airborne Asian hospitality for 27 years, an object of feminist ire and a primary reason her employer has vaulted to the forefront of the global aviation industry.'[14]

In January 2007, SIA invited bids for its advertising account, which had been held by Batey Ads, the creator of the Singapore Girl image since 1972. This led to heated debate in the press as to whether SIA should change or revamp the Singapore Girl image. The weight of opinion suggested that it would be harmful to remove or significantly alter an image that affords the airline effective differentiation, and that had been painstakingly built over the previous three-and-a-half decades. Although there was some criticism over the years that the image was 'sexist and subservient',[15] former SIA flight crew members commented that they felt proud to wear the trademark *sarong kebaya* uniform and to represent both SIA as well as Singapore to the world.[16] In March 2007,

SIA reassured the public that the Singapore Girl icon would remain, even if there were new ideas injected into the advertising.[17]

Young Aircraft Fleet

Maintaining a young fleet has been a core element of SIA's strategy since its inception. In the 1980s, it was able to maintain its fleet age at around 30 months. Over the past 15 years, though SIA's average fleet age has fluctuated between 58 and 77 months (see Figure 3.2), it remains less than half of the industry average, with various estimates at 158 months[18] or 177 months.[18,19] Despite a gentle upward slope in the average age of the fleet since 2003-2004, it is remarkable that SIA has been able to maintain a relatively young fleet in the face of difficult economic times such as the Asian economic crisis and the industry downturn following the September 11 terrorist attacks, when profits and cash flow were elusive for most other airlines, as well as the hike in oil prices from 2007 onwards. In 2008 SIA had a fleet of 98 planes (90 Boeing and eight

Figure 3.2
Size and age of SIA's fleet

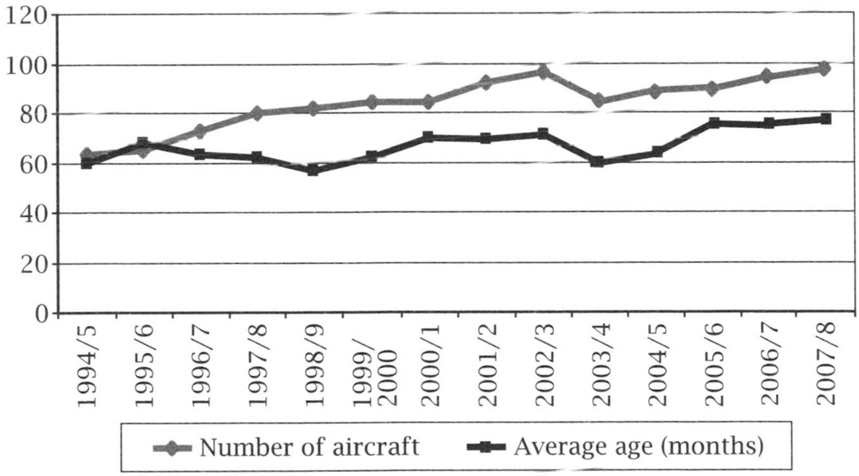

Source: Singapore Airlines Annual Reports.

Airbus) with an average age of 77 months. Seventy-six aircraft were owned and 22 were on operating lease (including three A380s). There were 80 planes on firm order, and 59 on option. Of the 80 planes on order, 55 were Airbus, including 16 A380s.

SIA derives several visible and apparent benefits from maintaining a young fleet. New aircraft, based on the latest technology, are more fuel efficient. Lower fuel costs help SIA outperform its rivals on a relative basis, especially during periods characterised by high oil prices. Further, young aircraft typically cost less to maintain and need only scheduled maintenance which can be carried out at the home base by SIA's own technicians. The superior reliability of SIA's fleet also means that it seldom needs to call in outside agencies to address technical problems in foreign locations, which can be an expensive proposition. Third, due to fewer breakdowns, SIA avoids the additional costs (such as meal vouchers, marketing inducements such as frequent flyer miles and sometimes overnight hotel stays for passengers) due to delayed flights or missed connections. Fourth, higher reliability of SIA's fleet also means better on-time performance, an important criterion for business travellers, which enhances SIA's differentiation. Finally, according to former CEO and chairman Dr Cheong Choong Kong, 'another benefit derived from newer, modern aircraft is enhanced passenger appeal, which is hard to quantify.'[20]

Many high profile aircraft acquisition orders help SIA to keep its fleet young. Even in its early days, SIA announced the largest aircraft acquisition orders in the history of the industry – including one for US$1 billion in 1978 and two orders, each amounting to US$1.4 billion, in 1981 and 1983. About ten years later (1994 and 1995), two more large orders were announced which would determine the structure of SIA's fleet over the next decade. During 2006–2007, SIA placed orders for 49 new aircraft (including nine A380s that took its total order of this aircraft type to 19) with both Airbus and Boeing, worth US$12 billion in terms of manufacturers' list prices.[21] SIA's fleet acquisition is aimed at meeting long-term demand projections and, typically, does not fluctuate in response to short-term issues. Former CEO and chairman J. Y. Pillay says, 'Short- and medium-term problems cannot blind us to the needs of the future. We have to ensure that when demand resumes its growth we shall be in a position to meet it.'[22]

While explaining the timing of aircraft acquisition orders, Dr Cheong Choong Kong says, 'A very important factor that cannot be overlooked is the timing of the order. The last big order was made in 1983, under recessionary conditions for airlines and airlines manufacturers. Orders for equipment were few and far between, and manufacturers were generous with concessions to get their production lines moving. Both Boeing and Airbus were eager to establish a foothold in Asia for their new aircraft – the B757 and the A310 respectively.'[23]

When examining SIA's fleet acquisition policy, we can see virtuous circles in operation, where consistently high profitability and positive cash flow from operations are key facilitating factors for SIA's aircraft acquisitions. These acquisitions, in turn, facilitate the achievement of high efficiency and the creation of differentiation through operating one of the youngest fleets of all major airlines (complemented by other factors such as innovation, service excellence and people development, which we will discuss in subsequent chapters).

Low Staff Costs and High Productivity

Some industry observers attribute the success of Asian airlines, such as SIA, to the fact that these airlines pay lower salaries to their employees than airlines in Western countries. It is also often argued that the higher wage costs of many Western country airlines are due to local labour laws, and, hence, outside their control. Conversely, the institutional environment of many Asian carriers (or airlines based in developing countries, in general) may not have as strict labour laws as in other environments such as the EU or the US (for example, regarding the level and costs of employee benefits including health insurance and annual leave) and hence offer a cost advantage.

However, wage costs constitute only one side of the equation; the other side is productivity. SIA's top managers have drawn attention to the role of the superior productivity of SIA's employees as a determinant of SIA's competitive advantage. SIA's former chairman Dr Cheong Choong Kong said in 1985, 'The fact is that SIA's staff costs are not low. It is true that in proportion to total operating costs, SIA's staff costs are a low 21%, compared to around 30% for most Western airlines, but this is attributable to higher productivity (staff costs here include the cost of the staff in the airport handling and engine maintenance subsidiaries, for proper comparison with other airlines) ... If SIA were to have the same productivity as British Airways, its staff numbers would have to rise and its staff costs as a percentage of total operating costs would be over 26% in 1983–1984. This percentage would rise further to 29% with SAS' productivity and 34.6% with Swissair's.'[24] In 2007–2008, SIA's staff costs were 16.6% of total costs.[25] Figure 3.3 shows the comparative figures of selected airlines.

Analysis by industry experts supports SIA's position with regard to the importance of labour productivity. Doganis' (2006) analysis, for example, showed that Asian carriers generally had higher output in terms of available tonne-km per US$1,000 of labour costs (see Figure 3.4).[27]

Figure 3.3
Labour costs as a percentage of total operating costs

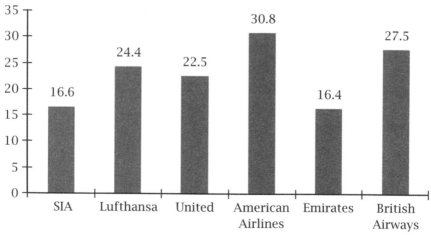

Source: *Annual Reports of the respective airlines.*[26]

Doganis' analysis also shows that there are significant variations in productivity across Asian carriers, with SIA having the second highest productivity after Korean Airlines.

There are several drivers of high employee productivity at SIA. Firstly, large investments in state-of-the-art equipment and training, as well as a culture of continuous improvement and cost consciousness, enhance employee productivity. Secondly, since 2000, the company has been granting stock options to employees at all levels. Due to its consistently

Figure 3.4
Differences in airline labour productivity

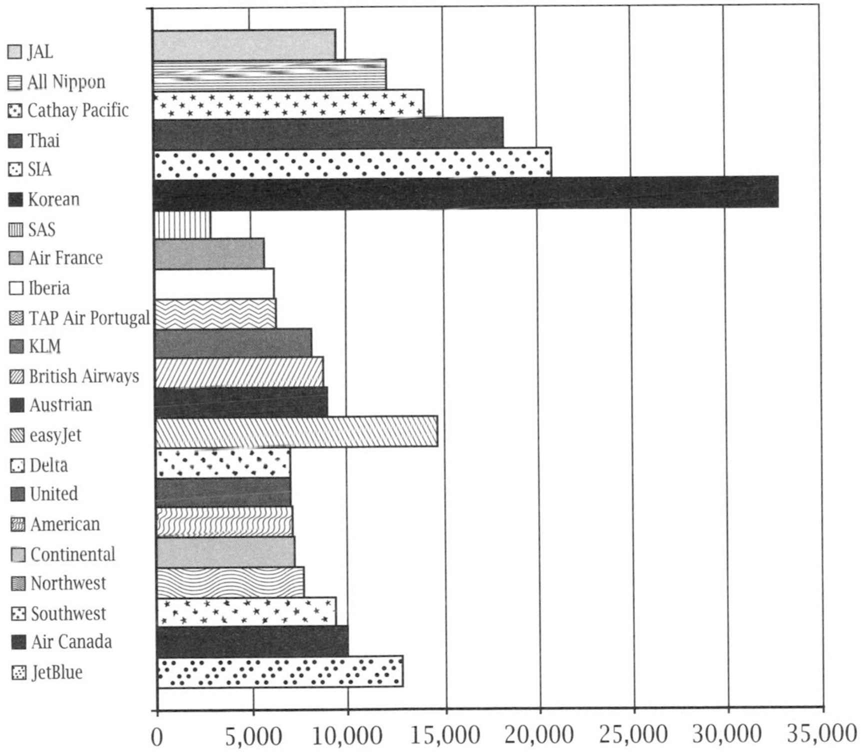

Source: Doganis, R. (2006) The Airline Business, 2nd edition, Routledge, p. 129. Figures are for 2002, and refer to available tonne-km per US$1,000 of labour cost.

71

Figure 3.5
Group staff strength and productivity

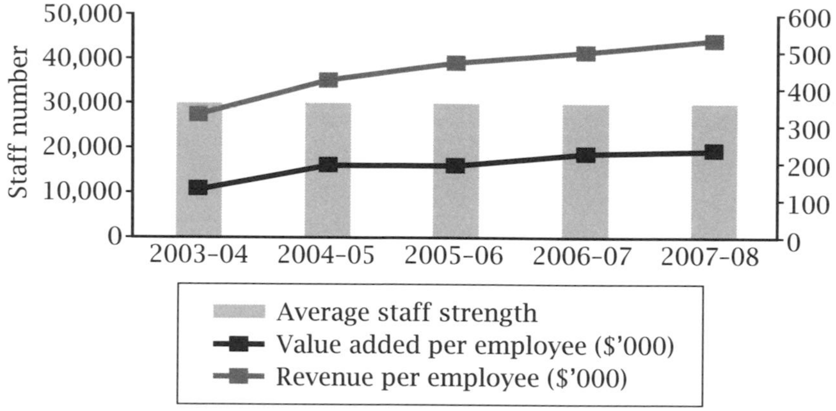

Source: Singapore Airlines Annual Report, 2007-2008.

superior financial performance related to its industry, these options are likely to be perceived as valuable by employees and hence act as a motivating factor.[28] Finally, staff turnover in SIA is relatively low. In 1996, Dr Cheong Choong Kong observed that 19% of SIA's employees had been with the company for more than 20 years.[29] As Figure 3.5 shows, the value added per employee and revenue per employee at SIA have been on a generally upward slope.

Early Exposure to Competition

In the highly regulated airline industry where decisions about forming airline companies and supporting them through the regulation of flight frequencies as well as direct subsidies are often driven more by national pride and hubris rather than economic soundness, SIA remains a notable exception. While SIA remains majority-owned by the government (through Temasek Holdings, which owns 55% of the airline[30]) to this day, there has been surprisingly little government intervention in SIA's operations. In 1993, Michael Tan, former deputy managing director (Commercial) and vice president (Marketing) for SIA, noted that 'right from the beginning, the Singapore government made it clear that we were to operate profitably or not at all. Singapore could not afford a national carrier for the sake of pride alone ... Singapore's skies were opened and foreign carriers welcomed. This policy has benefited Singapore, travellers and shippers, and established Changi as a key international and regional aviation hub, today served by 59 airlines to 109 cities. But it also meant that SIA had to compete at the outset as a commercial entity. Although the government is the majority shareholder and the Board is nominated by them [sic], it plays no direct role in running the company.'[31]

The lack of government protection and absence of subsidies turned out to be a blessing in disguise. Forced to compete with bigger and well-established airlines from other parts of the world, SIA developed one of the most efficient cost structures among all airlines, even as it aimed for industry-leading quality. Despite the low yields due to the stiff competition, SIA was able to be financially successful because its costs were even lower.[32] The substantial difference between yields and unit costs means that SIA generates significant positive cash flows, which are used to fund aircraft acquisition and product innovations, while avoiding debt financing which adds to the risk due to the cyclical nature of the industry (see Figure 3.6). The healthy cash flows can

Figure 3.6
Cash flow generation and capital expenditures by SIA

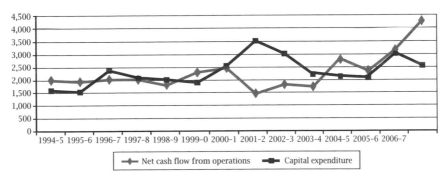

Source: Singapore Airlines Annual Reports. Figures refer to the SIA group and are in S$ millions.

also be used to time aircraft purchases during industry downturns (resulting in price discounts) as well as to fund the brand-building and service enhancement (such as improvement in inflight services) campaigns.

In sum, early exposure to competition encouraged SIA to invest, develop and refine core competencies of cost-effective service excellence, which support its strategy and, in combination with other factors, lead to sustainable competitive advantage (cost-effective service excellence at SIA will be further discussed in Chapter 4).

Global Revenue Base

Global presence in terms of its route network is another key strength for SIA, because it aids the geographic diversification of revenue and reduces economic risk. The company takes pride in the fact that it is not dependent on any one geographic region for its revenues. Even when the Asian region was growing much faster than the rest of the world (from the late 1980s till the Asian crisis in 1997, and subsequently after the economic recovery), SIA did not make the mistake of neglecting the rest of the world and former CEO and chairman J. Y. Pillay was able to assert that 'no country or route accounts for more than 15% of [SIA's] revenue.'[33] In 1991, the *Far Eastern Economic Review* noted that SIA earned twice as much outside Asia than Cathay Pacific, itself a high profile global airline.[34] Figure 3.7 shows the global distribution of SIA's revenues in 2002–2003 and 2007–2008, illustrating a well-balanced overall revenue composition with the prevalence of revenues from East Asia reducing slightly over the five-year period.

The benefits of a globally diversified revenue base are twofold. First, adverse economic conditions which might affect traffic patterns in a particular geographic region (for example, the Asian economic crisis or the decline in traffic to and from the US following the September 11 terrorist attacks) have less of an impact on SIA. SIA's diversified revenue base allows it to sustain its relative success in the affected regions at the expense of the geographically focused carriers (for example, Garuda during the Asian crisis). Second, a global presence enables SIA to offer

Figure 3.7
Global spread of SIA's revenues

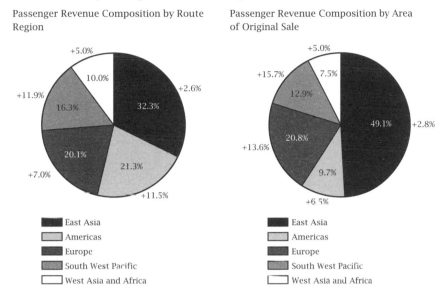

SIA's passenger revenue composition in 2002-2003

Passenger Revenue Composition by Route Region

Passenger Revenue Composition by Area of Original Sale

SIA's passenger revenue composition in 2007-2008

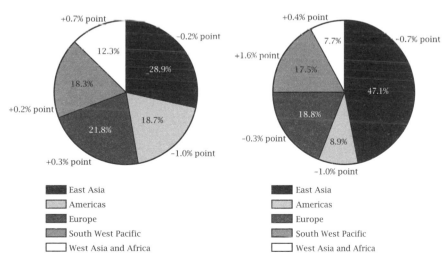

Passenger Revenue Composition by Route Region

Passenger Revenue Composition by Area of Original Sale

Source: Singapore Airlines Annual Reports 2002-2003 and 2007-2008.

75

the benefit of superior connectivity to customers and also aids its global brand-building investments.

Response to Crises

Since 1997, SIA has been through a number of crises. Interestingly, neither industry-wide crises such as 9/11, nor company-specific crises such as the crash of flight SQ006 in Taiwan, have forced SIA to dilute its strategy. In fact, it has emerged stronger after some crises. During the depths of the Asian crisis, a combination of low demand and depreciating currencies caused financial hardship for most Asian carriers; Cathay Pacific made the first financial loss in its history, Korean Air was worth less than three of its fleet of 45 jumbo jets (Boeing 747s) and Garuda witnessed a plummeting load factor (from 80% to 49%). SIA was able to remain profitable over this time period through a variety of measures, including belt-tightening measures such as capacity reductions, salary freezes and promotions (some jointly with hotels) to spur demand.

In the middle of the Asian financial crisis, on 11 September 1998, SIA announced its biggest-ever product launch, with brand new products and services being introduced in all three classes on its Boeing 747, Airbus A340 and Boeing 777 planes. The cost of the launch, which included mini suites, complete with seat-beds and retractable desks for first-class passengers, privacy dividers and increased pitch, width and height for business class passengers, improved seats enhanced with headrests and side ears for economy class passengers and improved cuisine for all classes, was estimated at S$500 million.

In October 2000, the first major accident in SIA's history occurred when one of its planes (747-400; flight SQ006) crashed in inclement weather at Taiwan's Chiang Kai Shek Airport. In an effort to do damage control, SIA was quick to offer a compensation of US$400,000 to the next-of-kin of those killed and US$20,000 to the survivors.[35] The former figure significantly exceeded the sum of US$75,000 specified under the Warsaw convention. Subsequently, SIA terminated the services of the two pilots involved in the crash and its reputation was (apparently) unscathed.

The terrorist attacks of September 11 severely impacted air travel in general, and travel to and from America, in particular. For the six months surrounding the event, SIA's earnings disappointed analysts. By January 2002, however, traffic had rebounded and within 12 months of the event, SIA had launched an improved business class service (including Spacebeds and a new inflight entertainment system) on selected routes and almost half of its aircraft fleet. According to industry analysts, the upgrades were driven by competitive pressures in the form of similar upgrades by rivals (such as British Airways and Qantas) and the need to enhance reputation, especially in the eyes of business class customers.

In March/April 2003, a pair of crises in the form of the US-led war in Iraq and the spread of the Severe Acute Respiratory Syndrome (or SARS) were impacting airlines. The eruption of SARS affected SIA in particular since Singapore as well as some key destinations (especially the Guangzhou province in China and Hong Kong to which SIA was flying 41 times a week) had a significant number of SARS cases. SIA responded with cutbacks in capacity to the affected regions, lay-offs and salary cuts. It also adopted customer-friendly policies such as allowing customers to re-route their flights without penalties or charges. Hedging contracts shielded the airline to a significant extent from the rapidly escalating oil prices during the Iraq war and also in the following two years when the oil price remained high.

While the scope and impact of each crisis was different, there are several key commonalities across SIA's responses to the different crises. First, SIA was not afraid to make large investments aimed towards improving customer service even during the depths of the crises. These investments often generated positive publicity for SIA and kept it in the public eye.[36] Its accumulated strengths (financial reserves and brand reputation) served it well during these difficult times, enabling significant investments when most of its competitors were cash-strapped. Second, SIA's single-minded focus on providing superior customer service helped it adopt appropriate customer-centric policies such as allowing penalty-free re-routing for affected customers during the SARS crisis. This focus might also explain its quick offer to the victims of the SQ006 crash in Taiwan. Third, SIA's top management often set the correct example in terms of sharing the pain in difficult times. During the SARS crisis, for instance, top managers took the lead by cutting their own salary by 7 to 15% before other employees. Fourth, while labour-management relations in SIA have experienced occasional hiccups, it is a credit to the company that the pay cuts during crisis periods have been restored quickly when performance improved. Within a year of the September 11 terrorist attacks, SIA had reversed the pay cuts implemented during the thick of the crisis.

Alliance and Acquisition Strategy

Historically, a highly regulated environment prevented airlines from undertaking controlling acquisitions, especially cross-border ones, and increased the incidence of alliances in the industry. SIA was no exception to this and had formed a network of alliances by 1995 to improve access to key markets. SIA has been cautious in forging alliances, especially in its early days, operating a relatively small network of alliances. This network included equity stakes of 5% and 2.8% in Delta Airlines and Swissair respectively (see Figure 3.8).

Over time, SIA's alliance network grew in terms of the number of partners as well as geographic scope. By 2000, the network included a number of high profile partners such as United, SAS and Lufthansa. Some of its earlier equity relationships (with Swissair and Delta) had been dissolved by 2000 and new equity relationships had been formed with Virgin Atlantic and Air New Zealand. The more recent relationships represented larger stakes that allowed SIA to participate actively in the decision making of its partners. Finally, many of SIA's alliances and acquisitions were driven by a need to extend SIA's geographic reach. In its acquisition of Virgin, for instance, SIA was seeking flying rights for the transatlantic routes.

Figure 3.8
SIA's alliance network in 1995

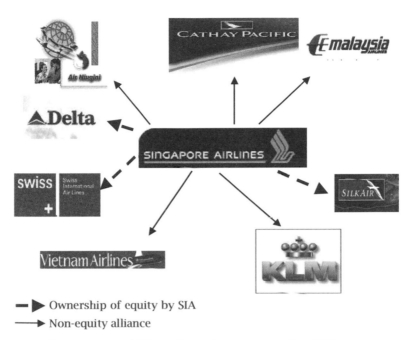

━▶ Ownership of equity by SIA
───▶ Non-equity alliance

Source: Airline Business, *Airline Alliance Survey, September 1995.*

Despite sound strategic logic, subsequent performance was not always as expected, and critics suggested that some acquisitions have not fared that well.[38] SIA bought 49% of Virgin Atlantic in 1999, and wrote off 95% of the investment soon after 9/11. In July 2007, it emerged that SIA was considering selling its stake in Virgin. In 2000, SIA acquired a 25% stake in Air New Zealand, which was subsequently seriously impacted by the collapse of its debt-laden Australian arm, Ansett Airlines; this investment was also written off. Despite these setbacks, SIA is focused on growth opportunities in the fast-growing markets of China and India.[39]

Tiger Airways was launched in 2004; apart from SIA's 49% stake, Temasek Holdings (the Singapore government's investment arm) owns 11%, with the rest owned by international investors such as Indigo

Figure 3.9
SIA's alliance network in 2000

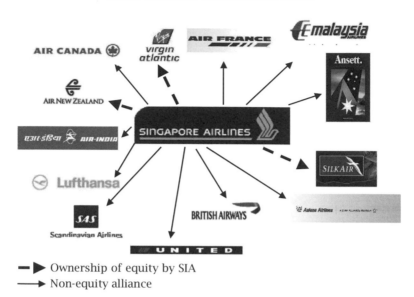

- ▶ Ownership of equity by SIA
- → Non-equity alliance

Source: Airline Business, *Airline Alliance Survey, September 2000.*[37]

Figure 3.10
SIA's alliance network in 2004

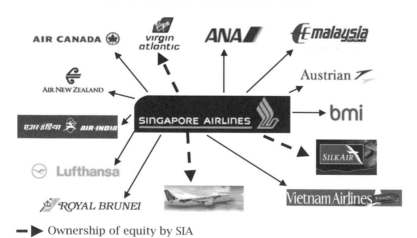

- ▶ Ownership of equity by SIA
- → Non-equity alliance

Source: Airline Business, *Airline Alliance Survey, September 2004.*

partners, as well as Ryanair. CEO Chew Choon Seng says, 'We intend to play in all the segments – SIA at the high end, Silk Air on middle ground and Tiger Airways at the low end.'[40] Figures 3.9 and 3.10 show the alliance structure of SIA in 2000 and 2004 respectively.

SIA has generally been cautious in its alliance formation. Its alliance network is far less extensive than some of its competitors such as Lufthansa (see Figure 3.11). SIA has been particularly conservative in forging code-sharing agreements since its hard-earned reputation might be dented due to unsatisfactory service on a partner airline's flight.

Figure 3.11
Alliance activity for SIA versus some key rivals

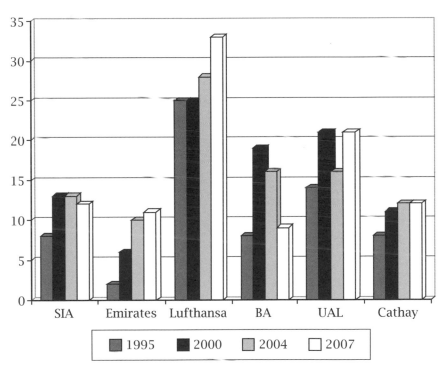

Source: Airline Business, *Airline Alliance Survey (1995, 2000, 2004, 2007). Figures pertain to number of alliance partners.*

81

In 2007 (as compared to 2004), SIA's alliance network did not include Vietnam Airlines, BMI and Austrian, and included four new alliance partners – Asiana Airlines, LOT Polish Airlines, South African Airways and US Airways – leading to an alliance network of around the same size, but one that evolved according to the strategic goals of SIA.

Service Excellence through Innovation and People Development

One key aspect of SIA's success is its ability to be a serial innovator, introducing many firsts in the airline industry, and sustaining this innovative orientation over several decades in the face of intense cost pressures, industry crises and the push towards commoditisation. SIA's approach to innovation involves the seamless combination of hard, structured, rigorous and centralised innovation on the one hand, and soft, emergent, distributed, but equally significant innovation on the other hand. In moving through the processes of idea generation, concept evaluation, design and development of new services, and managing new service launches, SIA is guided by a customer-oriented mindset. We will discuss in detail the innovation processes at SIA in Chapter 5.

Further, SIA is a role model in effectively adopting strategic human resource management in the sense of effectively aligning people to strategy. The strategic human resource management cycle at SIA includes stringent selection and recruitment processes, extensive investment in training and re-training, successful service delivery teams, empowerment of frontline staff to control quality, and motivating employees through reward and recognition. We will expand on these strategic human resource management processes at SIA in Chapter 6.

In conclusion, this chapter examined how SIA's strategic choices and resource deployment decisions have impacted its performance. A key conclusion that can be drawn from the above analysis is that SIA's superior performance is attributable to a complex array of strategic decisions which have been highly consistent over time, including such factors as the maintenance of a young aircraft fleet, sustained investments in brand-building and emphasis on training, leading to a high level of productivity and service excellence of its employees. There are also inter-relations among the factors which add to the individual stand-alone impact of some of these factors, as shown earlier in Figure 3.1. SIA's brand reputation, for instance, is enabled by investments in training and other strategic human resource management processes, as well as a young aircraft fleet. The young fleet, in turn, is supported by, and helps to achieve, low costs (high employee productivity and exposure to competition being two of the contributing factors). We believe that the sustainability of SIA's competitive advantage lies in the multitude of contributing factors and the inter-relationships among the factors, involving self-reinforcing virtuous circles. In other words, imitators would not be able to match SIA's competitive advantage or superior performance by copying individual aspects of its strategy such as the maintenance of a young fleet. We will present a more extensive view of virtuous circles at SIA in our discussion of the factors supporting cost-effective service excellence in the next chapter.

END NOTES

1. Chew Choon Seng, speech at the Global Brand Forum, Singapore, 17 August 2004.
2. http://www.airlinequality.com/StarRanking/5star.htm
3. http://money.cnn.com/magazines/fortune/globalmostadmired/2007/top50/index.html
4. Singapore Airlines Annual Report 2006-2007.
5. Singapore Brand Award, http://www.iesingapore.gov.sg/wps/wcm/connect/resources/file/eb651b04922587a/brand.pdf?MOD=AJPERES
6. Dr Cheong in a speech to the Young President's Organisation in Singapore on 8 February 1985, *Perspectives*, pp. 9-17.
7. Michael Tan at the Third World Advertising Congress held in Beijing, China, on 16-20 June 1987, *Perspectives*, pp. 26-29.
8. Richardson, M. (1993) The Singapore Girl, *International Herald Tribune*, 8 June.
9. *AsiaOne*, 9 March 2007, Singapore Girl Icon to Remain, Says SIA.

10. Singapore Airlines Annual Report, 2006-2007.

11. International Research Associates survey results cited in Singapore Airlines (A), HBS Case no. 9-687-022.

12. Staying Ahead of Competition, Thoeng Tjhoen Onn at the AIC Asia/Pacific Conference on Marketing Airline Services in Singapore on 26 August 1993, *Perspectives*, pp. 92-96.

13. Richardson, M. (1993) The Singapore Girl, *International Herald Tribune*, 8 June.

14. Arnold, W. (1999) For the Singapore Girl, it's Her Time to Shine. *New York Times*, 31 December.

15. Richardson, M. (1993) The Singapore Girl, *International Herald Tribune*, 8 June; MSNBC, 2007, Singapore Girl, Asia's Barbie, to Get New Look? 23 January.

16. MSNBC, 23 January 2007, Singapore Girl, Asia's Barbie, to Get New Look?

17. *AsiaOne*, 9 March 2007, Singapore Girl Icon to Remain, Says SIA.

18. Singapore Airlines Annual Report, 2007-2008.

19. Emirates Annual Report, 2007-2008. Emirates' average age of fleet during 2007-2008 was 67 months.

20. Dr Cheong in a speech to the Young President's Organisation in Singapore on 8 February 1985, *Perspectives*, pp. 9-17.

21. Singapore Airlines Annual Report, 2006-2007.

22. J. Y. Pillay in a speech at SIA's 28th anniversary gala dinner at the Shangri-La Hotel on 17 August 1974, *Perspectives* (Singapore: Communications Department, Singapore Airlines, 1998) pp. 7-8.

23. Dr Cheong in a speech to the Young President's Organisation in Singapore on 8 February 1985, *Perspectives*, pp. 9-17.

24. Dr Cheong in a speech to the Young President's Organisation in Singapore on 8 February 1985, *Perspectives*, pp. 9-17.

25. Singapore Airlines Annual Report, 2007-2008.

26. Sources: Singapore Airlines Annual Report, 2007-2008; Lufthansa Annual Report, 2007; United Airlines Annual Report, 2006; American Airlines Annual Report, 2007; Emirates Annual Report, 2007-2008; British Airways Annual Report, 2007-2008. The figures for Lufthansa include its non-airline operations.

27. Doganis, R. (2006) *The Airline Business*, 2nd Edition, Routledge.

28. The performance of SIA's stock has been inconsistent since the eruption of the Asian financial crisis (1997) with good periods alternating with challenging periods. Given its strong competitive position, however, barring

poor performance of the whole sector and strategic missteps, SIA is expected to outperform the industry in terms of stock price in the short- and medium-term.

29. *Perspectives* (1996) p. 69.

30. Singapore Airlines Report, 2006–2007.

31. Michael Tan to the Indonesian Business Association of Singapore on 18 March 1993, *Perspectives*, pp. 89–91.

32. Dr Cheong at the SIA World Marketing Conference on 16 November 1995, *Perspectives*, pp. 145, 'Both costs are yields dependent on stage length. SIA's average stage length is longer than most other airlines due to its emphasis on long-haul routes. What matters, in the final analysis, is that, accounting for stage length, an airline's yield should be greater than its costs.'

33. Guiding Principles, Stated by J. Y. Pillay in SIA's Annual Report (1990–1991), p. 30.

34. *Far Eastern Economic Review*, 24 June 1991, Profit Formation.

35. *Airline Industry Information*, 30 October 2002, Singapore Airlines to Face Lawsuits Over October 2000 Crash.

36. *Air Transport World*, August 2002, Asia's Class Divide, pp. 43–44.

37. While SIA was a part of the Star Alliance grouping in 2000, all the individual members of the Star Alliance are not shown in the above figure in the interest of simplicity.

38. *Airline Business*, 1 February 2004, Chew Choon Seng: Into the Spotlight.

39. *Airline Business*, 1 February 2004, Chew Choon Seng: Into the Spotlight.

40. *Outlook*, November 2004, quoted in Doganis (2006) p. 263.

4

ACHIEVING COST-EFFECTIVE SERVICE EXCELLENCE AT SIA[1]

Singapore Airlines (SIA) has found the holy grail of strategic success: sustainable competitive advantage. It has consistently outperformed its competitors throughout its more than three-and-a-half decade long history, after it broke away from the joint ownership between the Singapore and Malaysian governments in 1972. SIA has never posted a loss on an annual basis, and has achieved substantial and superior returns in an industry plagued by intermittent periods of disastrous under-performance.[2] SIA has achieved this feat by managing to navigate skilfully between poles that most companies think of as distinct and to deliver service excellence in a cost-effective way. With regard to service excellence, SIA's list of awards is long and distinguished, and the airline has won industry service awards year after year.[3] 'From the very first days of SIA, several things were clear in the mind of the brand owner: the airline was determined to be a highly profitable brand, and the best airline brand in the aviation industry. Quite a modest mission, would you not say, for the airline of one of the world's smallest nations!'[4] says Ian Batey, founder of Batey Ads, the agency that created and nurtured the Singapore Girl brand.

The Singapore Girl, an influential and potent brand carefully developed and safeguarded over the years, is known worldwide as the tangible embodiment of SIA's caring, professional service. According to Batey, every SIA advertisement features real Singapore Girls. Batey

The Singapore Girl has become synonymous with SIA over the years and personifies quality service.

Source: SIA photo bank.

Ads developed the image according to the following characteristics: 'Physically, she has the attractive, natural looks of most young Asian women, and her trim figure is ideal for the distinctive *sarong kebaya* uniform. Character-wise, she mirrors her Asian heritage – natural femininity, natural grace and warmth, and a natural, gentle way with people.'[5]

SIA has managed to integrate elements of a differentiation strategy (with regard to external positioning and service levels) and cost leadership strategy (with regard to the efficiency of the internal organisation), in a way that has been deemed impossible. In the following sections, we give an overview of SIA's business-level strategy and corporate-level strategy before we discuss in detail the five pillars of SIA's cost-effective service excellence. Collectively, these five pillars help us understand how SIA integrates elements of differentiation and cost leadership strategies.

SIA's Strategy and Planning Process

Since strategy professor Michael Porter's influential suggestion that differentiation and cost leadership are mutually exclusive strategies,[6] and that an organisation must ultimately choose where its competitive advantage will lie, stick to that choice and make the right investments to implement and support it, there has been fierce debate about whether cost leadership and differentiation strategies can be combined and sustained over the long term.[7]

Porter suggested that this combination is only feasible if the organisation's competitors are undecided between the two strategies, if cost is strongly affected by market share or inter-unit relationships, or if there is some technological or process innovation that allows this. He argued that all of these could only afford the organisation temporary advantage, however, until competitors imitated whatever factors afforded this advantage. The organisation would then have to make a clear choice about how to compete, otherwise it would risk achieving neither cost leadership nor differentiation, resulting in below-average performance.

SIA has managed to integrate elements of differentiation and cost leadership strategies for more than three-and-a-half decades, outperforming its competitors in the process. It is positioned as a premium carrier with high levels of innovation and excellent levels of service, and has made a clear strategic choice of giving priority to profitability over size. For 'full service' airlines and service organisations in general, delivering excellent service always comes at a cost. SIA on the other hand has managed to deliver premium service to some of the most demanding airline customers, who have sky-high expectations, at costs that are within the range of those of budget carriers. A usual measurement of airline costs is cents per available seat kilometre (ASK).[8] Flag carriers' costs per ASK tend to fall between US$0.09 and US$0.14, and those of budget carriers, between US$0.045 and US$0.075.[9] SIA's costs per ASK were US$0.058 in 2007–2008 and US$0.055 in 2006–2007,[10] which put it firmly within the budget airlines' cost efficiency bracket. Collectively, the five pillars of cost-effective service excellence we discuss below allow us to get a better understanding of how this is achieved.

At the corporate level, SIA follows a strategy of related diversification. The SIA group has 27 subsidiaries which are involved in all aspects related to the operations of an airline,[11] including Singapore Airport Terminal Services, SIA Engineering Company Limited and Singapore Airlines Cargo Pte Ltd. SIA also owns regional carrier Silk Air (100% ownership), and is a shareholder in budget carrier Tiger Airways (49%) and Virgin Atlantic (49%), and supports the key customer segments within the industry. According to CEO Chew Choon Seng, this is part of SIA's intention to participate in all the segments, with SIA, Silk Air and Tiger Airways catering to the high end, middle income and low end customer segments respectively.[12]

As part of its international business strategy, SIA joined the Star Alliance, one of the three major international airline alliances (the other two being Oneworld and SkyTeam) in April 2000. Prior to that, various divisions of the SIA group have been investing in China, India and other countries through strategic alliances with local organisations such as those dealing with cargo division, airport services, engineering services and catering. These partnerships add value to SIA's endeavours. The shareholders in Tiger Airways, for instance, include Temasek, the Singapore government's investment arm as well as SIA's majority owner, and Irelandia Investments, the private family investment vehicle of Anthony Ryan, the founder of Ryanair, one of the world's leading budget carriers. Getting Ryan as a shareholder was a smart move since SIA knew that managing a budget carrier effectively would require different competencies than those involved in managing a premium carrier.

The successful use of information technology (IT) is an essential feature of SIA's strategy to enhance customer service as well as increase efficiency. SIA's website is one of the most advanced and user-friendly in the industry, allowing customers to view schedules, buy tickets, check into a flight, manage their frequent flyer accounts, find out about promotions, and even choose their meal for their next flight. Given that agents' commissions can amount to 7.5% of total operating costs (with reservations and ticketing charges chalking up a further 5.4%)[13] effective use of IT can significantly reduce costs. When the current CEO took over in mid-2003, cost cutting was at the top of his agenda, with particular emphasis on cutting non-fuel costs by 20% within three years and outsourcing IT functions to IBM. The sustained drive for efficiency as well as quality has enabled SIA to increase the spread between the breakeven load factor and the actual load factor to 6.7%.[14]

Like other leading companies, SIA management takes strategic planning seriously, spending significant time and energy on it. The strategic planning process helps SIA to anticipate and deal with industry trends and competitor actions, as well as to develop contingency plans for unexpected events. Planning at the different levels is integrated, which enables the translation of strategic issues and their implications down to the operational level. The strategic planning process at SIA involves a structured annual rhythm complemented by frequent management meetings. It takes place at three levels: the board of directors, the management committee and the operating divisions. Mr Lee Lik Hsin, vice president of the Company Planning and Fuel Department, says, 'There are certain stages throughout the year where we engage in strategy planning sessions ... At the beginning of the year, we have a session with the board, which we call the strategic agenda setting session. At this session the board will discuss what they feel may be key strategic shifts that they see in the next one year or in the longer horizon ... The management committee will take the suggestions and comments from the board and provide inputs of their own ... At this point, things are fleshed out in a bit more detail. Typically, most of the operating divisions will participate in putting up proposal papers or discussion papers ... Then, some time around the middle of the year, we go back to the board again ... Basically, at the second board meeting, we present a report on what management has done in terms of planning around the issues that the board has raised as well as further thoughts that management may have had on other strategic issues that the board may not have raised but management feels that the board should also consider. So the objective of this session is really to seek the board's endorsement on the entire set of issues and plans and ways to move forward ... And finally, each operating division and department will present to management its own strategic and operating plans, which should take into account the issues that have been raised earlier.'

The Five Pillars of Cost-Effective Service Excellence

In common with many other organisations with a reputation for providing excellent service, SIA displays the characteristics of world-class service companies including top management commitment, customer-focused staff and systems and a customer-oriented culture. Dr Cheong Choong Kong, former CEO, says, 'Our passengers ... are our raison d'être. If SIA is successful, it is largely because we have never allowed ourselves to forget that important fact.' However, what distinguishes SIA's customer-oriented and cost-conscious culture is that these are not just abstract, motherhood statements. The values of cost-effective service excellence are enshrined in a unique, self-reinforcing activity system that makes the values real for all employees, who live them out in their every decision and action.

Figure 4.1
The five pillars supporting SIA's cost-effective service excellence

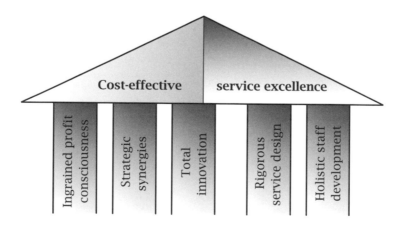

The five pillars of this activity system are rigorous service design and development; total innovation (integrating continuous incremental improvements with discontinuous innovations), profit and cost consciousness ingrained in all employees, holistic staff development, and reaping of strategic synergies through related diversification and world-class infrastructure.

These five pillars relate with one another to build an internally coherent business system that supports, enables and safeguards the central core competency of cost-effective service excellence at SIA (see Figure 4.1).

Rigorous Service Design and Development

Twenty-five years ago, marketing professor Lyn Shostack complained that service design and development are usually characterised by trial and error.[15] Unlike manufacturing organisations with their R&D departments and product engineers, systematic development and testing of services, or service engineering, was not the norm in the service industry. Things appear to have changed little since then. For SIA, however, product design and development has always been an important issue.

SIA has a service development department that hones and thoroughly tests any change before it is introduced. This department undertakes research, trials, time and motion studies, mock-ups, customer reaction assessment and whatever else is necessary to ensure that a service innovation is supported by the right procedures. Underpinning the continuous innovation and development is a corporate culture that accepts change not just as an inevitable fact of life but as a way of life. It is OK for a trial to fail or an implemented innovation to be removed after a few months. In some other organisations, personal reputations can be at stake and so pilot tests 'have to work'. At SIA a failed pilot test damages no one's reputation.

Service and product innovations sometimes live beyond their useful years because of political pressure or the lack of investment resources for further innovation and renewal. At SIA, however, it is expected that any innovation will have a short shelf life. One recent example is the discontinuation of FAST (Fully Automated Seamless Travel), a check-in system involving biometric technology which allowed customers to clear immigration within 1 to 3 minutes. This process was developed jointly by SIA and the Civil Aviation Authority of Singapore. While it worked well, the system was discontinued because usage was lower than anticipated given that the regular channels at the airport were also highly efficient.

SIA recognises that to sustain its differentiation, it must maintain continuous improvement, and be able to abort programmes or services that no longer provide competitive differentiation. Mr Yap Kim Wah, senior vice president of the Product and Service Department, says, 'It is getting more and more difficult to differentiate ourselves because every airline is doing the same thing ... the crucial fact is that we continue to say that we want to improve. That we have the will to do so. And that every time we reach a goal, we always say that we got to find a new mountain or hill to climb ... you must be able to give up what you love.'

These comments on the need to continually innovate raise the question of sustainability of competitive advantage. SIA has indeed sustained superior performance relative to its peers, but what is it that makes it so difficult to imitate SIA? The answer may lie in the holistic internal integration of the organisation: it is easier to imitate fragments of a business system rather than the whole system. If such a system is internally consistent and self-reinforcing, held together by robust, customer-focused processes and cultural values, it becomes almost impossible to imitate.

The stakes are raised for SIA, not only by its competitors but also by its customers. A company with a sky-high reputation attracts customers with sky-high expectations. SIA's research team has found that SIA attracts a disproportionately large number of very demanding customers who expect the best. Mr Sim Kay Wee, senior vice president of the Cabin Crew Department, elaborates, 'Customers adjust their expectations according to the brand image. When you fly on a good brand like SIA, your expectations are already sky-high. And if SIA gives anything that is just OK, it is just not good enough.'

SIA treats its customers' high expectations as a fundamental resource for innovation ideas. Weak signals are amplified. Written comments and verbal comments to the flight crew are taken seriously and reported to the relevant sections of the airline. Ms Lim Suet Kwee, senior rank trainer, explains, 'All feedback that is being given by customers is taken very seriously because we have to look into *why* the customer gave that particular comment and also are there ways to improve in that area?' An additional source of intelligence is SIA's 'spy flights', where individuals travel with competitors and report detailed intelligence on competitive offerings.

Lastly, SIA recognises that its competition does not just come from within the industry. As a rule, SIA sets its sights high and, instead of aiming to be the best airline, strives to be the best service organisation. To achieve this, SIA employs broad benchmarking not just against its main competitors but against the best-in-class service companies. Mr Yap Kim Wah elaborates, 'It is important to realise that [our customers] are not just comparing SIA with other airlines. They are comparing us against many industries, and on many factors. So when they pick up a phone and call up our reservations, for example, they are actually making a mental comparison, maybe subconsciously, to the last best experience they had. It could be with a hotel; it could be with a car rental company. If they had a very good experience with the hotel or car rental company and if the next call they make is to SIA, they will subconsciously make the comparison and say "How come you're not as good as them?" They do not say "You have the best telephone service system out of all the other airlines I've called". Our customers, albeit subconsciously, will benchmark us against the best in almost everything. The new ball game for SIA is not just to be the best of the best in the airline industry but to work at being the best service company.'

Total Innovation: Integrating Incremental Development with Unanticipated, Discontinuous Innovations

An airline has a multitude of sub-systems which facilitate the operation of components such as reservations, catering, maintenance, inflight services and entertainment. SIA does not aim to be a lot better but just a bit better in every one of them than its competitors. This not only means constant innovation but also total innovation – innovation in everything, all of the time. Importantly, this also supports the notion of cost-effectiveness. Continuous incremental development comes at a low cost but delivers that necessary margin of value to the customer. Mr Yap Kim Wah says, 'It is the total experience that counts, not the expense. If you want to provide the best food, you might decide to serve lobster on short-haul flights between Singapore and Bangkok, for example. However, you might go bankrupt. The point is that, on that route, we just have to be better than our competitors in everything we do. Just a little bit better in everything. This allows us to make a small profit from the flight, and to innovate without pricing ourselves out of the market. We want to provide excellent and all round value for money. This makes it much harder for our competitors. Therefore, in SIA, it's about coming up with new things all the time. We want to be a little bit better all the time in everything we do.'

Whilst cost-effective incremental improvements are an important basis for its competitive advantage, SIA also frequently implements major initiatives that are firsts in the industry. One example is its Outstanding Service on the Ground programme. This initiative was led by the managing director and involved working with many other organisations to ensure seamless, efficient and caring customer service before and after a flight. SIA's latest service excellence initiative, known as the Transforming Customer Service (TCS) programme, involves staff in five key operational areas – cabin crew, engineering, ground services, flight operations and sales support. The development programme aims at fostering team spirit among key operational staff to ensure that the customer's journey, from the purchase of the ticket onwards, is as pleasant and seamless as possible. SIA employs a total innovation approach captured in their '40-30-30' rule, ensuring a holistic approach to service improvement. SIA focuses 40% of its resources on training and invigorating its people, 30% on the review of processes and procedures, and 30% on creating new product and service ideas. Total innovation is about cost-effective service excellence based on the whole rather than just one aspect of customer experience.

SIA's reputation as a service innovator is boosted by its unanticipated inflight innovations, which are based on a deep understanding of the trends in customer lifestyles, and of the implications they have on the future of better inflight service. Mr Yap Kim Wah elaborates on this, saying, 'Most new changes that really secure the "wow" effect are those things that customers never expected ... we have a product innovation department that continuously looks at trends and why people behave in a certain manner, why they do certain things. And then we do a projection of 3–5 years of what is going to happen ... For the airline, it's not just about having a smoother flight from A to B. That will be taken for granted. It is really about what are the customers' lifestyle needs. Can you meet these lifestyle needs?' The seats in SIA's A380 business class and first-class suites are an example of such an innovation; compared to its competitors, SIA boasts the widest seats in these two categories.

SIA has made a clear strategic choice of being a leader and follower at the same time. It is a pioneer on innovations that have a high impact on customer service (for example inflight entertainment or flat-bed seats). However, it is at the same time a fast follower in areas that are less visible from the customer's point of view. For example, SIA's revenue management and customer relationship management (CRM) systems run on tried-and-tested technology that have existed in the market for some time – which ensures that it can be implemented smoothly and cost-effectively – rather than on the latest technology available, which would not only cost more, but also carry a higher implementation risk.

Batey describes the innovation climate at SIA in the following way, 'Captain Kirk of the *SS Enterprise* would be in his element working at SIA, because from the day they were born they've been tireless in their mission of exploring and bringing to their customers a continuous stream of new, breakthrough service ideas. It's all part of the airline's enduring core appeal to provide a unique travel experience.'[16] SIA's innovation capabilities are a key part of its competitive success and therefore of strategic importance. In Chapter 7 we return to this crucial theme, further expanding on the nature of 'strategic innovation', the reasons for which we regard SIA as a strategic innovator, and on how strategic innovation can be fostered in organisations.

Profit Consciousness Ingrained in All Employees

Although SIA is totally focused on the customer and providing continually improving service, managers and staff are well aware of the need for profit and cost-effectiveness. Every member of staff from the highest to the lowest level of the organisational hierarchy is able to handle the potentially conflicting objectives of excellence and profit. This is made possible by inculcating in the staff a cost and profit consciousness. 'It's drilled into us from the day we start working for SIA that if we don't make money, we'll be closed down,' says Mr Yap Kim Wah. 'Singapore doesn't need a national airline. Second, the company has made a very important visionary statement that "We don't want to be the largest company. We want to be the most profitable". That's very powerful.'

Any proposed innovation is analysed carefully on the balance of expected customer benefits versus costs. Station managers and frontline staff constantly trade off passenger satisfaction versus cost-effectiveness – the customer has to be delighted, but through cost-effective means. During the development of the A380, there was careful consideration of how the cabin configuration would affect profitability. According to Mr Sim Kim Chui, who led the A380 project, the ideas arising from focus groups with frequent flyers were ranked and the best suggestions were collated but their implementation was carried out with profitability in mind. 'It's important to look at all these ideas, and we shortlisted the better ones,' says Mr Sim, who is also the vice president of the Product Development Department. 'The next thing is, of course, at the end of the day, the aircraft must make money. I was reminded time and again that this aircraft is not to win awards per se ... Don't go win the best design award and at the end of the day we don't make any money.'

Profitability does not just come by controlling costs, but also by the ability to charge a premium price – which is the true test of differentiation. With regard to the A380 project, even though the manufacturer states that the aeroplane can carry 555 passengers, the final seat count on SIA's A380s is 471 passengers. Mr Sim Kim Chui explains, 'You see, the safe approach is to cram it with as many seats as possible, then you know the risks are lower, but I think it's important for the positioning of Singapore Airlines [to emphasise] that we are the premier carrier, we are not selling a commodity here. So this aircraft must be different from everybody else's, must offer the best, fit the customer expectations and then of course we will charge a premium.'

In everyday operations, SIA's staff keeps the importance of reducing wastage in mind without compromising customer service. Mr Patrick Seow, senior rank trainer, gives an example, 'We try to minimise the number of bottles of wine we need to open, by gauging the passengers' demand for it, rather than just automatically opening X bottles, which, at the end of the day, you have to throw away. In that sense, we do attempt to save costs. Through feedback collected from the passengers in survey forms, we find that because of the late departure of some of our flights, 30% of passengers choose not to eat inflight meals and so we feel that maybe we don't need to keep a full stock of meals for every passenger.'

According to Mr Sim Kim Chui, it is important to prioritise customer needs and spend only on the most important things, and to reduce wastage without affecting customer service. 'Firstly, why is it so important that we prioritise passenger needs? If I have $100 to spend I must spend it on what is important to the customer. No point giving me a shopping list and trying to do too many things. So you will find that SIA would deliberately not spend on certain things, especially things that are of a low priority to the customer, but what the customer perceives as very high priority is where we'll put the money ... Secondly, we try to really reduce wastage, which is what I can take away without affecting the customers. So prudent wastage reduction is what we do at SIA day in day out. And you'll be surprised how much we can reduce wastage. Keep your costs down without affecting your service in any way.'

Finally, and like many service organisations, SIA has a reward system that pays bonuses according to the profitability of the company. However, at SIA, everyone gets the same percentage bonus – the same formula is used throughout the company. As a result there is a lot of informal peer pressure from individuals within the organisation, and managers and staff appear to be open to challenging decisions and actions if they see resources being wasted or money being inappropriately spent.

SIA builds team spirit within its 6,600-strong crew through its 'team concept', where small teams comprising 13 crew members fly together for at least two years. The bond between the team members reinforces the culture of cost-effective service excellence and increases the peer pressure to deliver SIA's promises to its customers.

Developing Staff Holistically[17]

Senior managers say that 'training in SIA is almost next to pursuing godliness', but this statement does not capture the full extent of the value of training in SIA. Everyone, no matter how senior, has a training and development plan with clear goals. New cabin crew undergo training for four months, which is a longer training period than any other airline's. Crew members are trained not only in functional skills, but also in the soft skills of personal interaction, personal poise, and emotional skills of dealing with the consequences of serving very demanding passengers. Mr Patrick Seow, senior rank trainer at the SIA Training School, says, 'A large portion of cabin crew training is actually centred on soft skills. So you are correct in saying that SIA cabin crew look a certain way, act a certain way and have certain manners. We actually pay attention to how they should treat passengers, how they should position themselves when they come into contact with customers. For instance, you will see that in the aircraft environment, cabin crew always go down to the eye level of the customers.' SIA's training of the Singapore Girl is likened to the training at a finishing school. Mr Seow continues, 'The girls are transformed from the moment they enter the training programme, and by the time they complete it, they look totally different. Their deportment, the way they carry themselves … There's a great transformation there.'

In addition to such training, SIA also encourages and supports activities that might on the surface be seen as having nothing to do with service in the air. Crew employees have created groups such as the

Performing Arts Circle, staging full-length plays and musicals, the Wine Appreciation Group and the Gourmet Circle. These activities help to develop camaraderie and team spirit, as well as personal knowledge of the finer things in life, which enhances the personalised and exceptional service that the crew delivers in the air.

Development is continuous. As customers get more sophisticated and their expectations rise, the training that the Singapore Girl receives changes to accommodate this. Mr Sim Kay Wee says, 'While our Singapore Girl is our icon, and we're very proud of her and her achievements, we continue to improve her skills, we continue to improve her ability to appreciate wines and cheeses, for example, or our Asian heritage ... the enhancement must be continuous.'[18]

Cabin crew can select refresher courses, and on average spend three to four days a year attending such courses. Popular courses include those on basic and intermediate transactional analysis (a counselling-type course), leadership and European languages. The company is moving from a system of directing which courses cabin crew should attend, to one of self-directed learning, where staff take responsibility for their own development.

Even before development starts, substantial effort is spent to ensure that the company hires the right staff. For example, entry qualifications for cabin crew applicants include both academic achievements (cabin crew have to hold at least polytechnic diplomas, meaning that they have spent 13 years in school), as well as physical attributes. The recruitment process is extensive, involving three rounds of interviews, a 'uniform test', a 'water confidence test', psychometric tests and a tea party where management gets to interact with the prospective employees on a more informal basis. Over 16,000 applications are received every year, and the company hires around 500 to 600 new cabin crew each year to cover attrition rates of around 10%. This includes both voluntary and directed attrition. If, for example, a Singapore Girl becomes pregnant, she has to leave the airline. There is a scheme that allows these stewardesses to re-apply to join the airline. After the Singapore Girls start flying, they are carefully monitored for the first six months, and the management receives a monthly report by their inflight supervisor. At the end of the probationary period, 75% get confirmed, around 20% have to extend their probation period, and 5% leave.

Achieving Strategic Synergies through Related Diversification and World-Class Infrastructure

SIA utilises related diversification in the way it was intended: to reap cost synergies and at the same time control quality and enable transfer of learning. Subsidiaries serve not only as the development ground for well-rounded management skills and a corporate rather than a divisional outlook through job rotation, but also as sources of learning.

In addition, related operations (such as catering, aircraft maintenance, airport management) have healthier profit margins than the airline business itself because competitive intensity is lower, and industry structure is more favourable. SIA Engineering, for example, ensures that SIA does not have to pay expensive aircraft maintenance fees to other airlines; it sells such services to other airlines at healthy margins. SIA's fleet, the youngest in the world, ensures low maintenance costs,

An A340 plane from SIA's *Leadership* fleet, flying the world's longest non-stop commercial flight between Singapore and Los Angeles.

Source: SIA photo bank.

102

low fuel expenses and high flight quality, as achieved, for example, through the executive economy class and the non-stop flights to the US by SIA's *Leadership* fleet. SIA's Inflight Catering Centre produces SIA's inflight cuisine, ensuring high quality, reliability and responsiveness to customer feedback, and, at the same time, caters for other airlines at a healthy margin.

SIA's Singapore Airport Terminal Services (SATS) Group subsidiary manages Changi Airport, which is regularly voted as the best airport in the world. The excellent airport management and infrastructure entice passengers en route to Australia, New Zealand or other countries in the region, to pass through Changi Airport and to choose SIA as their carrier.

SIA's subsidiaries operate under the same management philosophy and culture that emphasises cost-effective service excellence. Even though they are part of the group, they are quoted separately on the Singapore Stock Exchange and are subject to market discipline with very clear performance expectations. In SIA, therefore, the conventional

Changi Airport's excellent infrastructure and facilities provide a wide variety of entertainment and leisure options for waiting or transit passengers.

Source: http://www.asiatraveltips.com/PicturesofSingaporeAirport.shtml.

wisdom of outsourcing 'peripheral' activities and focusing on what the organisation does best does not readily apply. External suppliers would not be able to offer the value that SIA's own subsidiaries can offer to SIA. Related diversification enables SIA to reap strategic synergy benefits in terms of reliability of key inputs, high quality, transfer of learning and, at the same time, cost-effectiveness.

Figures 4.2, 4.3 and 4.4 illustrate three broad airline business models at the corporate level. Essentially, the models differ on whether subsidiaries are within the corporate structure or not, with implications for performance expectations and market discipline. SIA follows the third model shown in Figure 4.4, which affords both a degree of control through substantial ownership, as well as market discipline through listing of the subsidiaries.

Figure 4.2
The traditional integrated airline model

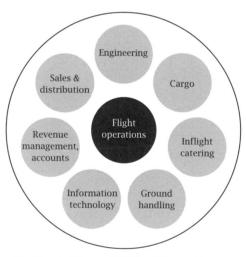

Traditional airline model: Self-sufficient, with most
functions and services within the corporate structure
(e.g., Delta, Iberia, Thai)

Source: Doganis, R. (2006) The Airline Business, *2nd edition. Abingdon: Routledge.*

Figure 4.3
The virtual airline model

Virtual airline model: Most of the functions and
services are outsourced (e.g., some low cost airlines)

Source: Doganis, R. (2006) The Airline Business, 2nd edition. Abingdon: Routledge.

Figure 4.4
Aviation business model

Aviation business model: Separate business units that serve the passenger
core but earn most of their revenue from external clients (e.g., SIA, Lufthansa)

Source: Doganis, R. (2006) The Airline Business, 2nd edition. Abingdon: Routledge.

Bringing It All Together: Building a Self-Reinforcing Activity System

How, specifically, do these elements lead to cost-effective service excellence? The five pillars of SIA's cost-effective service excellence are supported, operationalised and made real in everyday decisions and actions through a self-reinforcing activity system of virtuous circles. The cultural values of cost-effectiveness and service excellence (which also form SIA's core competence) are thus more than just abstract ideas. They are ingrained into the minds and actions of employees as well as organisational processes.

This may help to explain why SIA's competitive advantage has been sustained for decades. While it is easy to copy single elements, it is much harder to reproduce an entire self-reinforcing activity system. Many factors interrelate to produce virtuous circles within the self-reinforcing system (see Figure 4.5), shedding light on why competitors find it difficult to copy SIA. This system effects the quality of 'causal ambiguity';[19] competitors know that something great is happening at SIA, but are not exactly sure about the causes, interrelations and mechanisms through which this happens. Imitating one or two elements will not achieve the same result since the whole system would need to be imitated. Finally, the continuous improvement philosophy at SIA helps to ensure that even as competitors learn how some of SIA's internal processes operate, they will still find it difficult to catch up.

Achieving a Dual Strategy of Differentiation and Cost Leadership

Strategies of differentiation and cost leadership usually involve different and incompatible investments by companies so as to achieve organisational alignment supporting the strategy. As noted above, it has been argued that any such combination of incompatible generic strategies would at best be temporary and risks companies being stuck in the middle, having neither high levels of differentiation nor sustainable low cost.[20] In spite of arguments to the contrary,[21] cases

Figure 4.5

SIA's self-reinforcing activity system for developing cost-effective service excellence

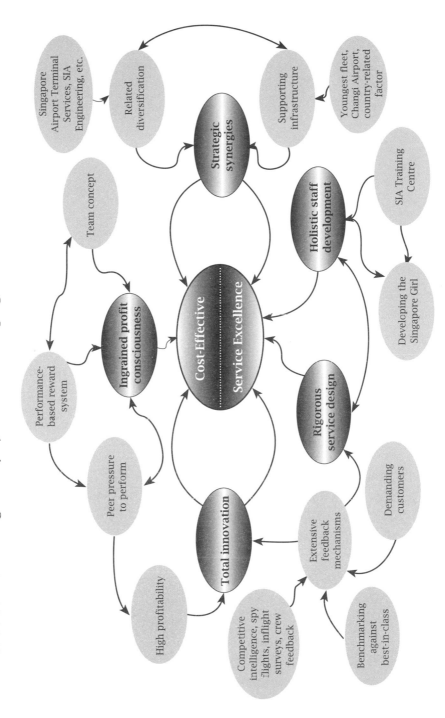

where organisations have successfully achieved a combination of differentiation as well as lower costs relative to competitors' costs have been rare.

A strategy of differentiation is usually associated with high-quality offerings, service excellence, investment in innovation and other organisational processes that support these, the ability to charge a premium price and, due to the higher level of investments, higher costs than average. Intriguingly, SIA is able to adopt a differentiation strategy without a cost penalty relative to its peer group. In fact, SIA boasts significantly higher efficiency than its peer group, the key feature of a successful cost leadership strategy; its efficiency levels in terms of cents per available seat kilometre are as high as that of a budget carrier. A cost leadership strategy also involves offering acceptable rather than superior quality, relatively low prices, and usually little investment in innovation. Surprisingly, SIA does not follow any of these elements.

This combined strategy has enabled SIA to consistently outperform its counterparts in the airline industry, a key measure of robust sustainable competitive advantage. Bear in mind that it is extremely tough to succeed in the airline industry in light of its disastrous business cycles, susceptibility to over-capacity, difficulty of differentiation, and high risk profile.[22] Table 4.1 outlines many of the elements discussed above in relation to the dual strategy of integrating differentiation and cost leadership.

In this chapter, we have addressed SIA's core competence, cost-effective service excellence, suggesting that SIA has managed to consistently deliver excellent service in an efficient manner. In addition to exhibiting key characteristics of leading service organisations, such as management commitment, customer-focused staff and systems, and a customer-oriented culture, our research has shown that SIA achieves this successful balance between integrated differentiation and cost leadership through five pillars that constitute its unique activity system: rigorous service design and development; total innovation (integrating continuous incremental improvements with discontinuous

Table 4.1
Elements of differentiation and cost leadership
strategies at SIA

Differentiation	Cost leadership
· Positioning of service excellence and superior quality, brand quality (marketing strategy) · Developing the Singapore Girl (HR development policies) · Inflight experience (young fleet, entertainment system, gourmet cuisine – operations strategy) · Cultural values and practice of constant innovation and learning · Changi Airport – one of the world's best (related infrastructure) · Premium pricing in Singapore and in business/first class, and higher load factor as differentiation indicators	· Young fleet (higher fuel efficiency, lower maintenance costs, effective fuel hedging, paying cash for planes) · Lower labour costs compared to major competitors (16.6% vs 30%); continuous drive for productivity, cost-reduction programmes · Related diversification through efficient subsidiaries that contribute to bottom line · Cultural values: cost consciousness, obsession with reducing wastage · Innovations not only increase differentiation but also efficiency · Changi Airport – one of the world's most efficient (related infrastructure)

innovations); profit and cost consciousness ingrained in all employees; holistic staff development; and reaping of strategic synergies through related diversification and world-class infrastructure. We have suggested that these five pillars of SIA's cost-effective service excellence are supported, operationalised and made relevant to everyday decisions and actions through a self-reinforcing activity system of virtuous circles, fine-tuned through continuous improvement, which makes it even more difficult for competitors to imitate SIA's sustainable advantage. We then summarised the elements that allow SIA to achieve and sustain this dual strategy.

109

APPENDIX 1

Research Project on SIA's Competitiveness

This chapter is based on a research project which started in 2001. The project examined SIA's strategy and competitiveness over the years, in particular, its competencies of service excellence, efficiency and innovation. Both primary and secondary data were gathered. In addition to library and database research on SIA and the airline industry in general, we conducted a total of 20 interviews with 16 executives and cabin crew members, each lasting between 45 minutes and 90 minutes, from 2001 to 2008. We recorded, transcribed and analysed most of these interviews (and took extensive field notes when the recording of interviews was not allowed) with a view to getting a deeper appreciation of how SIA has managed to achieve a sustainable competitive advantage and outperform other airlines in its peer group for decades, both in terms of financial performance as well as industry service.

APPENDIX 2

Performance Comparisons Between SIA and Its Top 20 Competitors

The performance comparisons shown in Figures 4.6 and 4.7 compare SIA's performance in terms of net profit margin and return on assets (ROA) against the weighted average for the top 20 airlines by market capitalisation (as at 15 May 2004), for the period between 1992 and 2004. The 20 airlines were Southwest Airlines, SIA, Cathay Pacific, Japan Airlines, Lufthansa, British Airways, All Nippon Airways, Qantas, Air France, Ryanair, JetBlue Airways, China Southern Airlines (A shares), China Eastern Airlines (A shares), Thai Airways, American Airlines, Malaysian Airlines, Scandinavian Airlines System, China Airlines, WestJet Airlines and Alitalia.

Figure 4.6

SIA's net profit margin vs that of the top 20 airlines by market capitalisation (1992-2004)

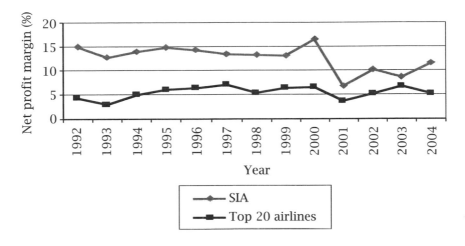

Figure 4.7

SIA's ROA vs that of the top 20 airlines by market capitalisation (1992-2004)

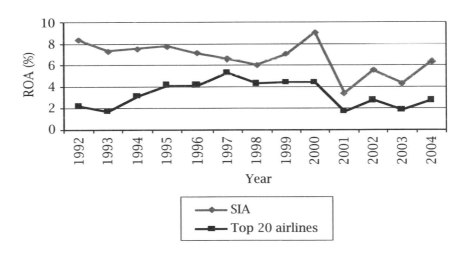

END NOTES

1. This chapter draws from Heracleous, Wirtz and Johnston (2004) Cost Effective Service Excellence: Lessons from Singapore Airlines, *Business Strategy Review*, Spring, pp. 33-38; Heracleous and Wirtz, Strategy and Organization at Singapore Airlines: Achieving Sustainable Advantage through Dual Strategy, Working paper; and Wirtz and Heracleous, 2005, Biometrics Meets Services, *Harvard Business Review*, February, p. 48. See Appendix 1 for further information on our broader research project on SIA's competitiveness.

2. See Appendix 2 for performance comparisons of SIA vs the top 20 airlines by market capitalisation for the period 1992-2004. See also Chapters 1 and 2 for information on the airline industry's performance and analysis of relevant industry factors.

3. http://www.singaporeair.com (see "about SIA").

4. Batey, I. (2002) *Asian Branding: A Great Way to Fly*. Singapore: Prentice Hall, p. 123.

5. Batey, I. (2002) *Asian Branding: A Great Way to Fly*. Singapore: Prentice Hall, p. 120.

6. Porter M. (1985) *Competitive Advantage*. New York: Free Press.

7. For example, see Hill, C. W. (1988) Differentiation versus Low Cost or Differentiation and Low Cost: A Contingency Framework, *Academy of Management Review*, 13, pp. 401-412.

8. Available seats multiplied by distance flown.

9. Binggeli, U. and Pompeo, L. (2002) Hyped Hopes for Europe's Low-Cost Airlines, *McKinsey Quarterly*, 4, pp. 86-97; Doganis, R. (2006) *The Airline Business*, 2nd edition. Abingdon: Routledge.

10. Singapore Airlines Annual Report 2007-2008. Currency conversions conducted on 5 September 2008.

11. See Singapore Airlines Annual Report 2007-2008.

12. *Outlook*, November 2004, quoted in Doganis, R. (2006) *The Airline Business*, 2nd edition. Abingdon: Routledge, p. 263.

13. Doganis, R. (2006) *The Airline Business*, 2nd edition. Abingdon: Routledge.

14. Singapore Airlines analyst presentation, http://www.singaporeair.com/saa/en_UK/content/company_info/investor/analysts.jsp, accessed on 19 June 2007.

15. Shostack G. L. (1984) Designing Services that Deliver, *Harvard Business Review*, 62 (1), January-February, pp. 133-139.

16. Batey, I. (2002) *Asian Branding: A Great Way to Fly.* Singapore: Prentice Hall, p. 136.

17. In addition to the named quotations, this section draws from in-depth interviews with Choo Poh Leong, senior manager of crew services, and Toh Giam Ming, senior manager of crew performance.

18. Chapter 6 presents a more detailed discussion of SIA's human resource management policies.

19. For example, see Reed, R. & DeFilippi, R. J. (1990) Causal Ambiguity, Barriers to Imitation and Sustainable Competitive Advantage, *Academy of Management Review*, 15, pp. 66-102.

20. Porter M. (1985) *Competitive Advantage.* New York: Free Press.

21. For an example, refer to Hill, C. W. (1988) Differentiation versus Low Cost or Differentiation and Low Cost: A Contingency Framework, *Academy of Management Review*, 13, pp. 401-412.

22. Costa, P. R., Harned, D. S. and Lundquist, J. T. (2002) Rethinking the Aviation Industry, *McKinsey Quarterly* (Risk and Resilience Special Issue), pp. 89-100. See also Chapters 1 and 2 for detailed information and analysis on the airline industry.

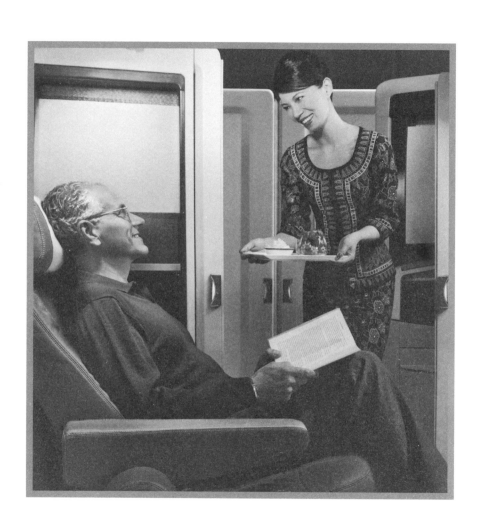

5

INNOVATION AS A KEY TO SUSTAINED SERVICE EXCELLENCE[1]

This chapter explores the role of service innovation in Singapore Airlines' (SIA's) ability to sustain cost-effective service excellence and competitive advantage for over three-and-a-half decades. This chapter presents the senior management's perspective of the key challenges it faces in delivering sustained cost-effective service excellence. Our research has shown that SIA's main approaches to these challenges are mostly related to constant innovation, redesign and new service development. The main body of the chapter focuses on SIA's approaches to innovation; we shed light on SIA's ability as a serial innovator to introduce many firsts in the airline industry over the years, and to sustain this innovative orientation over decades in spite of intense cost pressure, industry crises and the push towards commoditisation. SIA's approach to innovation involves the seamless combination of, on the one hand, hard, structured, rigorous and centralised methods and, on the other hand, soft, emergent, distributed but equally significant ones.

The Key Challenges of Delivering Service Excellence

Three key challenges SIA faces stood out in our interviews with senior management. It is important to understand these challenges to be able to appreciate the drive behind SIA's amazing innovation capability.

Specifically, in this section, we will discuss the following three key challenges SIA's senior management staff highlight repeatedly and from different angles throughout our interviews:

- How to consistently satisfy the sky-high and continuously rising expectations of SIA's demanding customer base.

- How to balance standardisation and personalisation of its services, and overcome the tension between offering standardised service (i.e., consistently delivering the brand promise) that is at the same time personalised.

- How to manage a large number of services and their support sub-processes in totality to attain excellence in all processes and sub-processes.

Dealing with Sky-High and Ever Rising Customer Expectations

Having an international reputation for service excellence makes delivering outstanding service a continuous challenge, because customers tend to adjust their expectations according to the reputation and brand image of the company. Mr Yap Kim Wah, senior vice president of the Product and Service Department, explains, 'We have a high reputation for service and that means that when someone flies with us, they come with high expectations. Still, we want them to come away saying "Wow! That was something out of the ordinary".'

Furthermore, SIA understands that customers' expectations are also influenced by the service standards of other airlines as well as service firms in other industries. Customers expect SIA, being a 'full service' premier carrier, to provide a service standard that is tangibly better than that of most of its competitors in the aviation industry. However, they will also compare SIA's service standards with leading service firms from other industries. Mr Yap Kim Wah adds, 'This is a fantastic challenge for us. We have to look at everything we do. This means that the food we place on board and our food and beverage service has to be the best. So we serve the best champagne, and even when we serve local dishes such

116

as chicken rice, it has to be the best when compared to the local market. If we can't achieve this with a dish, we just have to drop the item.'

In order to deliver an extraordinary service that delights its customers despite their high expectations, SIA places a lot of importance on the 'wow' effect and occasionally surprising its customers. Mr Yap Kim Wah says, 'It's the new things that create the "wow". The things that customers never expected. There is a whole realm of things that customers don't know they want! We try to study the trends ... We try to follow both the short- and long-term trends.' Besides analysing trends, SIA also uses feedback from its staff, information about other airlines, and customer compliment/complaint analysis and major traveller surveys to help generate new ideas. The new ideas gathered from the various sources enable the airline to constantly identify all possible opportunities to delight its customers through the introduction of new services.

Mr Yap Kim Wah adds, 'It's very easy to love what we do, and that's the danger. It's easy to say that the customers will surely want what we do. To be a winner, we have to continually strive to provide the very best service when compared with any industry. That's why it's so challenging. Whatever we do, we are in search of excellence and are

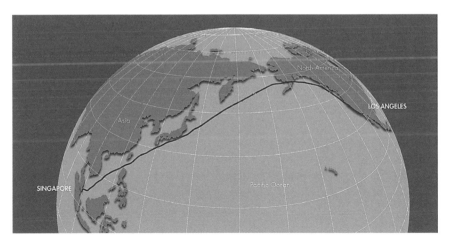

SIA's direct flyer to Los Angeles: A world's first for ultra long-haul flights.
Source: Courtesy of Singapore Airlines.

never willing to settle for what we have already achieved. It's good to be passionate, but I think you must be able to say "I'm willing to kill it with a better program". And that is a huge challenge internally. We have to be able to tell ourselves that, "I love this new thing that I've developed and we'll make sure that it's well implemented". However, we also have to kill it with a better product in X number of months. It could be six months, it could be 12 months, it could be 20 months. But you have got to kill it because the lifestyles of our customers are continuously evolving … This means constant innovation and constant development in all the things that we do.'

SIA therefore clearly sees constant innovation and the 'wow' effect it provides as a key factor in addressing the sky-high and ever rising expectations of its passenger base. Of great importance in enhancing the 'wow' effect is the delivery of the innovation, as experienced by passengers through interaction with the cabin crew. Mr Patrick Seow, senior rank trainer at the SIA Training School says of the new recruits he trains, 'Besides teaching them functional skills, I always try to seek the opportunities to get them immersed in our culture … it's our culture that makes us stand out.' Furthermore, according to Ms Lim Suet Kwee, a fellow senior rank trainer at the SIA Training School, during the initial training period, 'the crew, … other than learning about the correct ways to serve and all that, spend a lot of time learning how to communicate with the passengers and among themselves. Communication, of course, covers eye contact, the correct usage of words and the tone of voice as well.' As Chapter 6 further elaborates, sustaining high customer satisfaction is supported by the development of such a customer-oriented mindset through continuous training and development of employees, as well as internal policies such as SIA's reward and evaluation system.

Balancing Standardisation and Customisation of Service

Mr Sim Kay Wee explains, 'The challenge in service is that there has to be consistency. When you buy a product, it's very different from buying a service. If you buy a piece of soap, for example, it's just a piece of soap, manufactured by the same process day in and day out. A service, however, is more human, with the potential for inconsistency.' Mr Choo Poh Leong, senior manager of the Crew Services Department, shares how the airline ensures that its passengers get the same consistent level of excellent service on each trip, 'All of our procedures are very finely honed and tested before we introduce any change.' Ms Betty Wong, acting vice president of the Inflight Services Department, adds that her department will 'carry out research and trials, time and motion studies, make mock ups, see how long things will take, assess customer reaction, and do whatever is necessary to ensure that it is the right procedure.'

SIA recognises that whilst all the components of a service are important, there is an important difference between hygiene and enhancing factors. Mr Sim Kay Wee explains, 'We have a long list of the things that passengers expect when it comes to good service: flight schedules, punctuality, seat comfort, and for flight staff to have technical skills such as safe piloting and the ability to pour a cup of coffee without spilling it all over the place. But these are just technical requirements and I think a lot of airlines can master them. These are all "hygiene" factors – you must have them. Mind you, there are some airlines that don't have them and are still in business! The enhancing factors are the softer skills, such as warmth, care and the ability to anticipate needs.' SIA's strategy is to ensure that hygiene factors, which are expected by most travellers, are consistently delivered, whereas the enhancing factors are personalised and can be more variable, which helps the airline give service that is personalised to the needs of each individual, especially in the premium classes.

SIA recognises that the biggest challenge in delivering consistent yet personalised service is the management of people. Mr Sim Kay Wee says, 'The additional complication is that while striving for consistency, we need people who can be flexible. I know this is a contradiction, but the worst thing about service delivery is when everybody just follows the book. I want the staff to be flexible and creative. In Singapore, there is a tendency for people to be too regimented in their thinking. If a passenger asks for his vegetarian meal and we do not have it on board, for example, we want the member of staff to go back to the galley, think on the spot and create a solution, such as putting together a plate from all the fruits and vegetables, rather than annoy the customer by telling him it was not catered for so he can't have it.' Mr Sim Kay Wee continues, 'Instead of being too regimented in their thinking, SIA wants its staff to have a good relationship with the customer, and not just follow the rule. The challenge is to encourage and harness staff–customer rapport to present a different kind of service image, and for staff to be very positive towards the passenger.'

In order to manage this constant struggle between offering standardised service that is at the same time personalised, SIA places a lot of importance on testing all procedures to ensure that they can be consistently delivered, and the participation of employees from all levels in the innovation processes as this helps foster creativity, flexibility and a mindset geared towards personalisation to customer needs. When staff master the basic processes extremely well and can deliver them consistently, they then have the mental capacity to look out for opportunities to personalise, anticipate needs, and to regularly create the 'wow' effect that will surprise and delight the customers, instead of merely satisfying them.

Focus on Excellence in All Processes and Sub-Processes

SIA understands that customers are buying the total travel experience. Service excellence means that all of its service components have to be excellent. This includes everything that the customers encounter during the journey, all processes and sub-processes ranging from reservations and ground service, inflight service and food and beverages to seats and leg rests and services related to its frequent flyer programme. Mr Yap Kim Wah elaborates, 'A flight has many, many sub-components. By being better at every one of these sub-components we give our competitors a hard time. By the time they copy, we would already have moved ahead. This means constant innovation, and constant development in all the things we do. We don't just put the best seat in business class and sit back. We want the best inflight service, the best food, the best service on the ground, as well as the best seats.' Summarising SIA's perspective on totality, he continues, 'It is better to be 1% better in 100 things than 100% better in one thing.' To provide a service that is excellent in all aspects and better than its competitors in many areas is a challenge, as many people and much technology are involved. Yet it is precisely this complexity that allows SIA to gain a competitive edge based on its processes and focus on totality. The airline needs to constantly improve its processes and sub-processes to ensure it maintains this edge, and keeps pace with customers' changing needs and expectations.

SIA's focus on totality also shows in its approach to launching new services. SIA makes sure that each launch is a complete and integrated package in itself. Mr Yap Kim Wah explains, 'It is a stronger proposition to our customer than to say I have a better cup. We say that the cup comes with better coffee, better delivery and better design.'

Therefore, in order to approach a large number of services and support sub-processes in totality to attain excellence in all of them, SIA engages in constant innovation and fine-tuning. In addition, as we discuss in the next chapter, an important aspect of this is the mindset developed by staff training and development, job rotation and teamwork, which ultimately support the development of self-reinforcing virtuous circles at the organisational level, as discussed in Chapter 4.[1]

SIA's Approaches to Continuous Improvement and New Service Development

SIA's approaches to overcoming its key challenges in delivering sustained service excellence are in one way or another linked to constant innovation and improvement. It is the company's amazing ability to innovate that has enabled it to sustain its service excellence and cement its service leadership position over decades. Unlike many other service firms that tend to rely heavily on centralised R&D departments to develop new services, SIA's approach to new service development involves the seamless combination of both hard, structured, rigorous and centralised methods, headed mainly by the Product Innovation Department, and soft, emergent, distributed but equally significant ones, mainly headed by

SIA has the widest business class seats in the world, folding out to become 6-foot beds. With only four seats per row, all seats have direct access to the aisle.

Source: Courtesy of Singapore Airlines.

different functional departments. SIA understands that the importance of regularly introducing discontinuous, substantial innovations that wow the customer and position it as a service leader in the eyes of its passengers, such as the launch of the first inflight entertainment system on demand in all classes, the suites in the A380, the flat beds in business class and, more recently, the widest business class seats in the world.

At the same time, SIA also knows that it is necessary to initiate a large quantity of incremental, cost-effective innovations across all its operating units to ensure the airline is constantly improving its service standards and productivity levels. Using distributed innovations effectively means that a large quantity of incremental innovations are produced by individual functional departments, which gives SIA an edge over its competitors and helps it to sustain excellent standards for all aspects of its services. As Mr Timothy Chua, senior manager of the Inflight Services (Projects) Department, notes, 'Innovation is not just thinking about new ideas but looking at old ideas and thinking about how to make them better.' Hence sustaining service excellence through constant innovation is not about employing some geniuses and getting them to innovate, but more about encouraging the staff to look at all processes constantly to search for opportunities to improve. SIA aims to improve just a little bit, all the time, in everything, making it very difficult for competitors to copy. In the following sections, we will discuss SIA's centralised new service design, followed by its distributed innovation capabilities.

Centralised Innovation – SIA's Approach to Designing Major Service Breakthroughs

Centralised innovations are mainly hard and highly structured innovations and include many major, discontinuous innovations such as the recently launched non-stop service between Singapore and New York with upgraded business and executive economy classes, or the design of the A380 cabin. SIA's Product Innovation Department consists of a small group of people, augmented by staff from all departments on one-year placements, whose key task is to conceive innovative ideas and to take

The executive economy class cabin provides passengers with affordable comfort on SIA's ultra long-haul flights between Singapore and Los Angeles, and Singapore and New York.

Source: Courtesy of Singapore Airlines.

selected ones through the development cycle to commercial introduction. Mr Sim Kim Chui, vice president of the Product Development Department (2000–2007), says, 'Within the Product Innovation Department there is what we call the innovation lab, where resources are on a one-year basis. This person who comes in can be from anywhere in the company, be it the cabin crew or the engineering division or elsewhere. They would be asked to come into this idea lab, where they will spend one year coming up with ideas. No holds barred so they can come up with ideas on any aspect of the airline business ... Their KPI is how many good ideas they can come up with. It's not easy, it's very challenging actually.'

The Product Innovation Department follows a well-defined innovation framework that guides activities such as new service development processes including opportunity identification and selection, concept evaluation, design and development, and new service launches. At the very preliminary stage, there must be abundant useful information that provides the company with some valuable insights on where it should start. The information can come from various sources including benchmarking surveys run by the International Air Transport Association (IATA), which compares SIA's performance with that of other airlines, surveys conducted with random sampling of passengers on about 10% of SIA's flights, focus groups, and listening to its frontline staff. After the opportunities have been identified, evaluated and approved by the management committee, the design and development processes begin, followed by the launch (see Figure 5.1).

At a broad level, SIA's innovation is heavily driven by customer needs. Mr Yap Kim Wah says, 'SIA is a profit-generating organisation. We are not an institute of technology, and whatever we do must make business sense. That is the guiding principle. To support the guiding principle, we have to make a profit and customers must want to return. Therefore all innovations, in one way or another, must be something that customers need, although sometimes, customers may not know what they need!' SIA conducts workshops and focus groups with customers asking them to identify what new services they would like to see on an aeroplane. These services are prioritised in SIA's list of potential innovations. Mr Sim

Figure 5.1

SIA's three-step centralised innovation process

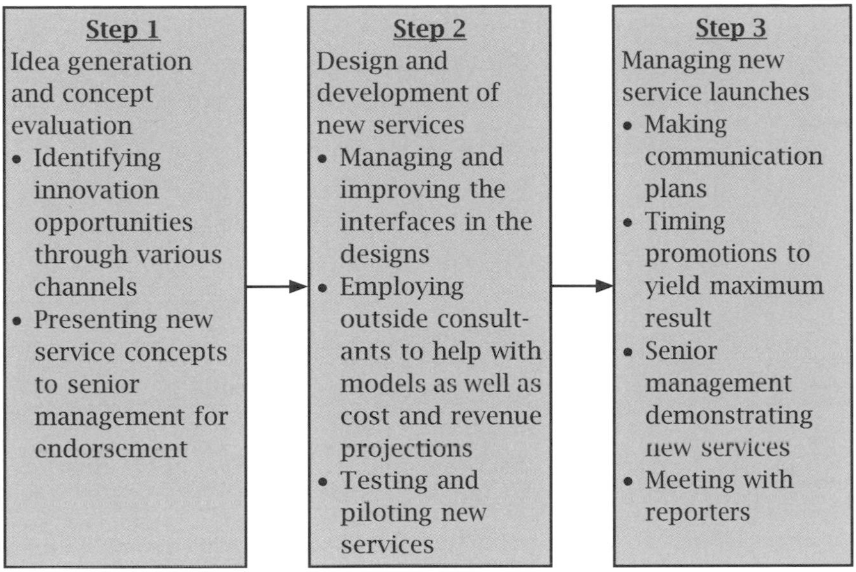

Step 1	Step 2	Step 3
Idea generation and concept evaluation • Identifying innovation opportunities through various channels • Presenting new service concepts to senior management for endorsement	Design and development of new services • Managing and improving the interfaces in the designs • Employing outside consultants to help with models as well as cost and revenue projections • Testing and piloting new services	Managing new service launches • Making communication plans • Timing promotions to yield maximum result • Senior management demonstrating new services • Meeting with reporters

Source: Authors' interpretation based on interviews with SIA management.

Kim Chui elaborates, 'The most important is what is important to the customer. So from that list ... what we are interested in would be the key needs, the top 5, the top 10, the ones that everybody wants.'

Idea Generation and Concept Evaluation

Besides identifying innovation opportunities through the feedback gathered from customers and frontline staff, the Product Innovation Department also tries to generate innovation ideas from other sources of information, such as the study of lifestyle trends and competitor analyses. Members of the staff are constantly searching for new ideas. They surf the Net, attend conferences, process feedback gathered from customers, and are constantly in contact with designers worldwide.

Apart from searching for ideas outside the airline context, SIA also closely monitors competition. According to Dr Yeoh Teng Kwong, senior manager of the Product Innovation Department, knowing what competitors are offering and what they are not gives SIA a better knowledge of what might work for the organisation. A research department that tracks and compares competitors' and SIA's products and services has been set up. This presents SIA with very good opportunities to explore the needs that are not yet satisfied or not fully satisfied by existing service offerings. For instance, whenever a competitor offers a new service, SIA would send its people to try it out. After exploring a new service, SIA would evaluate it and see if it would make sense to introduce that service as well, or to come up with something that is even better than the competitor's offerings. To track competition more closely, SIA also subscribes to an IATA market research tool known as the Global Airlines Performance Survey (GAP). From this survey, SIA identifies airlines with significant improvements or airlines that are particularly strong in certain aspects. Those are the airlines SIA will study in more depth to see what can be learned from them.

SIA also knows that sustaining service excellence means aiming to be a bit better at everything compared to its competitors; it constantly benchmarks itself against its competitors to try to achieve this. Dr Yeoh Teng Kwong notes, 'One of the things we can do in terms of innovation is not necessarily always coming up with new ideas. If somebody can do [something] very well, we can emulate them and do better if we can.'

Although sustaining service excellence may mean emulating competitors and doing better than them, SIA also recognises the fact that it needs to come up with new ideas that differentiate the brand in order to cement its service leadership position as, ultimately, it is the new ideas that will wow customers. Mr Yap Kim Wah explains, 'Idea generation within SIA is, to a large extent, governed by the need to differentiate, in other words, to stay ahead as we are a premium carrier. Therefore, there will be ideas that we always come up with that are uniquely different from others.'

Although major and substantial innovations are the Product Innovation Department's mainstay, a soft, flexible and unstructured innovation process co-exists to allow individuals in the department to pursue less orthodox ideas, let them simmer and be incorporated at a later point into the formal new service development process, or be handed over to the operational units for development.

Over the last few years, to encourage employees to participate actively in the opportunity identification process, all of SIA's employees have been given a chance to join a programme called Future Works. Future Works is like an annual mini boot camp that consists of some 50 executives from various departments. Dr Yeoh Teng Kwong elaborates, 'The concept is to bring together a group of people from different departments and backgrounds, lock them up for a few days … and do brainstorming.' Participants will have a chance to let their imagination run wild. At the end of the workshop, they will be given a chance to present their ideas to the Venture Board, a selected group of SIA's senior vice presidents. Funds will be provided to develop ideas if the board endorses them. (Future Works has recently been superseded by the programme which places staff from various departments of the company into the innovation lab for a year to come up with new ideas and to involve others in developing and testing them.)

A simple tool known as the central electronic log enables everyone in the Product Innovation Department to participate and contribute in the innovation process. Dr Yeoh Teng Kwong explains that whenever a staff member of his department finds an exciting new idea or technology on the Internet, in the newspapers or elsewhere, they are encouraged to capture the idea in the electronic log. So at any one time, the department can have about tens of ideas in this log, many of which are wild and preliminary. Meetings are held every few weeks to discuss these ideas.

SIA's success in getting employees from all levels to participate and contribute to idea and concept generation can be credited to the conducive processes that the organisation has instilled and developed. Dr Yeoh Teng Kwong adds, 'SIA makes innovation possible and easy by using the oxymoron called "systematic innovation".'

Design and Development of Innovations: Bringing Innovative Ideas One Step Closer to Customers

After identifying and selecting innovative ideas, and getting the endorsement from the management committee, an innovation has to be carefully developed before it can add real value to SIA and its passengers. Development consists of the creation of everything from the design to the marketing of a new service.

As customers' interest is always SIA's top priority, a lot of time is spent to ensure that any innovation is extremely user-friendly. Various models and combinations are tried, modified and subjected to detailed testing. Mr Timothy Chua says, 'We focus very much on simplicity and ease of use; we are constantly reviewing the interface and deleting what is unnecessary to make the innovation as simple as possible ... Because, ultimately, if we have something that's not easy to use, it doesn't serve the purpose.' SIA also brings in third-party consultants to help with the models and projections. 'Some of the modelling things are a little bit tricky, even for our own people,' says Dr Yeoh Teng Kwong. For instance, a consulting firm assisted in the development of A380 cabin concepts using various analytical tools, including conjoint and financial analyses, to help optimise the cabin design. Third-party consultants are also employed to assess the ideas, processes and projected quantities developed by SIA's staff because they represent the objective view of outside experts.

Because of the cross-functional nature of airline operations, every new service development team has to have the right mix of people. Dr Yeoh Teng Kwong explains that the senior staff in his department tend to be the project drivers, but each team has an approximately equal number of people from other relevant departments to ensure a cross-functional perspective to a project.

After the product development proposals are drawn up, much time is spent fine-tuning and identifying potential failure points by asking what can go wrong and why. The different failure points are connected to get a coherent picture of the underlying problems which the team then

128

proceeds to address. Testing and piloting come after the design and engineering stages. Mr Timothy Chua explains that instead of going into large-scale implementations and investing lots of capital, SIA prefers to conduct small trials, often with a small group of priority customers, to test a new service.

Finally, the SIA team will try to synergise all new services as much as possible with its famous cabin crew. Mr Sim Kim Chui, vice president of the Product Development Department, says, 'I say we leverage on our strength because crew service is our key strength ... at the end of the day it's about cabin crew service. So I always emphasise to my team that the hardware that we develop must leverage on the software; only then can we get the maximum out of it.' He adds that the decision to provide flexibility to passengers flying in the A380 suites – who could choose to have complete privacy by closing the doors or leave them open if they prefer the flight crew to attend to them – was based on providing passengers constant available access to the airline's key strength, cabin crew service.

Managing New Service Launches

After the piloting, testing and trials, new services meeting management approval are introduced and marketed to its customers. Promotional activities are launched to encourage the adoption of the new services and to increase their usage. During the initial launches, SIA organises media events, in which a senior member of staff, such as Mr Yap Kim Wah, meets with reporters and demonstrates a new service. After the initial launches, SIA often runs various types of promotions, including lucky draws and offers for double frequent flyer points to encourage customer adoption as well as special deals for flying on new routes, using the SMS-based check-in service, the Internet for frequent flyer service transactions and conducting online redemptions of frequent flyer rewards. This final phase of new service management is important as it helps educate customers about the benefits of new products and how they are operated and used, so as to facilitate customer adoption.

In March 2008, SIA commenced its four-times-weekly flights to Houston via Moscow, making the airline the first to provide direct flights to the Russian capital.

Source: Courtesy of Singapore Airlines.

Distributed Innovation – SIA's Approach to Continuous Improvements and Major Redesign of Processes Throughout the Organisation

Besides the hard and centralised approach, SIA also adopts a softer new service development approach, which is perhaps best described as distributed innovation, a process that truly differentiates the company's innovation and new service development approaches from those of many other companies. While the centralised innovation undertaken by the Product Innovation Department follows a well-defined innovation framework involving a number of key fixed points (for example, initial senior vice president endorsement, development of a robust business case, and senior management approval), distributed innovation is overseen by individual functional departments. It is primarily an unstructured, emergent process that focuses on continuous improvement, and tends to be fluid and flexible. In addition, the budget for distributed innovation is often absorbed in the individual department's operating expenses. Dr Yeoh Teng Kwong explains, 'I would not consider my department as the central product development unit as this would give the impression that we drive all new developments in SIA. Far from it. The culture of innovation is so pervasive in the company that most functional departments have the innovation objective as part of their mission. SIA strives to excel in a multitude of areas so that our competitors find it a near insurmountable task to try to rival us.'

SIA's culture encourages a stream of new ideas from its various functions, such as inflight services, ground services and loyalty marketing. The ideas are developed and implemented by people in those functions in a decentralised, distributed manner, using department budgets at least for the initial stages of development. The recently redesigned Internet check-in service is an example of distributed innovation. This service was conceptualised, developed and implemented by the Ground Services Department after it noticed the high customer acceptance and utilisation of telephone and SMS check-in services. Distributed innovation is especially important in sustaining service excellence – which requires all the components of a service encounter (the totality) to be excellent, as it helps to ensure that all functional departments focus on improving their respective services.

The fluid process of distributed innovation enables and encourages specific departments to take ownership of their innovations and continuously monitor and develop them, based on staff and customer feedback. Continuous enhancements to the SMS check-in process, for example, were made to improve functionality without sacrificing ease of use. Other improvements which have resulted from distributed innovation include the now commonly available ability to choose one's seat through the Internet or via SMS, and the unique book-the-cook service which allows business and first-class passengers to order their favourite dish before their flight.

Distributed innovation guards the company against blindly following technological fads because it involves the people who are close to the actual processes and who therefore can more easily see hype for what it is. For example, at the height of the WAP (wireless application protocol) craze, the Ground Services Department made a conscious decision to focus on SMS check-in technologies instead because SMS was considered more user-friendly and the infrastructure was readily available to most of its passengers.

In addition, the influence and direct involvement of operations staff in the innovation process means that the ability to consistently and seamlessly deliver, a cornerstone of SIA's success, is not compromised by the introduction of innovations that sound good but cannot be delivered reliably. One example of such an innovation is the proposed idea of passengers ordering inflight drinks through KrisFlyer, SIA's inflight entertainment system. Eventually, SIA decided not to pursue this as it could foresee the ability to deliver the drinks to passengers within a reasonable time and with the necessary level of customisation would be compromised. This operational ownership of innovations at the department level is crucial for SIA, reinforcing its key competency of the operational ability to deliver consistent and reliable service every time, in every customer transaction.

The soft distributed innovation process also has a hard edge. Functional departments undertake major new service developments that are mainly within their areas of control. While minor adjustments can be made almost anytime, expensive and significant changes are subjected to key fixed point checks also adhered to by the Product Innovation Department. However, these developments are carried out independently of the Product Innovation Department, and are generally overseen by the senior vice presidents of the respective divisions.

Table 5.1 outlines the features of the hard, structured service development process as well as the soft, unstructured service development process at SIA.

132

Table 5.1
A summary of the features of the service development process

New service development process	New service development organisational activity	
	Centralised, Product Innovation Department	Distributed, functional departments
Hard, highly structured new service development process	Well-defined and structured innovation framework with a number of fixed points, focusing on major, usually high-cost, innovations.	Major new service development conducted within the departments' areas of control but subject to the same key fixed points. Structured assessment of customer feedback and rewards for innovation.
Soft, flexible, unstructured, emergent process	Flexible process allowing individuals to pursue less orthodox ideas before the ideas are fed into the formal new service development process or handed over to operational units for development.	Primarily unstructured, emergent process focusing on continuous improvements. Budget often absorbed in operating expenses.

Source: Adapted from Heracleous, L., Wirtz, J., & Johnston, R. (2005) Kung Fu Service Development at Singapore Airlines. Business Strategy Review, Winter issue, pp. 25–31.

The Role of Feedback in Driving Service Innovation

It is important to note that one key driver behind SIA's distributed innovation competence is the high importance given to customer feedback. To encourage the customers (both internal and external) to voice out their comments, SIA takes both compliments and complaints seriously.

133

Mr Sim Kay Wee elaborates, 'There is a vice president responsible for compliments and complaints and every letter must be acknowledged, investigated and followed up, even letters of compliment.' In addition to analysing customer complaints, compliments and suggestions, SIA collects around 12,000 questionnaires a month on all its routes and travel classes to reliably understand strengths and weaknesses system-wide, by geographic region, by station, by route and by travel class. The detailed and comprehensive analysis allows SIA to pinpoint any weaknesses in its service delivery system and to understand its strengths and work on cementing them better.

Through its integrated customer feedback system, SIA gathers a lot of feedback from its customers. A large proportion of customer feedback is verbally given to its frontline staff, especially the cabin crew. Mr Yap Kim Wah explains, 'We take verbal reports very seriously. In order for someone to sit down and write, he or she has to be either very happy or very angry. But there are always lots of little, less extreme things that people don't bother to write down. If a customer mentions to a member of crew, for example, that a meal is a little too salty, the member of crew will pass on the comment to their manager. The manager will contact our food and beverage manager who will inform the caterer ... So if you don't listen to the crew, you've let an opportunity to improve your service quality pass, which is crazy!'

SIA's feedback system is geared to gather and process feedback from its employees, including the cabin crew, ground staff, and back-office employees. In addition, SIA listens very attentively to its overseas staff as the company knows the importance of local country and culture-specific knowledge, especially for a globally operating firm with customers from all over the world and offices in many countries. SIA's elaborate feedback mechanisms help it not only listen to customers, but also to understand them better. Mr Yap Kim Wah adds, 'SIA understands that the frontline staff are very important because they are in intimate contact with the customers. The management listens sincerely to the crew of every flight that the airline operates and they know that the management takes their feedback very seriously. If the company does not respond to the feedback given by the crew members, they will be disheartened.'

At SIA, customer feedback is recorded and transferred to the relevant departments for immediate consideration, and to a central unit that tabulates, analyses and maps trends before reporting on an aggregate level back to the departments. As a result, individual departments have plenty of first-hand opportunities to introduce small but significant improvements continuously. Besides providing useful insights for individual departments and reinforcing SIA's distributed innovation competence, the comments and feedback also help the Product Innovation Department to identify opportunities to wow and surprise its customers.

Understanding customers is not easy, however. Mr Sim Kay Wee elaborates, 'Sometimes, passengers can't tell you what they will need, they cannot anticipate. We have to do this for them ... For example, we noticed the changing tastes of passengers. They were becoming more health conscious about their food, so we made the food lighter and more nutritious. We study data and observe customers in order to understand them really well, so that we can anticipate their needs.' He goes on to cite the introduction of the flight alert service as an example of the importance of anticipating customers' needs, 'We developed our mobile phone services largely because we believed that there would be a demand for them. Some people were sceptical. We were the first to introduce the alert service, which sends an SMS informing the customer of flight arrivals and delays.' He gives another example, saying, 'There was some scepticism when we launched our e-mail service in the air. Some people said that the aircraft is about the only sanctuary they have, away from their work and their bosses. They didn't want all that connectivity! However, the feedback that customers gave really showed that they really appreciated it. So, we provided that facility. If you don't want it, you don't have to use it. But I think business people will enjoy the flight more if they have cleared their e-mails! Often, business people feel very stressed in the last hours before they leave the office, so we can say to them, "Relax, you don't have to be so frantic. You can take your time on board to deal with those last-minute problems". We study the trends and try to be proactive.'

It is worth noting that the inflight e-mail service was discontinued in 2006 because of insufficient demand. The pricing imposed by Boeing, the developer of the technology, was relatively steep, between US$10 and US$27, for different durations within a single flight.[2] What the discontinuation of the service shows is that even with extensive consumer research and robust planning and implementation, there is always a risk that innovations will not be accepted as anticipated. It also shows the value of experimentation and the need for flexibility to remove innovations that do not deliver as expected.

SIA – A Master of Innovation

SIA has shown in the past 30-plus years that it can deliver sustained cost-effective service excellence and competitive advantage powered significantly through its innovation capabilities. SIA seems to have the ability to combine hard and soft aspects of innovation. This unique approach to new service development involves the seamless combination of both structured, rigorous, centralised innovation, led mainly by the Product Innovation Department, with emergent, distributed, but equally significant innovation led by different functional departments. This process is supported by SIA's integrated customer and frontline staff feedback systems that provide valuable insights for both the Product Innovation Department and other functional departments.

END NOTES

1. This chapter is partly based on interviews with the following SIA executives and staff (in alphabetical order) from 2001 to 2008. Since the interviews were conducted over a number of years, the designations of some interviewees have changed. The list of interviewees below shows the title of the individuals during the interview, and any subsequent changes in designation since then are indicated in parentheses:

- Mr Choo Poh Leong, Senior Manager, Cabin Crew Performance (now Senior Manager Crew Services)
- Mr Timothy Chua, Project Manager, New Service Development (now Senior Manager Inflight Services (Projects))
- Ms Lim Suet Kwee, Senior Rank Trainer, SIA Training School
- Ms Lim Suu Kuan, Commercial Training Manager
- Mr Seow, Patrick, Senior Rank Trainer, SIA Training School
- Mr Sim Kay Wee, former Senior Vice President, Cabin Crew
- Mr Sim Kim Chui, Vice President, Contracts (from 2000-2007, Vice President, Product Development)
- Ms Betty Wong, Senior Manager, Cabin Crew Service Development (now Acting Vice President, Inflight Services)
- Mr Yap Kim Wah, Senior Vice President, Product and Service
- Dr Yeoh Teng Kwong, Senior Manager, Product Innovation (currently with another company)

2. Figure 6.6 in Chapter 6 gives a summary of the above discussion in the context of strategic human resource management.

3. *Times Online*, 17 August 2006, Boeing Scraps In-Flight Broadband, http://business.timesonline.co.uk/tol/business/industry_sectors/engineering/article611892.ece

6

MANAGING PEOPLE EFFECTIVELY TO DELIVER SUSTAINED SERVICE EXCELLENCE[1]

'The only resource that the country has is its people. And therefore, there's no option but to be the best ... At the end of the day it's the software, people like us, who make the real difference.'

Patrick Seow, senior rank trainer,
Singapore Airlines Training School, and senior flight steward

'In Singapore, we always want to be the best in a lot of things. SIA is no different. ... a lot of things that we have been taught from young, from our Asian heritage ... filial piety, the care and concern, hospitality, and of course the most important part is trying, if we can, to do whatever we can to please the customer. And how do we do it? Sometimes, people just wonder "how do you guys manage to do it with limited time and resources on a flight", yet we manage to do it somehow. Call us magicians.'

Lim Suet Kwee, senior rank trainer,
Singapore Airlines Training School, and senior flight stewardess

Behind most of today's successful service organisations stands a firm commitment to the effective management of human resources (HR), including recruitment, selection, training, motivation and retention of employees.[2] Leading service firms are often characterised by a distinctive culture, strong service leadership and role modelling by top management. It is probably harder for competitors to duplicate high-performance human assets, and the associated mindset and values than any other corporate resource. In addition, service staff can be crucially important for a firm's competitive positioning, because the frontline:

- **Is a core part of the product.** As soon as frontline staff are involved in a service process, it tends to be the most visible element of the service, delivers the service and significantly determines service quality. This is exemplified in the case of SIA where its frontline staff – the Singapore Girl – has become synonymous with SIA, personifies quality service,[3] and is one of the airline industry's most instantly recognised figures. This affords the airline a key competitive advantage since none of the other airlines have managed to 'brand' and promote their cabin crew as successfully as SIA.
- **Is the service firm.** Frontline staff represent the service firm, and from a customer's perspective, are the firm. Frontline staff at SIA are empowered to make appropriate decisions that customise service delivery as needed and take corrective actions instantaneously during service recovery.
- **Is the brand.** Frontline staff and service are a core part of the brand. It is the staff that determine whether the brand promise gets delivered or not. SIA understands that and places enormous emphasis on all aspects of the selection, training and motivation of its staff in general, and its frontline staff in particular.

In this chapter, we will focus on the people side of SIA's sustained service excellence. Specifically, we will:

- Expand on the five key elements behind SIA's effective HR management, and how each of the five elements reinforces SIA's service excellence strategy
- Outline how SIA manages to effectively address three key service-related challenges: how to deal with sky-high customer expectations; how to achieve balance between service standardisation as well as personalisation; and how to approach a large number of services and support sub-processes in totality to attain service excellence

- Address the industrial relations challenges posed by the need to cut costs due to the difficult operating environment, and the steps SIA took to address them

The Five Key Elements of SIA's HR Management

Based on our interviews with SIA's senior management, we identified five interrelated and mutually supportive elements that together constitute SIA's strategic HR management. Together with the leadership and role-modelling of its top management, these five elements are an important part of the explanation of how SIA has managed to consistently deliver cost-effective service excellence for over three decades through the effective development and management of one of its greatest assets, its human resources (see Figure 6.1).

Figure 6.1
The five elements behind SIA's effective HR management

Source: This model was derived from the authors' interviews with SIA's senior management and service personnel.

141

As seen in Figure 6.1, the five elements behind SIA's effective HR management include stringent selection and hiring of people, followed by extensive training and re-training of employees, formation of successful service delivery teams, empowerment of the frontline, and employee motivation. Such elements are highlighted in successful HR management, especially in the 'strategic HRM' field, and they have been shown to lead to higher company performance.[4] However, many service firms have not been able to implement them successfully. Now let us take a closer look at how the five elements work and complement each other at SIA.

Stringent Selection and Recruitment Processes

As Jim Collins says, 'The old adage "People are the most important asset" is wrong. The right people are your most important asset.' We would like to add to this: '… and the wrong people are a liability.' Getting it right starts with hiring the right people. To support its service excellence strategy, SIA adopts a rigorous system and process for staff selection and recruitment.

Cabin crew applicants, who must be under 26 years old, are initially assessed on both academic and physical attributes. If they meet baseline requirements on these, then they go through an extensive recruitment process that involves three rounds of interviews, a 'uniform test', a 'water confidence' test, psychometric tests and a tea party. Out of 16,000 applications received annually, around 500 to 600 new cabin crew are hired to cover turnover rates of around 10%, which include both voluntary and directed attrition. When the cabin crew start flying, they are carefully monitored for their first six months through a monthly report by the inflight supervisor. At the end of the probationary period, around 75% get confirmed for their initial five-year contract, around 20% get an extension of the probationary period, and around 5% leave.

Due to the special social status and glamour that SIA's cabin crew enjoy, many young and educated women and men from all over Asia apply every year to join the ranks of SIA. Ms Lim Swet Kwee, senior rank trainer at the SIA Training School, who joined SIA in the late 1980s,

The Singapore Girl created in 1972 has since been the leading figure of SIA's international marketing and advertising campaign.

Source: Courtesy of Singapore Airlines.

says, 'It was like everyone was talking about SIA. It was the most hip word you heard around ... The commercials played a very great part ... [For many] girls at the time, ... [and even] today, being a stewardess at SIA has been the ultimate. You know, we just want to fly with this airline that everybody has been talking about and ... [to be] part of it.'

Because of SIA's brand reputation as a service leader in the airline industry and as a company that develops its staff in an extensive and holistic manner, it can have its pick of talented young people. Many prospective employees in Asia, especially school leavers and university graduates, see SIA as an excellent company to work for, often opening the door to more lucrative jobs in other companies. In order to provide a richer sense of what is involved in SIA's selection and recruitment process, we quote Mr Choo Poh Leong, senior manager of crew services.

143

According to Mr Choo, SIA looks for cabin applicants 'who have that empathy with people.' He says, 'We try and see whether the person is cheerful, friendly, humble, because we don't want him or her to fly and then … give … [passengers] a bad time on board the airline.'

After SIA receives the job applications, successful candidates are shortlisted and then brought in for an interview. Applicants go through several rounds of interviews: first a group interview, an initial preliminary round where the interviewers look at the applicants' overall looks and personality and their spoken English. Typically, in that round, applicants will be asked to introduce, talk about themselves, and then read a passage for interviewers to assess their standard of English. In this initial round, interviewers look at applicants purely to determine whether they have that SIA look and overall personality. At this point, the interview is not very in-depth. If an applicant is successful in the initial round, he or she moves on to a more in-depth one-on-one interview. Here, the interviewer will ask more in-depth questions to try and assess whether applicants have the core values and competencies SIA desires in its cabin crew. If an applicant succeeds in this second round, he or she will then take a psychometric test. The result will be given to a senior management panel at the end of the process. This test complements the selection exercise in confirming the results of the in-depth interviews. After this test, applicants move on to what SIA calls a 'uniform check'. Applicants will actually put on the *sarong kebaya* (SIA's uniform for female cabin crew), and at this stage mostly female interviewers will assess how an applicant looks in the *sarong kebaya* in terms of posture, gait and general looks. Successful applicants in this round then move on to a water confidence test. At SIA's training pool at its flight safety wing, applicants, wearing a life jacket, are asked to jump from a three-metre height into the pool; since successful applicants will later as part of their training learn how to help passengers when doing an evacuation on water, SIA cannot have cabin crew with a fear of water or heights. The next round of interviews is what SIA calls the management round. Here, the senior vice president of cabin crew and one of the senior staff of cabin crew services interview all those who have been shortlisted from all the earlier rounds. Here, it is a two-on-one interview. This round is again very in-depth, because SIA wants to ensure that it picks the right applicants. After this round, the final assessments will be made at a tea party with the successful applicants. Mr Choo Poh Leong says, 'We mix with them, we talk to them ... in case during the two-on-one round, we have certain doubts about them, ... or we may have made certain judgement about them [which] we like to reconfirm in the management tea party round. So once you get through that, then you are selected.' This rigorous selection process ensures with reasonable certainty that SIA hires the cabin crew it desires, and eliminates less suitable candidates. The result is that only 3–4% of applicants are hired in each recruitment drive.

Extensive Investment in Training and Re-Training

When a firm has good people in the first place, investments in training and re-training can then yield outstanding results. Service champions show a strong commitment in words, dollars and action towards training. As Schneider and Bowen put it: 'The combination of attracting a diverse and competent applicant pool, utilising effective techniques for hiring the most appropriate people from that pool, and then training the heck out of them would be gangbusters in any market.'[5]

Our interviews with SIA's senior management clearly show that SIA places great emphasis on training, so much so that it is one of its focal points in its HR and service excellence strategy. Ms Lam Seet Mui, senior manager for HR development, says, 'SIA invests huge numbers of dollars in infrastructure and technology but, ultimately, you need people to drive it. At SIA, we believe that people actually do make a difference, so the company has in place a very comprehensive and holistic approach to developing our human resources.'

Although training is regularly highlighted as a key component in the cycle of success for service firms,[6] SIA seems to put a relatively greater emphasis on the training of its frontline staff. For example, a newly recruited batch of cabin crew staff are required to go through an intensive four-month training course, which is considered to be the longest

SIA's pilots will only be allowed to take off and land upon completing 29 months of comprehensive training.

Source: Courtesy of Singapore Airlines.

and most comprehensive training programme in the airline industry,[7] being twice the industry average. In addition, flight crew are also required to go through 29 months of comprehensive 'online training' before being promoted to First Officer.[8]

The aim of SIA's training is to provide gracious service reflecting warmth and friendliness, while maintaining an image of authority and confidence in the passengers' minds. Each month, thousands of prospective cabin crew employees apply for the airline's rigorous and holistic course that encompasses not only safety and functional training, but also beauty tips, discussions on gourmet food and fine wines, and the art of conversation.[9] Mr Choo Poh Leong elaborates, 'During the four months of training, of course, there are several courses you go through. Typically, you'll have to go through modules like the SIA Way [in which] they teach you what we expect of you in SIA, passenger handling skills, food and beverage skills, service attributes, grooming. We pay a lot of attention to grooming and deportment. And then you also go through various safety training courses which are conducted by our flight safety department ... [where you learn] about first aid, ... safety equipment [and] procedures, evacuation procedures [and] how to handle unruly passengers. So it's quite a comprehensive training course and [after]

146

you pass the course, then you fly. And then you go on probation for six months ... But training doesn't stop there, there's continual training, so even operating crew are brought back down to the ground for further training.'

The development of soft skills is crucial. Mr Patrick Seow, senior rank trainer, comments, 'Making eye contact to us is very important, body language, how we should greet, the words we should use [are all very important].' Further, new recruits are being taught the importance of going the extra mile. Ms Lim Suet Kwee, senior rank trainer, adds, 'Apart from the standard procedures that you have to know, all the "extra miles" come from within. So we always tell ... [the staff], "If you think you can go the extra mile, you want to give more to make a very happy passenger, ... please go ahead and do it." We always say that we do not expect any form of reward or anything from our customers when we give excellent service. The only thing that is most pleasing to our ears is, you know, [when] someone getting off the plane ... [says to us] "thank you for your wonderful job, I want to come back and fly with you guys again. It's been a wonderful experience." This is the thing that we love to hear. We don't need anything else.'

Because of SIA's reputation for excellent service, coupled with its aim of continuous improvement, SIA's customers tend to have very high expectations and can be very demanding, which can put considerable pressure on its frontline staff. According to Ms Lim Suu Kuan, commercial training manager, SIA has a motto: 'If SIA can't do it for you, no other airline can ... The challenge is to help the staff deal with the difficult situations and take the brickbats'. Although SIA staff are very proud and protective of the company, the company still has to help them deal with the emotional turmoil of having to satisfy and even delight very demanding customers, without feeling that they are being taken advantage of.

According to Dr Cheong Choong Kong, 'to the company, training is forever and no one is too young to be trained, nor too old.' And Mr Yap Kim Wah, senior vice president of product and service, adds, 'We believe that there is no moment, regardless of how senior a staff is, when you cannot learn something. So all of us, senior vice presidents included, are sent for training regularly. We all have a training path. You can always pick up something. If you have completed quite a number of programmes, then you go on sabbatical. You go and learn a language, do something new and refresh yourself.' Such continuous training and re-training have been vital to SIA's sustained service excellence, because it helps staff have an open mindset, accept change and development, and deliver the new services that SIA introduces regularly.

SIA's extensive training equips its frontline staff with the skills and attitude required for delivering warm, friendly as well as competent service.

Source: Courtesy of Singapore Airlines.

SIA's Training Centre was set up in January 1993 and consists of the Management Development Centre (MDC) plus four other training departments: Cabin Crew Training, Flight Crew Training, Commercial Training and IT Training. General management training is offered by MDC, which is under the purview of the HR Division. It provides executive and leadership programmes for staff from all parts of the company to generate effective administrators as well as visionary managers. This training is centralised so that engineers get to meet IT experts, marketing people, and so on. This purposeful mixing of its staff enhances mutual understanding and a more integrated and holistic view (and management) by all divisions. MDC's programs are divided into three broad areas:[10] firstly, management development programmes focusing on the changing priorities and skills required at various levels of the managerial hierarchy; secondly, management skill programmes which are functional or skill-related ranging from the art of negotiation to the learning of other cultures; and thirdly, self-development programmes in areas such as social etiquette.

SIA trains about 9,000 people a year and is well known for its dynamic and committed approach to training. Ms Lam Seet Mui says, 'About 70% of SIA's courses are in-house, and one of SIA's recent service excellence initiatives, called Transforming Customer Service (TCS), involves staff in five key operational areas – cabin crew, engineering, ground services, flight operations and sales support. To ensure that the TCS culture is promoted company-wide, it is also embedded into all management training. The MDC has put together a two-day management training programme entitled TCS Operational Areas Strategy Implementing Synergy (OASIS) ... The programme is also about building team spirit amongst our staff in key operational areas so that together, we will make the whole journey as pleasant and seamless as possible for our passengers. One has to realise that it is not just the ticketing or reservations people and the cabin crew who come into contact with our passengers. The pilots, station managers and station engineers have a role in customer service as well, because from time to time, they do come into contact with the passengers

... But TCS is not just about people. In TCS, there is the "40-30-30" rule – a holistic approach to people, processes (or procedures) and products. SIA focuses 40% of its resources on training and invigorating our people, 30% on the review of process and procedures, and 30% on creating new product and service ideas.' SIA thus looks at the totality rather than focus on just one aspect of the customer experience, which enables the airline to deliver a service that is excellent in all aspects.

One of the main forces behind the success of SIA's training and re-training programmes is its leadership, as well as the relationship management builds with staff. Mr Timothy Chua, product manager of the New Service Development Department, says, 'I see myself first as a coach and second as a team player.' Instead of positioning themselves as managers or superiors, SIA's management staff often view themselves as mentors and coaches, guiding and imparting knowledge and experience to new recruits and new department members.

To assure its management understands the big picture, SIA trains all management staff through job rotation. Managers are rotated between departments every few years. This policy has a number of benefits. Managers acquire an understanding of the workings of more of the organisation than they would otherwise. It also promotes a corporate outlook, reduces inter-departmental disputes, and creates an appetite for change and innovation as people constantly bring fresh perspectives and new ideas to their new positions.

Building High Performance Service Delivery Teams

The nature of many services requires people to work effectively in teams, often across functions, if they want to deliver seamless customer service. Effective teams facilitate communication and knowledge sharing among team members, thus enabling the members to understand and learn from each other.

SIA understands the importance of teamwork in the delivery of service excellence, and has always worked hard to create esprit de corps among its cabin crew. SIA's approach to developing teamwork among its diverse group of cabin crew involves the 'team concept', which entails dividing the 6,600 crew into teams, small units with a team leader in charge of about 13 people. Members of the team will be rostered to fly together as much as possible. Flying together as a unit allows them to build camaraderie and get to know each other. The team leader also gets to know each member's strengths and weaknesses well, and will become their mentor and their counsellor, someone whom they can turn to if they need help or advice. The 'check trainers' oversee 12 or 13 teams and fly with them whenever possible, not only to inspect their performance, but also to help the teams develop.

Senior vice president of the Flight Crew Department Mr Sim Kay Wee says, 'The interaction within each of the teams is very strong. As a result, when team leaders do a staff appraisal, they really know the staff. You would be amazed how meticulous and detailed each staff record is, even though there are 6,600 of them. We can pinpoint any staff's strengths and weaknesses easily. So, in this way, we have good control, and through the control, we can ensure that the crew deliver on what they promise … If there are problems, we will know about them and we can send them for re-training. Those who are good will be selected for promotion.'

Mr Toh Giam Ming, senior manager of the Crew Performance Department, adds, 'What is good about the team concept is that despite the huge number of crew, people can relate to a team and have a sense of belonging. They can say, "This is my team." And they are put together for one to two years and rostered together for about 60–70% of the time, so they do fly together quite a fair bit … New people will find that they have fewer problems adjusting to the flying career, no matter what their background is, because once you get familiar with the team, there will be support and guidance on how to do things.' Mr Choo Poh Leong adds, 'The individual, you see, is not a digit or a staff number, because if you don't have team-flying, you have 6,000-odd people; it can be difficult for you to really know a particular person.'

Even when members of the usual team do not fly together, the team spirit is still alive. Mr Patrick Seow notes, 'As far as we are concerned, on every flight, we work as a team whether you are from "my" team or not. Whatever team you come from, you have to work as a team because it's how we get things done. We cannot work individually, there is no way we can do that.' Further, teamwork extends much beyond the flight itself, 'we see that the crew on the flight is a team, and we are also a part of a bigger team. We have to work and have good relationships with the ground services, the engineering ... Because we are a team among all divisions, that's why we are successful.'

SIA also has a lot of seemingly unrelated activities in the cabin crew division. For example, there is a committee called the Performing Arts Circle made up of talented employees with an interest in the arts. During the biennial Cabin Crew Gala Dinner in 2004, SIA cabin crew raised over half a million dollars for charity.[11] In addition to the Performing Arts

Extracurricular activities give SIA crew members the opportunity to do charity work while fostering team spirit.

Source: http://www.singaporeair.com, accessed on 3 March 2005.

Circle, SIA also has a gourmet circle, language circles (such as a German and French speaking group), and even sports circles (such as football and tennis teams). As Mr Sim Kay Wee notes, 'SIA believes that all these things really encourage camaraderie and teamwork.'

Empowerment of the Frontline Staff to Control Quality

Over time, the soft skills of flight crew and other service personnel get honed, leading to service excellence that is difficult to replicate, not only in terms of how the service is delivered, but also in terms of the mindset that supports this delivery. Ms Lim Suet Kwee says, 'Through the years, we have learnt how to anticipate the [needs of our] customers ... [by watching them as we walk] through the cabin. Sometimes they nod their head a little bit or move their hands a little bit and somehow, from the corner of our eye, we notice that and we just walk over to them and ask, "Can I help you, sir? Is there something I can do for you?" ... You never know if someone needs some help somewhere. And if we can help, we do. So we try, sometimes we crack our heads a little bit to try and help a passenger solve some problems that he or she may have encountered somewhere. And if we can't do that, that's when we start to liaise with the ground staff anywhere else in the world to take over the problem from us so that this person may be helped.' This customer-oriented mindset contrasts markedly with the mindset of flight crew from many other airlines, who are neither as engaged nor display too much interest or care in their passengers and any problems they might be facing. In fact the media regularly reports service lapses and mistreated customers in the airline industry.

Virtually all outstanding service firms have legendary stories of employees who recovered failed service transactions, walked the extra mile to make a customer's day, or averted some kind of disaster for a client. Mr Toh Giam Ming shares two such recent stories about SIA staff: 'This particular wheelchair passenger in her eighties was very ill and suffering from arthritis ... She was travelling from Singapore to Brisbane. ... What happened was that this stewardess found the elderly passenger gasping for air due to crippling pain. [The stewardess] used her personal hotwater bag as a warm compress to relieve the passenger's pain, and then she knelt beside her to massage her [swollen] legs and feet for 45 minutes ... The stewardess stayed with the passenger and offered her a new pair of flight support stockings for her swollen feet ... without asking her to pay for it. Basically she cared for her through-out the seven- to eight-hour trip. This old lady was so grateful when she got back to Brisbane ... her son was so thankful that he called the hotel where the crew were staying to try and track down this particular stewardess to thank her personally. This was followed up with a letter to us. I don't know if training is part of it, or if it was a personal thing. You can't find people to do this just purely from training, I think. We find the right people, give them the right support, give them the right training, which enable them to do this kind of things.' Such actions are part of the culture at SIA. According to Mr Choo Poh Leong, the crew members 'are very proud to be part of the SIA team, very proud of the tradition and very proud that SIA is regarded as a company that gives excellent care to customers. So they want to live up to that.'

Employees have to feel empowered in order to engage in such discretionary efforts. Employee self-direction has become increasingly important, especially in service firms, because frontline staff frequently operate on their own, face-to-face with their customers, and it tends to be difficult and also unproductive for managers to constantly closely monitor their actions.[12] Mr Patrick Seow says, 'The most important thing is that crew must have situational awareness ... We don't have a set procedure for each and every situation that we encounter. We say "what would I like to see happen if I were the passenger?" So the crew will look at it from that angle.'

However, one of the biggest issues many service organisations face when it comes to empowerment is that they talk a lot about empowerment without taking concrete actions to achieve it. According to SIA's senior management, staff must have a clear idea of what is within their authority, and it is the responsibility of management to articulate and make it clear what they mean by empowerment. In SIA's case, for example, whereas the usual baggage allowance is 20 kg, frontline staff are empowered to increase the baggage allowance to 25 kg, 30 kg and even 50 kg, as long as the staff feel that it is a right decision. However, such a decision by a frontline staff must be recorded and justified. Mr Yap Kim Wah elaborates, 'For a department to implement the empowerment guidelines, it should give all its staff empowerment two levels up. If you are a clerk, you should know what your officer and your senior officer could do. If these two guys are not around, then go up to their limit.' Empowerment of the frontline staff is especially important during service recovery processes. Mr Timothy Chua comments, 'We strive for instantaneous service recovery. I think that is one of SIA's biggest differentiators. When something goes wrong, we react quickly, and I believe we generally do it in a very fair way.'

The empowerment of the frontline staff to control quality is consciously considered in SIA's innovation processes. According to Mr Sim Kim Chui, vice president of product innovation, cabin crew service is the key strength of SIA, and when developing new services this fact is taken into account so that these new services can be developed in a way that is as much as possible synergistic with SIA's famous inflight service. Further, cabin crew contribute to cross-functional task forces to address specific challenges, and can participate in processes such as the 'innovation lab', where employees from all departments get transferred for a year to work full-time on generating ideas and developing and testing innovations.

Motivating People through Rewards and Recognition

Once a firm has hired the right people, trained them well, empowered them and organised them in effective service delivery teams, how can it ensure that they will deliver service excellence? Staff performance is a function of not only ability but also motivation. Reward systems are the key to motivation, and service staff must receive the message that they will be recognised and rewarded for providing quality service. Motivating and rewarding strong service performers is also one of the most effective ways of retaining them.

Understanding that many service businesses fail because they do not utilise the full range of available rewards effectively, SIA employs several forms of reward, including interesting and varied job content, symbolic forms of recognition and performance-based share options. SIA recently introduced equity-linked incentives for staff, and linked more variable components of pay to the individual staff contribution as well as to the company's financial performance.[13] SIA's employees also continuously receive praise and motivation through the international accolades for excellence that have been awarded to the airline over the years, which include several 'best airline', 'best cabin crew service' and 'Asia's most admired company' awards.

To further spur the desire of its employees to deliver excellent service, the company believes in effective communication. Corporate-wide business meetings and briefings are held regularly to keep staff informed of the latest developments. Corporate newsletters and circulars help to promote information sharing. Interaction between staff and management is encouraged through regular staff meetings. As Ms Lim Suu Kuan notes, 'It's about communication. For example, if we add a new service at check-in, we will talk to the people involved before, during and after implementation. We will discuss the importance and the value of it, and make sure everyone is aware of what we are doing and why. It helps to give staff pride in what they do.' Communication is also important in celebrating service excellence. According to Ms Lim Suu Kuan, 'the company uses other non-financial rewards to encourage good service. The newsletters are used to share and recognise good service.' Ms Lam Seet Mui adds, 'We try to recognise members of staff who go the extra mile. Every year there is the Deputy Chairman's Award. This is a way for the top managers to show appreciation.' Sim Kay Wee also comments on the importance of recognition at SIA: 'We know that a pat on the back, a good ceremony, photographs and write-ups in the newsletters can be more motivating than mere financial rewards, hence we put in a lot of effort to ensure that heroes and heroines are recognised for their commitment and dedication.' SIA's performance management system is quite sophisticated and comprehensive; an outline of this system with regard to cabin crew, supplied by SIA, is described in the appendix.

In response to our query of what makes SIA cabin crew so special that other carriers try to imitate it, Mr Choo notes, 'Here, there are some intangibles ... I think what makes it special is a combination of many things. Because first, you've got to ensure you find the right people for the job you want and then your training matters a great deal; the way you nurture them, the way you monitor them and the way you reward them. It need not necessarily be money, the recognition you give, and I think another very important ingredient is the overall culture of cabin crew, and the fact that you have people who really are very proud of the tradition. A lot of our senior people, and it rubs off on the junior crew as well, take pride in that they have helped build up the airline; they are very proud of it and they want to ensure that it remains that way.' Mr Toh adds, 'Amongst other contributing factors is a very ingrained service culture not just among the cabin crew but in the whole company, ... I think it goes back to 35 years ago when the airline was set up. Very, very strong service culture throughout the whole organisation, very strong commitment from top management; we take every complaint seriously ... We react to every complaint ... we try to learn from the feedback, it's a never-ending process.'

Dealing With Service Delivery Challenges

The combined effect of the strategic HR management processes discussed above is that SIA manages to effectively address three key service-related challenges: how to deal with the sky-high and ever-rising expectations of its customers; how to achieve balance between standardised and consistent, yet personalised service; and how to approach a large number of services and support sub-processes in totality to attain excellence in all of them. We discussed these challenges in Chapter 5 from the perspective of innovation. Figure 6.2 summarises the challenges and how SIA deals with them, additionally drawing from the discussion in this chapter on issues such as people training and development, and customer-oriented mindset.

Figure 6.2

How SIA deals with three key challenges of service delivery

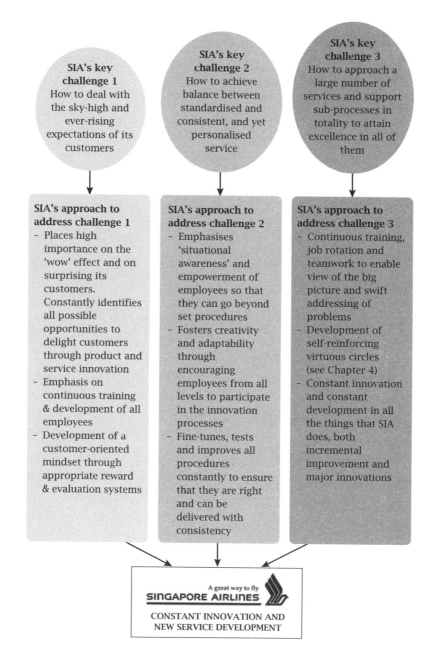

SIA's key challenge 1
How to deal with the sky-high and ever-rising expectations of its customers

SIA's key challenge 2
How to achieve balance between standardised and consistent, and yet personalised service

SIA's key challenge 3
How to approach a large number of services and support sub-processes in totality to attain excellence in all of them

SIA's approach to address challenge 1
- Places high importance on the 'wow' effect and on surprising its customers. Constantly identifies all possible opportunities to delight customers through product and service innovation
- Emphasis on continuous training & development of all employees
- Development of a customer-oriented mindset through appropriate reward & evaluation systems

SIA's approach to address challenge 2
- Emphasises 'situational awareness' and empowerment of employees so that they can go beyond set procedures
- Fosters creativity and adaptability through encouraging employees from all levels to participate in the innovation processes
- Fine-tunes, tests and improves all procedures constantly to ensure that they are right and can be delivered with consistency

SIA's approach to address challenge 3
- Continuous training, job rotation and teamwork to enable view of the big picture and swift addressing of problems
- Development of self-reinforcing virtuous circles (see Chapter 4)
- Constant innovation and constant development in all the things that SIA does, both incremental improvement and major innovations

A great way to fly
SINGAPORE AIRLINES
CONSTANT INNOVATION AND
NEW SERVICE DEVELOPMENT

Cost-Cutting Measures Leading to Industrial Relations Challenges

The cost-cutting measures necessitated by the company's first-ever quarterly loss of S$312 million in the quarter ending July 2003 brought about by the SARS (severe acute respiratory syndrome) period and the challenges posed by the market entry of a multitude of low cost carriers across Asia have exerted pressure on SIA. On 19 June 2003, SIA's CEO Chew Choon Seng announced the retrenchment of 414 Singapore-based employees (1.5% of the company's staff), comprising office staff, airport workers and engineering personnel. SIA initiated the retrenchment exercise as a last resort in response to the difficult operating environment, following earlier moves towards stringent cost management that included deferring discretionary spending, freezing recruitment, asking management to accept wage cuts of up to 27.5%, and introducing compulsory no-pay leave for cabin crew.[14] Mr Chew Choon Seng announced, 'We have always said that we would consider retrenchment as a measure of last resort. I am sad to say that we are now at that point. It is unfortunate, but there is no alternative if we are to ensure that the company survives this downturn and to position ourselves to compete effectively in the marketplace of the future.'

In addition to retrenchments, SIA staff were asked to accept pay cuts and take unpaid leave. What followed was a public debate of labour-management positions in the pages of the *Straits Times*, Singapore's major daily newspaper. A survey of three of the four SIA unions showed lower staff morale and a perceived change in the 'family atmosphere', for which the carrier was known, to one of 'accountability' in which workers feared losing their jobs.[15] Tension between pilots and the airline escalated after pay cuts were implemented in June 2003, and the situation worsened when the pay cuts continued after SIA posted a profit of S$306 million in the following quarter. Leaders of three unions – SIA Staff Union (SIASU), the Singapore Airport Terminal Services Workers Union (SATSWU) and the SIA Engineering Company Engineers and Executives Union (SEEU) – were asked to provide feedback on SIA labour-management relations and several areas that needed to be addressed were cited.[16]

Even though SIA's labour productivity is high and rising (as noted in Chapter 3), it will be a challenging balancing act to keep raising SIA's already high labour productivity while at the same time retaining and retooling its hitherto highly successful HR management. While we were impressed by SIA's rapid response to the crises, the stringent cost-cutting measures that were required to cope with these challenges inevitably affected morale with the potential to challenge the company's service-oriented culture, despite SIA's efforts to offer support services to retrenched staff such as training programmes and workshops that included courses on managing emotions, financial planning and career guidance.[17]

SIA has recognised the tensions raised by the cost-cutting measures, and has taken steps to restore morale and smooth relations between unions and management. Managerial and supervisory staff have been advised to be more sensitive to the needs of their staff, and top management has been receiving regular feedback to keep apprised of the situation on the ground.[18] Further, two organisational climate surveys were conducted (in 2005 and 2006) to gain understanding of employee perceptions on various organisational areas and what needs to be addressed; two workshops were held in early 2007 between the SIA unions, management and the national trade union congress (NTUC), which identified several initiatives aiming to improve the SIA group's competitiveness as well as staff welfare; and in April 2007 the Singapore Airlines Group Union-Management Partnership was launched as a way of sustaining attention to these issues.[19]

In conclusion, for over three-and-a-half decades, SIA has managed to achieve what many others in the aviation industry can only dream of: cost-effective service excellence that is reinforced by effective HR management and a positive company culture and image and accompanied by superior and stable financial performance. In this chapter, we discussed the role of SIA's leadership and the five key elements constituting SIA's HR management (that is, stringent selection and hiring of people, followed by extensive training and re-training of employees, formation of success-ful service delivery teams, empowerment of frontline staff, and employee motivation), which helped SIA to build and sustain service excellence at levels consistently above the competition. We also outlined how these processes enable SIA to deal with three central challenges of service delivery. The recent crises, the emergence of budget carriers, security concerns and high oil prices mean that SIA needs to sustain its focus on achieving cost-effective service excellence and keep re-examining and enhancing its recipe for success.

APPENDIX

Cabin Crew Performance Management (PM) Questions

1. **How is the cabin crew area structured and how does this influence the PM system?**

   Our crew are formed into 36 groups known as wards, each headed by a ward leader who monitors the performance of the crew. The ward leader, in turn, reports to a Cabin Crew Executive (CCE). Each CCE has six ward leaders under his or her charge and also oversees other aspects of crew administration/management such as communication, welfare, etc.

2. **Describe the performance management tool/process that you use to monitor your cabin crew.**

   The performance of a crew member is measured through 'on-board assessments' (OBA) carried out by a more senior crew member on the same flight. Elements assessed in OBA are:

   a) *Image* – on grooming and uniform turnout

   b) *Service Orientation* – crew's interaction and passenger handling capabilities

   c) *Product Knowledge and Job Skills* – crew's performance with the various bar and meal services and crew's familiarity with procedures/ job and product knowledge

   d) *Safety and Security* – knowledge and adherence to safety and security procedures

   e) *Work Relationship* – to assess crew's general attitude and teamwork/ team-spirit

   f) *People Management Skills* – supervisory and man-management skills, development of junior crew; ability to plan and co-ordinate the various services

   g) *Pre-Flight Session* – Effectiveness of the pre-flight briefing
      **Sections f & g are only applicable to the crew-in-charge

3. **How frequently do the assessments occur?**

   It varies from rank to rank and is tracked over a Financial Year (FY).

   a) *New Crew on Probation* – six OBAs during the six-month probation period

      In addition, there is also a 'closed assessment', which is carried out in conjunction with the OBA. In the closed assessment, we look at crew's attitude, interest towards the job and biases/apprehension towards certain passengers

   b) *Flight Steward/Stewardess* – minimum four per FY

   c) *Supervisory Crew* – three to four times per FY

   d) *Crew-in-Charge* – twice per FY

4. **What level of feedback is given to the individual – at the time of checks and cumulatively, that is, during the quarterly review, annual review, etc.? How do you manage a good quality of interaction rather than just making sure the meeting happens?**

   The OBA is an open appraisal and the appraiser discusses the strengths and weaknesses with the appraisee. Appraisee views and endorses the OBA. All returned OBAs are scanned and flagged out for the ward leader's monitoring if the scores fall outside our pre-determined thresholds. If necessary, the ward leader will go on the appraisees' flight to check out the crew personally. The ward leader can (and often does) call in the crew for a discussion at any time if deemed necessary.

   Concerted effort is made for the ward leader to fly with each crew member in his ward at least once a year. The ward leader will take this opportunity to review/discuss the records of the crew. In addition, the ward leader is required to carry out an annual assessment of all crew in his ward before finalising the annual appraisal score.

   The annual appraisal is weighted as follows:

Elements	Weightage %
OBA	60
Discipline	15
Attendance Record	10
Passenger Feedback	10
Ward Leader Assessments	5

163

5. **What degree of alignment is there between the company values and the areas assessed?**

   The company's core values are embedded in the elements assessed in the OBAs, such as service orientation & product knowledge (pursuit of excellence), safety & security (safety) and work relationship & people management (teamwork).

6. **How do you train assessors and what level of on-going training occurs to ensure rater consistency?**

   All crew promoted to supervisory rank have to attend a one-day appraisal workshop where they are taught the basics of assessment and coached on the use of the OBA form. There's also an on-going process to review all OBAs that have been improperly done and pick out appraisers who habitually give extreme ratings for follow-up by the ward leaders.

END NOTES

1. This chapter draws from Wirtz, J., Heracleous, L., and Pangarkar, N. (2008) Managing Human Resources for Service Excellence and Cost Effectiveness at Singapore Airlines, *Managing Service Quality*, 18(1): 4-19. The conceptual underpinning of this chapter and many of the management theories referred to were taken from Christopher H. Lovelock and Jochen Wirtz (2004), *Services Marketing: People, Technology, Strategy*, 5th edition. Upper Saddle River, New Jersey: Prentice Hall. Much of the material on SIA discussed in this chapter is based on interviews conducted from 2001 to 2008 with the following SIA executives (in alphabetical order). Since the interviews were conducted over a number of years, the designations of many interviewees have changed. The list of interviewees below shows the title of the individuals during the interview, and any changes in designation since then are indicated in parentheses:

   - Leong Choo Poh, Senior Manager, Cabin Crew Performance (now Senior Manager, Crew Services)
   - Timothy Chua, Project Manager, New Service Development (now Senior Manager Inflight Services (Projects))
   - Dr Goh Ban Eng, Senior Manager, Cabin Crew Training (now Senior Manager, Human Resource Development)
   - Lam Seet Mui, Senior Manager, Human Resource Development (now Senior Manager, Cabin Crew Training)
   - Lim Suet Kwee, Senior Rank Trainer, SIA Training School
   - Lim Suu Kuan, Commercial Training Manager
   - Seow, Patrick, Senior Rank Trainer, SIA Training School
   - Sim Kay Wee, former Senior Vice President, Cabin Crew
   - Mr Sim Kim Chui, Vice President, Contracts (from 2000-2007 Vice President, Product Development)
   - Toh Giam Ming, Senior Manager, Crew Performance
   - Betty Wong, Senior Manager, Cabin Crew Service Development (now Acting Vice President, Inflight Services)
   - Yap Kim Wah, Senior Vice President, Product and Service

2. Schneider, B. and Bowen, D. E. (1995) *Winning the Service Game*. Boston, MA: Harvard Business School Press, p. 131.

3. Chan, D. (2002) Beyond Singapore Girl: Brand and Product/Service Differentiation Strategies in the New Millennium, *Journal of Management Development*, Vol. 19, Issue 6, p. 515.

4. Huselid, M. A., Jackson, S. E. and Schuler, R. S. (1997) Technical and Strategic Human Resource Management Effectiveness as Determinants of Firm Performance, *Academy of Management Journal*, 40, pp. 171-188.

5. Schneider, B. and Bowen, D. E. (1995) *Winning the Service Game.* Boston, MA: Harvard Business School Press, p. 131.

6. Schlesinger, L. and Heskett, J. L. (1991) Breaking the Cycle of Failure in Service, *Sloan Management Review*, Vol. 31 (Spring), pp. 17-28.

7. Kingi, S. G. and Dutta, S. (2003) *Customer Service at Singapore Airlines.* Hyderabad, India: ICFAI Center for Management Research.

8. Singapore Airlines press release, January 2005, Crew Training.

9. Chan, D. (2000) The Story of Singapore Airlines and the Singapore Girl, *Journal of Management Development*, Vol. 19, Issue 6, p. 456.

10. Singapore Airlines press release, January 2005, Human Resources.

11. Singapore Airlines Cabin Crew Collect Over Half A Million Dollars For Local Charity, 25 September 2004, http://www.singaporeair.com/saa/app/saa?dynamic=PressReleases/NE_4904.html, accessed on 1 December 2004.

12. Yagil, D. (2002) The Relationship of Customer Satisfaction and Service Workers' Perceived Control-Examination of Three Models, *International Journal of Service Industry Management*, 13, no. 4 pp. 382-398.

13. Labour-Management Relations in SIA, 1 March 2004, http://www.singaporeair.com/saa/app/saa?dynamic=PressReleases/NTE_1504.html, accessed on 15 December 2004.

14. SIA Group to Retrench 414 Staff, 19 June 2003, http://www.singaporeair.com/saa/app/saa?dynamic=PressReleases/NTE_2603.html, accessed on 1 February 2005.

15. Mecham, M. (2004) Adapt or Die, *Aviation Week & Space Technology*, Vol. 160, Issue 9.

16. Labour-Management Relations in SIA, 1 March 2004, http://www.singaporeair.com/saa/app/saa?dynamic=PressReleases/NTE_1504.html, accessed on 15 December 2004.

17. SIA Group to Retrench 414 Staff, 19 June 2003, http://www.singaporeair.com/saa/app/saa?dynamic=PressReleases/NTE_2603.html, accessed on 1 February 2005.

18. Labour-Management Relations in SIA, 1 March 2004, http://www.singaporeair.com/saa/app/saa?dynamic=PressReleases/NTE_1504.html, accessed on 15 December 2004.

19. Singapore Airlines Annual Report 2006-2007, pp. 24-25.

7

HOW TO WIN IN CUT-THROAT INDUSTRIES I: ACHIEVING STRATEGIC ALIGNMENT

We undertook this study in order to gain a deeper understanding of the factors that can help a company achieve sustainable success in extremely tough industries. Our findings are based on a detailed study of the strategy and organisational features of a company that has achieved just that. In the next two chapters, we outline some strategic lessons from this study that we believe can be applied to any company that wants to achieve sustainable advantage. We do not aim to provide silver bullets (and in any case silver bullets are not possible since the right strategic decisions depend on the specific circumstances and challenges of each organisation) but rather to suggest useful strategic principles and to help executives ask the right questions. This is in our mind the only avenue to effective strategic thinking.

In this chapter, we address one of the most important findings and also a key principle for success: achieving strategic alignment, and recognising and dealing with misalignments before they become destructive. We begin with a reminder of why it is so hard to be successful in the airline industry and proceed with a discussion of the nature of strategic alignment, as well as the main misalignments that companies should be vigilant of. One important message of this chapter is that achieving strategic alignment is a pre-condition for achieving sustainable competitive advantage.

Why Is It so Hard to Be Successful in the Airline Industry?

We have discussed the airline industry features and dynamics in detail in Chapters 1 and 2. It is worth briefly reminding ourselves, however, of the main characteristics of this industry, and why it is so hard to be successful in it. At first sight, the airline industry might seem relatively healthy, since the service is widely available and demand enjoys reasonable growth in several markets. Over the last 20 years, airline revenue-passenger kilometres have been growing at over 5% annually, passenger numbers at 4.2%, and world gross domestic product at 3.5%. In some countries such as India and China, growth has been exceptional. Airline revenue growth has been lower, however, at around 2.8%, and industry net profits have been negative over half of the years.[1] The lower rate of revenue growth indicates a squeeze in prices charged and a squeeze in margins, which airlines have tried to deal with by seeking efficiency increases. These pricing pressures reflect the effects of supply increases brought about by deregulation that closely match demand. The industry suffers from significant over-capacity, where on average one quarter of airplane seats and almost half of cargo capacity are unutilised. The bargaining power of buyers, in addition, has been increasing due to technological advances allowing customers, who have low switching costs, to have high transparency of prices and choices through buying on the Internet. These factors have fostered a commoditisation of air travel, where in the absence of significant differentiation, many buyers make purchasing decisions in terms of price.

The rivalry among established firms has risen substantially, often degenerating in vicious price wars that ultimately make the whole industry worse off in terms of returns. High barriers to exit, the entry of low cost rivals, over-capacity and the maturity of the industry in most parts of the world only serve to raise rivalry to unsustainable levels. Airline alliances such as Star Alliance, SkyTeam and Oneworld, offering the options of more destinations with less hassle to passengers, often achieve little in terms of granting competitive differentiation to incumbents, since most major competitors belong to such an alliance. To make things worse, in many cases structural inertia due to regulatory or nationalist constraints does not allow industry consolidation that could raise industry efficiency and control rivalry. Finally, many suppliers can squeeze airlines and also pose uncontrollable cost fluctuations, such as the oil prices and charges of leading airports where demand outstrips supply. All of the above factors can shed light on the abysmal performance of the airline industry in terms of returns on investment. Even among the low cost carriers, only a handful have been relatively profitable (Ryanair, easyJet and Southwest Airlines).

In this challenging context, Singapore Airlines (SIA) has not only never made a loss on an annual basis, but has delivered superior returns to its competitors consistently over the years. We have aimed to understand more about SIA's exceptional performance, and offer our own interpretation of its success in this book. We suggest that one key reason for SIA's success has been its high levels of strategic alignment, and vigilance in identifying and dealing with misalignments before they become destructive. We have offered one representation of SIA's tight alignment in terms of the activity map presented in Chapter 4. We will discuss SIA's alignment further in terms of the ESCO model (environment, strategy, core competencies and organisation) as well as the McKinsey 7-S model in this chapter.

What Is Strategic Alignment?

There is no shortage of management ideas and frameworks that aim to help managers achieve strategic alignment in their companies. These include ideas about adapting strategy to the competitive environment, configuring organisational functions to implement or operationalise the strategy, or developing the right organisational and people competencies that support the strategic direction. The well-known McKinsey 7-S model, Kaplan and Norton's balanced scorecard and Michael Porter's value chain are all implicitly or explicitly about strategic alignment.

The idea of strategic alignment is simple, but the challenges it raises are numerous and frustrating. One useful and straightforward way to diagnose the level of alignment in any organisation is to distinguish between and map four levels: the environment (at various levels such as the competitive, macro-economic and institutional), the strategy of the company (at the business or corporate levels depending on the purposes of the analysis and the level of application), the organisational core competencies supporting the strategy, and the organisational functions and processes that should work in an integrated manner to deliver these core competencies. We have labelled this the ESCO model (environment, strategy, core competencies and organisation) (see Figure 7.1).

This sort of analysis can easily be paralysed by information overload unless a proper perspective is kept. Even though there are many potentially relevant aspects of the environment, many facets of strategy, many kinds of competencies needed and several minutiae of operations, it is important to be able to distinguish the wheat from the chaff, look at the big picture, and ask what are the key issues involved.

Figure 7.1
The ESCO model

- Competencies must be aligned with the strategy, and the organisational configuration must be aligned to deliver the desired competencies
- All of this must support the strategy, which must be right for the competitive environment

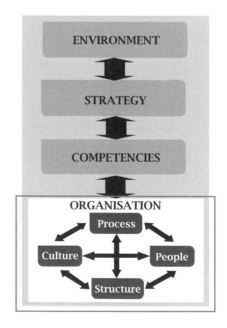

Even though it is far from easy to achieve, leading companies exhibit effective strategic alignment that they can sustain over time in the face of industry shifts, competitor actions and changing customer demands. It is no surprise that these companies also consistently outperform most of their competitors. If we apply the ESCO model to SIA (see Figure 7.2), we can see (as elaborated in Chapter 4) that its strategy is aligned to its environment, the right core competencies support the strategy, and the organisational five pillars give rise to these competencies.

Figure 7.2
Strategic alignment at SIA

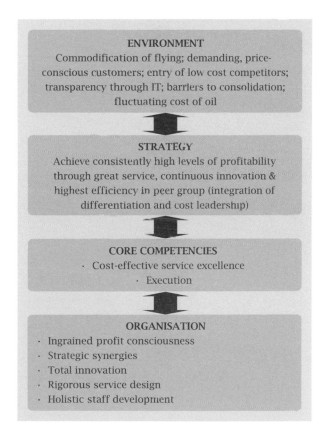

ENVIRONMENT
Commodification of flying; demanding, price-conscious customers; entry of low cost competitors; transparency through IT; barriers to consolidation; fluctuating cost of oil

STRATEGY
Achieve consistently high levels of profitability through great service, continuous innovation & highest efficiency in peer group (integration of differentiation and cost leadership)

CORE COMPETENCIES
· Cost-effective service excellence
· Execution

ORGANISATION
· Ingrained profit consciousness
· Strategic synergies
· Total innovation
· Rigorous service design
· Holistic staff development

We can also apply the ESCO model to an airline such as Ryanair (see Figure 7.3), a pioneer in the European budget segment, which has also outperformed its segment, exhibiting high levels of strategic alignment.

Figure 7.3
Strategic alignment at Ryanair

ENVIRONMENT
Commodification of flying; demanding customers; environmental concerns; low cost competitors; value-based high end competitors; IT creates transparency; fluctuating cost of oil

STRATEGY
Aggressive growth orientation through market/product development & market penetration; targeting budget conscious segment with attractive pricing; good levels of service in its class

CORE COMPETENCIES
· Efficiency
· Execution

ORGANISATION
Exploiting Internet technologies (direct ticket sales, sales of ancillary services); targeted advertising of website; operating from secondary airports, using only Boeing aircraft; frequent flights on short-haul routes; focus on crew productivity and plane utilisation; employee stock option plan

More elaborate frameworks can also be used to represent alignment, such as the classic McKinsey 7-S framework. In Figure 7.4, we apply the 7-S model to SIA.

In addition to the ESCO model and the McKinsey 7-S model, we can also employ the value chain to examine strategic alignment. If we consider strategic alignment at IKEA, arguably the world's most successful furniture maker, all the elements of the value chain are mutually consistent in support of a business strategy of cost leadership. Figure 7.5 portrays the value chain of IKEA in the bottom two rows as compared with the value chain of many traditional furniture manufacturers in the top two rows, competing with a business strategy of differentiation.

The crucial point to note from the perspective of the sustainability of competitive advantage is that whereas it is easier to copy isolated elements of a successful system, it is much more difficult to copy the whole system and the synergies that arise from the way the various processes interact and interconnect. A highly aligned system arises through a mixture of effective execution of plans, evolution and fine-tuning of the organisation design and processes, and even opportunism, as managers address misalignments, integrate systems and processes, remove elements that are outdated or do not fit desired arrangements, and generally resolve issues as they arise. What underlies this process is an attitude and culture of continuous improvement, and a continuous search for better and more efficient ways to do things.

Further, it is beneficial to employ different frameworks so that a variety of perspectives can be gained. What matters even more, however, is asking the right questions: Given what is happening in our environment, do we have the right strategy? If not, how does it need to change? Do we have the right core competencies at both the organisational and people levels to pull our current or intended strategy off? Do our operations deliver the organisational core competencies we need in an integrated, mutually supporting manner? Finally, where are the key misalignments and what can we do about them? These questions are inevitably hard to answer, and involve difficult choices, uncomfortable evaluations and political battles. But there is no alternative than to ask

Figure 7.4
Strategic alignment at SIA through the McKinsey 7-S model

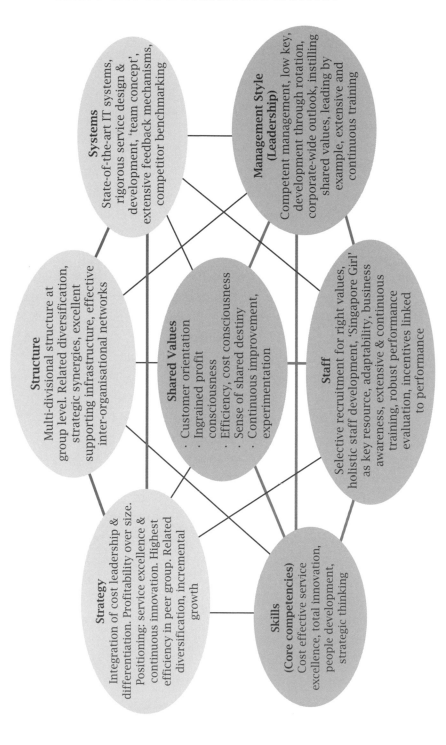

Systems
State-of-the-art IT systems, rigorous service design & development, 'team concept', extensive feedback mechanisms, competitor benchmarking

Management Style (Leadership)
Competent management, low key, development through rotation, corporate-wide outlook, instilling shared values, leading by example, extensive and continuous training

Structure
Multi-divisional structure at group level. Related diversification, strategic synergies, excellent supporting infrastructure, effective inter-organisational networks

Shared Values
· Customer orientation
· Ingrained profit consciousness
· Efficiency, cost consciousness
· Sense of shared destiny
· Continuous improvement, experimentation

Staff
Selective recruitment for right values, holistic staff development, 'Singapore Girl' as key resource, adaptability, business awareness, extensive & continuous training, robust performance evaluation, incentives linked to performance

Strategy
Integration of cost leadership & differentiation. Profitability over size. Positioning: service excellence & continuous innovation. Highest efficiency in peer group. Related diversification, incremental growth

Skills (Core competencies)
Cost effective service excellence, total innovation, people development, strategic thinking

Figure 7.5

Strategic alignment at IKEA vs traditional furniture makers

	Design	Parts	Assembly	Logistics	Marketing	Service
Traditional furniture makers	Independent designers	High levels of work-in-progress	Labour intensive	Relatively inefficient supply chain	Fragmented across geographies	'Full service'
	Complex, tailored designs	Handicraft, custom manufacture	Built to order	Transport costly, bulky finished product	Expensive, high-street display	Small lot delivery to customers
IKEA	In-house designers	Modular, inter-changeable parts	Minimal assembly by company	Computerised/ efficient	Leverage Scandinavian image	Self-service
	Simple designs	Cheaper materials, mass production	Assembly by customer	Transport modular parts	Cheap out-of-town display	Customer transports home

Source: Adapted from Kumar, N., Scheer, L. & Kotler, P. (2000) From Market Driven to Market Driving. European Management Journal, 18 (2), pp. 129–142.

and address them, otherwise inertia and even chance would be allowed to play a dangerously influential role.

Commonly Found Misalignments

If there are so many frameworks to help us diagnose and map the levels of alignment in organisations, why are misalignments so common and why do they persist? What are the main types of misalignments we find, and what can we do about them? Virtually all organisations have some misalignments; what is important is to regularly identify them and address them before they have the chance to become destructive. Strategic alignment is a simple idea to grasp, but it is surprising how difficult it is to get it right in practice, or how many misaligned or even conflicting activities and practices can be observed in organisations.

Strategic Misalignments

We outline below six of the most common types of misalignments that can be found in organisations, and offer examples of each.

Strategy Is Out of Line with External Competitive Environment

In some organisations there are high levels of alignment internally (among operations, core competencies and strategy), but all of this is misaligned with the demands and features of the competitive environment. For example, many Western brewing giants rushed into the Chinese beer market in the mid-1990s, collectively investing billions of dollars in building state-of-the-art factories, and producing premium beer sold under their global brand names for around five to six times the price of locally branded beer, which sold as cheaply as soft drinks. These new entrants painfully discovered that the premium segment of the beer market was only around 5% of total demand and was too small to support so many simultaneous new entrants, consumers were fiercely loyal to their local brands, local competitors were quick to engage in predatory price competition, the weak transport infrastructure made it harder to transport beer to other regions efficiently and therefore to build up demand and achieve capacity utilisation, and finally local bureaucrats were not always transparent or easy to deal with.

While these global competitors had high levels of internal alignment, there was a critical misalignment between their strategy of differentiation (high quality, premium price, state-of-the-art factories, global branding) and the competitive environment. What they offered was neither consistent with what the market wanted or could support, nor with the institutional environment. The result was that most of them had to exit the China market, unable to keep sustaining huge losses year after year, and had to sell their newly built factories to local competitors such as Tsing Tao at bargain basement prices.[2]

However, South African Breweries (now SAB Miller) was successful in China, by employing a strategy that was in many ways the opposite of the strategy of other multi-national beer companies, and that was highly aligned with the demands of the competitive environment. SAB got it right because it was able to learn from prior experience in other emerging markets such as sub-Saharan Africa and Eastern Europe, environments that posed many similar challenges, and could then effectively transfer that learning to its China operations. Further, SAB gave high priority to strategic alliances as a means of gaining local knowledge, entering local networks and getting a deep understanding of local consumer behaviour. This enabled SAB to keep its capital commitments manageable by not having to build new factories but investing to upgrade its partners' existing factories. Further, SAB realised that rather than offering global brands at premium prices, the market at that point would best support local brands at local prices, and that a China-wide expansion strategy would be much less realistic than a phased geographic expansion based on regional strongholds. Therefore, SAB entered the China market with a cost leadership/localisation strategy, which was aligned with the environment, rather than a differentiation/globalisation strategy, which was not.

Organisation and Competencies Fail to Support Strategy

This form of misalignment occurs when operational configurations and the competencies they exhibit do not support or operationalise strategy adequately, and they even create contradictions or tensions between strategy and operations. For example, a European firm in a service-oriented industry has over the last few years exhibited double-digit growth, but its customer service capability lagged behind, causing tensions with its customers, and creating the danger of distorting the firm's differentiated market positioning and jeopardising further growth. The firm identified this misalignment and dealt with it by increasing investment in its customer care function.

Further, a successful professional services firm with exceptional annual revenue growth rates (in the mid-20s) had a traditional functionally-based organisation design and a reward system that did not distinguish between levels of performance, both of which created difficulties in supporting this growth, in particular the efficient delivery of bigger and more complex projects. This firm took steps to review its organisation design, adopting a matrix design and changing some of its processes such as aligning reward to individual performance and instituting a more robust governance system. These steps enabled the organisation to support the strategy of rapid growth.

Incompatibilities and Tensions Within the Organisation Level

This form of misalignment occurs when operational configurations and processes are mutually inconsistent in their orientations and goals. This can occur at both the functional or departmental level as well as at the corporate or cross-divisional level. Examples at the functional level are the classic conflicts between internally-oriented functions such as production or operations and externally-oriented ones such as marketing or sales. At the corporate level, there may be conflicts among divisions that have to compete for funding from head office, or between the head office and divisions when there are differing views about the appropriate degree of centralisation/decentralisation. At the corporate level, tensions across divisions arise especially when corporate budgets get allocated across divisions largely based on financial performance without sufficient attention to cross-divisional synergies or longer term potential; or for cultural, historical and organisational design reasons, which could be harmful to competitive advantage.

When Carlos Ghosn took over the reins at Nissan in 1999, and was trying to diagnose the key issues that needed to be addressed to reverse the company's decade-long decline and imminent bankruptcy, he referred to a 'culture of blame' where various departments and regions blamed each other for the company's woes instead of taking responsibility and acknowledging their own contribution to the problems. The engineering department had been all powerful, leading to cars that were over-engineered and not necessarily aligned to what the market wanted.

The historical difficulties of achieving rapid development and global roll-out of innovations in multi-national giants such as Procter & Gamble (P&G) indicate less than ideal levels of cross-divisional alignment. P&G's mode of global expansion after the setting up of the overseas division in 1948 involved extensive duplication of operations and processes in several new markets, in effect creating a smaller P&G clone in each market, which enjoyed high levels of operational independence. This allowed and even fostered insufficient levels of cross-national coordination on processes such as new product development, lower levels of efficiency, development of a 'not invented here' syndrome and fierce independence of international operations. In the 1980s concerted efforts begun to address these issues through increasing cross-national integration and coordination of key functions. By the 1990s the international division was replaced by four regional organisations structured through a matrix organisation (regions/product categories), and global category executives were appointed, but innovation and diffusion were still too slow. This prompted a change programme initiated in 1998 labelled 'O2005', which was seen as the most fundamental and dramatic organisational change in P&G's history. The historically decentralised corporate design of P&G and associated culture of independence therefore led to low levels of cross-divisional and cross-national alignment, among other things impacting the innovation and global roll-out of new products, and efforts to address these issues took decades.

Rewarding One Thing but Expecting Another

One classic and widespread form of misalignment is 'the folly of rewarding A while hoping for B'.[3] In academia, for example, one receives the rewards that matter such as tenure or a full professorship in a world-class university mainly for one thing (research quality and productivity as evidenced in quality journal publications), yet great teaching, student mentoring and earnest performance in administrative duties are also hoped for. Further, we have seen service organisations rewarding employees based on strict quantifiable measures of individual performance (for example, sales figures), yet hoping for teamwork and sharing of culture; or rewarding managers purely based on specific measures of the firm's financial performance, yet hoping that these same managers work to create a climate where customers receive a great experience in their use of the service and in their interactions with the company. Of course great customer experience and financial performance ideally go together and are part of a desirable virtuous circle, but exclusive emphasis on just one element of a desirable gestalt can lead to distortions in emphasis and behaviours that undermine the other elements. This is why, for example, if a manager at General Electric hits the numbers but does not exhibit the company's desired values through their behaviours, they would still be in trouble.

Failure to Realign Strategy and Organisation with Environmental Changes

This form of misalignment occurs when a company has a highly aligned model across the four ESCO elements of operations, core competencies, strategy and environment (thus having high alignment both internally and externally), but it does not keep in touch with external changes, or does not appreciate their implications and impact. For a variety of reasons, such companies are too inertial to adapt their strategy and internal operations, and as a result do not realign effectively when the environment changes. Inertia can arise from organisational cultures that do not value rigorous debate or constructive dissent, are hostile to diversity, encourage groupthink, dwell on history and past successes, tolerate unproductive politics, or are characterised by a sense of invincibility that leads to complacency.

One example of failing to adapt to environmental change is Wang Laboratories, founded in 1951, and once the leader in network enterprise computing. One problem was that Wang failed to appreciate the extent to which the arrival of the personal computer (PC) would encroach on its market, and that it would in fact be cheaper for companies to buy several PCs for their employees rather than Wang's expensive mainframe-based system that tied companies to the provider in terms of regular maintenance costs. Mainframes would still be needed by the market, but to a much smaller extent than before. Other issues included lack of compatibility of Wang's systems with other available software because of their proprietary standards, and questionable senior appointments in the company that led to several senior managers leaving in protest. During its last couple of years the company undertook significant restructuring and started focusing more on software than hardware, but the effort to realign was too late; it filed for bankruptcy in 1992.

The situation of Eastman Kodak is also instructive. For the last five years the company has been remaking itself into a digital giant through a process that many believe has started too late. This has been a massive process of realignment of operations, core competencies and strategy prompted by an environment where digital technologies have not only cannibalised Kodak's traditional film business but also offer high returns for companies that can compete effectively in it. The realignment process has cost Kodak over $2.5 billion in restructuring costs, and a further loss of 27,000 jobs (to about 50,000 employees, down from 145,000 in 1988).

A company that managed to realign successfully is IBM. Under Gerstner's leadership, the company realised that most segments involving hardware were gradually becoming commodified and unattractive in terms of current and future profitability. IBM then gradually reduced its investments and operations in mass-market, commoditised hardware manufacturing and increased its capabilities in high-end servers, software, services and consulting, realigning itself with market trends and re-focusing on high-growth and high-return segments.

Lou Gerstner took over in 1993, after IBM had lost US$16 billion between 1991 and 1993. He had initially refused the job of IBM CEO, concerned that he lacked the technological background to lead IBM, but what is noteworthy is that his decisions about the future of the company were based not on technology but on the customers' perspective. This is what led him, for example, to make a U-turn on a momentous plan to break up IBM into smaller businesses, since from the customer's point of view it is more efficient and desirable to buy technology from an integrator rather than to buy from several different suppliers. He strived to change IBM's culture from an inward-directed, politically charged one where divisions were behaving like fiefdoms, to a customer-focused, integrated one, committed IBM to open technology standards and led the focus on services rather than hardware.

Misguided Strategic Actions Leading to Even Greater Misalignments

This final form of misalignment is the most regrettable one. It occurs when managers mistakenly take actions believing that the result would be greater alignment with a new strategy or a new environmental imperative. Their actions however destroy a company's capabilities and create even greater misalignments. One example is how the managers of Schlitz beer, once the second largest selling beer in the US, tried to reduce costs by using cheaper, synthetic ingredients in the production process and shortening the production cycle. This was promptly leaked to the market, and its market share started to fall. Even after the company decided to reinstate all production processes to their former mode, it was too late – the brand had already been tarnished and the company went bankrupt. A further common example of inadvertent destruction of competencies is re-engineering or re-structuring efforts handled poorly, where morale is destroyed, and productivity and profitability are only temporarily enhanced. Longer term problems occur since the company's capability base is depleted when the most capable employees feel unsure about their future in the company and are snapped up by competitors.

Why Do Misalignments Persist and What Can Be Done About It?

Why then do misalignments persist, despite so many tools to help managers achieve alignment, and despite the time and energy spent on this issue?

Organisational Inertia

One reason is the inertial pressures brought about by the influence of dominant ways of thinking and cultures that discourage debate and reward blind conformity. In BMW, inertia and groupthink are fought by a culture where vigorous debate and constructive conflict are encouraged by the company's leaders, particularly in new product development processes, with the assumption that once a decision is taken everyone commits to it even if they had previously held different views. On the other hand, inertia due to the dominance of accepted ways of thinking was a factor that arguably delayed Kodak's investment in digital technologies to the point where its very survival was at stake. Performance management systems that are fully focused on the numbers without taking into consideration issues such as what values are exhibited by executives, do not tolerate mistakes as learning opportunities and do not allow a reasonable timeframe for investments to pay off, tend to exacerbate the level of organisational inertia by fostering a culture of risk aversion and potential massaging of performance-related figures.

Flawed Strategic Planning and Unbalanced Resource Allocation

Linked to the disease of inertia is flawed strategic planning. This was a significant factor leading to the demise of foreign competitors in the Chinese beer industry, since it led to a misalignment between global brewers' strategy and environmental conditions. The impact and implications of the salient features of the environment such as the price sensitivity and patriotism of consumers, likely response of incumbents, weak infrastructure and red tape in each region were not fully appreciated. Further, Kodak's woes could be seen as resulting from less than fully effective environmental monitoring and assessment of the implications and impact of environmental/technological trends. A related issue is the unbalanced resource allocation that results from flawed planning, especially from lack of attention to issues of alignment, for example, a misalignment between growth in demand and the required investment in customer support capabilities.

Organisational Politics

Politics is another significant factor that leads to the creation or persistence of misalignments. A strategic re-orientation is often held back by a culture of fiefdoms rather than an overall corporate outlook, populated by individuals who believe they would lose out in a new order of things because of a lower level of resources allocated to their empire, a reduction in the numbers of their subjects, or new roles and responsibilities for themselves that they would feel uncomfortable with. As a result they either actively sabotage or passively resist any changes, making any organisational realignment harder. Such political issues were key among the factors that fostered performance problems that necessitated P&G's efforts to increase global integration and the speed of new product roll-out from the early 1980s onwards, IBM's turnaround in the mid-1990s, and Nissan's turnaround in the late 1990s.

What Can Be Done about Strategic Misalignments?

In terms of immediate action, cross-functional teams can conduct a review to identify the main misalignments and debate potential solutions. This should be adequately resourced in terms of time, perhaps the presence of an effective facilitator or organisation development practitioner, as well as the involvement of the right people. The six kinds of misalignments mentioned above could be used to help managers evaluate the extent of misalignments in their own organisation.

For each kind of misalignment, a rating can be given (1 for low, meaning that there is high alignment, to 5 for high, which would indicate the need for swift action). There may be a few relevant aspects for each broad type of misalignment, as well as a few potential solutions that may become obvious only after extended debate. These are simple questions but if taken seriously, they can foster meaningful conversations that address important strategic issues.

Type of misalignments   Rating (1 to 5)   Comments   Potential solution

1. Is there alignment between strategy and environment? _____

2. Do the organisation and competencies support strategy? _____

3. Are there any misalignments within the organisational level? _____

4. Is the reward system consistent with expected behaviours? _____

5. Is there adaptability to environmental change? _____

6. Are any actions taken that may create greater misalignments? _____

Leaders and senior teams must be vigilant since misalignments can creep up unnoticed. The boiling frog syndrome is a reality in many organisations. Small, incremental changes in the environment are often either not perceived or their collective implications remain un-appreciated, until crisis conditions develop when it may be too late to react effectively. An active strategic thinking, planning and operationalisation process that challenges managers' mindsets and helps them ask the right questions can minimise the chance that environmental changes and their implications go unnoticed. Diversity of thinking and questioning of the status quo can also minimise the influence of inertial and dominant strategic paradigms at the very times when fresh thinking is needed. Creative, out-of-the-box ways of strategising may be useful here.[4] Finally, leaders must make sure that politics are kept to a manageable, constructive level and swiftly address any destructive politicking.

In this chapter, we suggested that tight strategic alignment is a precondition to achieving sustainable competitive advantage, and offered examples of highly aligned firms such as SIA, Ryanair and IKEA. We then examined the main types of misalignments that can be found in companies, as well as the reasons for which misalignments persist and finally what leaders can do to identify misalignments and debate corrective actions. Achieving and maintaining alignment requires clear thinking, discipline, seamless execution and constant vigilance in monitoring external changes, fine-tuning and, if necessary, realigning to maintain a winning position.

END NOTES

1. See the ICAO and IATA figures cited in Chapters 1 and 2.

2. For a detailed discussion see Heracleous, L., The Demise of Foreign Competitors in the Chinese Beer Industry, in Singh, Pangarkar & Heracleous (2004) *Business Strategy in Asia*, 2nd edition, Thomson Learning.

3. Kerr, S. (1995) On the Folly of Rewarding A while Hoping for B, *Academy of Management Executive*, 9(1), pp. 7-14.

4. Heracleous, L. & Jacobs, C. (2005) The Serious Business of Play, *MIT Sloan Management Review*, Fall, pp. 19-20.

8

HOW TO WIN IN CUT-THROAT INDUSTRIES II: STRATEGY, COMPETENCIES, INNOVATION AND CULTURE

In this final chapter, we continue our discussion of the lessons that can be learned from our study of Singapore Airlines' (SIA's) competitive success. In particular, we suggest that strategic leaders need to be clear about the company's generic strategy and make the necessary investments to support it, and that a combination of elements of generic strategies is possible, potentially leading to a winning combination. Secondly, leaders should carefully identify, nurture and invest in capabilities and core competencies that support their company's strategy, and they should strive to foster strategic innovation that can either deliver competitive differentiation or support a strategy of cost leadership. Finally, we examine the enabling role of the institutional environment, as well as the pivotal role of culture, which should both be carefully considered when a company aims to develop sustainable advantage.

Selecting Generic Strategies

A first step to understanding how SIA's exceptional performance has been achieved is to consider its generic strategy. Michael Porter has argued that firms have to make a clear choice between a cost leadership and differentiation strategy (as well as whether to go for a niche or for a broad market), and make appropriate investments to execute their chosen strategy, otherwise they risk being 'stuck in the middle.'[1] According to Porter, 'the fundamental basis of above-average performance in the long run is sustainable competitive advantage ... there are two basic types of competitive advantage a firm can possess: low cost or differentiation ... combined with the scope of activities for which a firm seeks to achieve them lead to three *generic* strategies'.[2] Further, '... achieving competitive advantage requires a firm to make a choice ... Being "all things to all people" is a recipe for strategic mediocrity and below-average performance, because it often means that a firm has no competitive advantage at all'.[3]

Porter accepted that there can be three possibilities where a firm can achieve both cost leadership and differentiation: if competitors are stuck in the middle (that is, they have not really achieved any of these strategies), if cost is strongly affected by the market share of inter-company relationships (where a company can produce a high quality product, and if it has a high market share then it will also enjoy lower average costs), and lastly, if a firm pioneers a major technological or process innovation. However, he believes that all these situations are temporary, since such advantages can be swiftly imitated by competitors, and that a firm will at some point still have to make a clear choice: 'A firm should always aggressively pursue all cost reduction opportunities that do not sacrifice differentiation. A firm should also pursue all differentiation opportunities that are not costly. Beyond this point, however, a firm should be prepared to choose what its ultimate competitive advantage will be and resolve the trade-offs accordingly'.[4]

Porter's conviction that a firm has to ultimately make a choice is based on the different and often conflicting organisational and investment requirements that a successful strategy of cost leadership or differentiation entails. A cost leader would aim to cut costs at all elements of the value chain, standardise their offerings, build a culture of leanness and minimal waste, and compete on the basis of an acceptable product offered to the mass market at low prices. Companies such as Ryanair, Suzuki or Bic would be apt examples of this strategy. A differentiator, on the other hand, would be very careful about quality at every stage of the value chain, invest in innovation and customer service, build a culture of customer and market orientation, target specific value-added market segments and compete on the basis of superior quality products sold at premium prices. Companies such as Rolex, BMW or Harley-Davidson are good examples. Achieving both strategies would indeed involve incompatible organisational choices for most companies.

If we examine SIA from this lens, however, we can see elements of both these generic strategies, successfully intertwined (as outlined in detail in Chapters 3 and 4). *Differentiation* at SIA is achieved through such factors as service excellence and superior quality; premium pricing for business/first-class travel, as well as for economy, particularly when originating a trip from Singapore; high levels of brand equity in terms of the caring and elegant Singapore Girl; high investments in human resources development; young fleet enhancing the flight experience; continuous innovation; having Changi Airport, arguably one of the best airports in the world, as its base; and finally, the cultural values emphasising constant innovation and customer orientation.

As noted in Chapter 4, this is surprisingly achieved without a cost penalty (in terms of cents per available seat kilometre) as compared to SIA's peer group. SIA's young fleet is more fuel efficient and has lower maintenance costs than older fleets; buying planes in cash gives higher negotiating power; SIA has significantly lower labour costs compared to its major competitors, largely due to high levels of labour productivity; at the corporate level SIA engages in related diversification through efficient subsidiaries that are under market discipline, and that offers both quality services as well as contributes to the bottom line; makes effective use of technology that increases efficiency (for example, encouraging frequent flyer transactions via the Internet, selecting seat designs that are less likely to malfunction); exhibits an obsession with reducing wastage; cultural values of cost and profit consciousness that permeate the airline; and Changi Airport is one of the most efficient in the world.

All the above factors allow SIA to exhibit a successful combination of elements of differentiation (as far as the customer and external positioning are concerned) and cost leadership strategy (as far as internal organisation is concerned). Indeed, both superior quality as well as high levels of efficiency have been ingrained in the goals and objectives of SIA since its founding: firstly, to deliver the highest quality of customer service that is safe, reliable and economical; secondly, to generate earnings that provide sufficient resources for investment and satisfactory returns to shareholders; thirdly, to adopt human resource management practices company-wide that attract, develop, motivate and retain employees who contribute to the company's objectives; and fourthly, to maximise productivity and utilisation of all resources.

One lesson here is that it is possible to combine elements of differentiation and low cost strategies. It is not just SIA, but other companies such as Dell and Intel that have achieved this integration of elements of both generic strategies. In each case, the precise elements of implementation have varied, but the result is the same; an unbeatable strategic combination. Therefore, leaders have to ask: What is our company's generic strategy? Is it possible to integrate elements of both differentiation and low cost? How can we implement this integration?

The Role of Capabilities and Core Competencies

The resource-based view of strategy, introduced to the field around 25 years ago,[5] has focused attention on internal company-related factors, as opposed to planning prowess (the strategic planning view) or the selection of specific industry niches (the industrial organisation view), as crucial for competitive success. In the resource-based view, companies can win if they have access to resources or if they can develop certain capabilities that are valuable to the customers, rare or unique, hard to imitate, and hard to substitute for other capabilities. Capabilities make all the difference as to how a given set of resources is managed, and consequently organisations with broadly similar sets of resources can achieve markedly different outcomes and performance.

If we compare Kmart and Wal-Mart, for example, and look for the reasons for which Wal-Mart won the competitive battle, we can see that the differentiating capability that helped it overtake Kmart was logistics efficiency, which reduced costs by 2–3%, a significant advantage in retailing. Wal-Mart pioneered the process of cross-docking, and invested in a private satellite communications system and dedicated truck fleet at the time when most of its competitors were outsourcing these as non-core functions. Dell has been a market leader with a relatively healthy performance in personal computer hardware, at a time when the industry is saturated and commoditised, and most competitors are losing money. Dell's success can be explained by its differentiating capability of mass customisation, real-time market monitoring, and high levels of efficiency at all stages of the value chain. IBM's deep pockets were not able to make up for Dell's distinctive capabilities; trying to copy Dell would have entailed high levels of strategic risk since to achieve similar levels of efficiency the whole value chain would have to be imitated, creating conflicts with IBM's existing business model. IBM therefore progressively exited the computer hardware market and instead focused on service-related offerings that have higher margins.

All companies have resources, tangible and intangible, and all companies have various capabilities, or the ability to organise resources effectively and efficiently to realise strategy. Capabilities are intangible, embedded in people, processes and culture; they are much harder to copy than tangible resources, where it is often simply a matter of money to imitate successfully. However, few companies have capabilities that satisfy the four criteria of being valuable to customers, rare, hard to imitate and hard to substitute. Such capabilities can be referred to as core competencies that lead to sustainable competitive advantage, and companies that have them are more likely to achieve superior performance than their competitors in the longer term. Figure 8.1 displays this chain.

There are three main classes of capabilities: operational excellence, customer orientation and innovation. If we examine any world-leading company, we can see that it excels at one or more of these capabilities, to such a high degree that cannot be easily copied such that they become

Figure 8.1
Resources, capabilities, core competencies and sustainable advantage

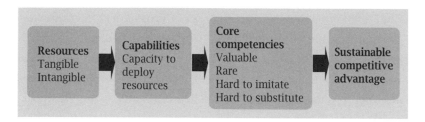

Table 8.1
Types/modes of core competencies and company examples

	Operational excellence	Customer orientation	Innovation
Mode 1	Efficiency – similar output cheaper than competitors	Creating emotional associations with customers	Continuous product or service innovation
Mode 2	Consistency – reliability, predictability, near zero mistakes	Tailoring products/services to customer niches	Efficiency or value added through process innovation
Mode 3	Exceptional levels of quality and continuous improvement	Consistently exceeding expectations	Business model innovation that is hard to imitate
Company examples	SIA, Zara, McDonald's, Toyota, Louis Vuitton, Bose	Harley-Davidson, Coca-Cola, Apple, eBay, Disney, BMW	3M, Samsung, Amazon, First Direct, Dell, IKEA

core competencies of that company. Capabilities are multi-dimensional, and companies can excel at different dimensions, as Table 8.1 shows.

One mode of operational excellence, for example, is efficiency, achieving similar outputs at lower cost than the peer group (for example, SIA or Zara). A second mode is consistency, reliability, predictability, and near zero mistakes (for example, McDonald's or Toyota). A third mode is the achievement of exceptional levels of quality and continuous improvement (for example, Louis Vuitton or Bose).

If we consider customer orientation, we can see that it is also a multi-dimensional concept. One mode is the ability to create emotional associations with the customer (for example, Harley-Davidson, Coca-Cola). A second mode is the ability to effectively tailor products and services to specific customer niches through a deep understanding of the customer (for example, Apple, eBay). A third mode is the ability to consistently exceed expectations (for example, Disney, BMW).

Lastly, we can consider innovation. There are companies that excel consistently at offering new products and services, either in an incremental fashion or a combination of incremental and ground-breaking ones (for example, 3M, Samsung). A second mode is process innovation, allowing higher organisational efficiency or value added to customers, or both (for example, Amazon, First Direct). A third mode of innovation however, more strategic in nature, is the ability to develop a new business model, a new organisational architecture (including systems, processes and values), that can be sustained in the longer term as a differentiating factor (for example, Dell, IKEA).

It is not just the structural aspects of the business model that offer sustained success, since these can be copied by competitors, but rather the detailed internal systems, processes, inter-relationships and cultural values that are developed over time. In Chapter 4, for example, we depicted the activity systems map of SIA, illustrating the internal fit and coherence of various organisational aspects that operationalise and enshrine the core competency of cost-effective service excellence. In Chapter 7, we offered an analysis of SIA's internal arrangements using the McKinsey 7-S model. We elaborated in Chapters 5 and 6 on SIA's innovation processes and its human resource management systems. Even if competitors copy parts of these, for example, the 'holistic staff' development' or the 'strategic synergies', they will only have a part of the puzzle, and they will also lack the specific cultural values that glue together these organisational arrangements.

If we had to select one of the three competencies where SIA excels, it would be operational excellence, given the seamless execution of strategy in an efficient and consistent manner, the tight and coherent inter-connections among various organisational processes, and the consistently superior levels of service. Having said that, operational excellence alone cannot explain SIA's sustainable advantage.

We would indeed argue that SIA has developed all three competencies to a higher level than most of its peer group, which would go some way towards explaining its outstanding performance over the years. With regard to operational excellence, we discussed in earlier chapters several factors that give SIA an edge over competitors in terms of efficiency as well as consistent superior quality. With regard to customer orientation, we discussed SIA's ingrained customer-oriented mindset, attention to prioritising and delivering services that customers want, and to gathering, analysing, utilising and responding to customer feedback to keep in touch with its market. With regard to innovation, we saw how SIA engages in continuous service as well as process innovation and maintaining a unique internal activity system that competitors find it almost impossible to copy.

Capabilities and core competencies are thus embedded in people, processes and culture. Companies have to be clear whether they have any capabilities that satisfy the four criteria (that is, are valuable to the customer, rare, hard to imitate and hard to substitute) and can therefore be seen as their core competencies. If there is no clarity on this, then the links with strategy will also be unclear, and strategic alignment may be compromised. Further, core competencies as differentiating factors can slowly be eroded if competitors invest in building similar competencies; thus a company has to continuously monitor competition and improve its own competencies to stay ahead.

It is also worth noting that investments in developing capabilities and competencies are often hard or impossible to evaluate in advance, using conventional criteria of return on investment and other financial measures. This is because these innovations may be ground-breaking with no benchmarks to compare with, and the time frame needed for the investments to bear fruit may be long. When SIA decided in 1972, for example, to break from industry norms and compete on service excellence, the assumptions involved to calculate costs and returns would make any numerical calculation at best incomplete and inaccurate, and at worst irrelevant.

What is needed is rather a conviction, from the highest levels, that this is the right thing to do; and the ability to mobilise the organisation in a coherent manner to actualise the vision. According to J. Y. Pillay, first chairman of SIA, when referring to SIA's decision to focus on superior service in an industry where service was lacklustre,[6] 'those were the days when most airlines in the region and around the world were heavily subsidised by their governments. SIA capitalised on that myopia. A subsidised entity is, almost by definition, a flaccid, supine organisation. SIA, therefore, did not really have to face severe competition until the authorities in more and more countries got religion, the religion of the market economy. Then SIA had to work more strenuously. A great advantage SIA enjoyed three decades ago was the ability to cock-a-snook at the competition. The major carriers in the industry, together with their camp-followers, suffered from a self-imposed constraint, through IATA, the International Air Transport Association, to offer uniform standards of service and fixed tariffs. Not being a member of IATA, SIA led the way in pioneering quality innovations in the cabin, allied to flexible pricing in the marketplace. That policy attracted the customers, boosted revenue and profit, and enabled SIA to modernise its fleet faster than the competition ... The competition eventually got wise to SIA's formula for success, and sought to emulate it. SIA's lead was attenuated, but by no means eliminated. That lead persists because of the high quality of internal dynamics within the organisation. Organisational strategy plays no less important a role than corporate strategy.'

One important lesson is therefore the need to critically examine the company's capabilities, and apply stringently the four tests (valuable to customers, rare, hard to imitate, hard to substitute), to find out whether the company has any capabilities that qualify as core competencies and that can provide competitive advantage. Executives are often asked to think about such issues during executive development work: what are their companies' core competencies, if any; are these aligned with the market, strategy and operations; and will their companies be success-ful in future with these competencies? These are always interesting issues to consider, but never simple or uncontentious ones to answer.

Understanding Strategic Innovation

We discussed in Chapters 4 and 5 SIA's innovation processes, but this is not the whole story of SIA's success as a serial innovator. Extending the theme of innovation as a capability, we can now ask: what is it that makes innovation 'strategic'? 'Strategic innovation' can be seen as a different answer to the three basic questions of strategy: what, who and how.[7] 'What' relates to both product or service offered, as well as to positioning or a unique selling proposition. 'Who' refers to the segments targeted, and 'how' refers to delivery channels as well as to the business model involved. Table 8.2 gives examples of strategic innovation in the airline and banking industries; in each case, budget airlines and virtual banking at one time presented different, novel answers to these basic questions of strategy, and created significant headaches for the incumbents.

Is SIA a strategic innovator? If we begin by considering its early days, SIA did provide a different answer to the dominant industry approach in 1972, when Malaysia-Singapore Airlines split up into two parts, Malaysian Airline System and Singapore Airlines. The dominant industry approach involved offering low levels of service (constrained by stringent IATA rules) and emphasised issues such as safety and infrastructure robustness. According to Ian Batey, founder of Batey Ads, the company that developed and nurtured the Singapore Girl brand icon, at the time most Asian airlines 'bowed under the pressure of the popular global commentary and consumer research in the early 1970s.' He adds, 'Both

200

Table 8.2
Strategic innovation in the airline and banking industries

Strategic innovation dimensions	Airlines: Dominant answer	Airlines: New answer	Banking: Dominant answer	Banking: New answer
What? (product – service)	'Full service' air travel	Budget air travel	High street banking	Virtual banks
What? (positioning)	Differentiation, service levels	Low cost, no frills	Differentiation (brand, reliability)	Differentiation (service levels, convenience)
Who?	All segments	Primary target budget conscious travellers	All segments	Primary target educated professionals
How? (channels – delivery)	Air & ground infrastructure	Air & ground infrastructure	Branches, Internet, telephone	Internet, telephone
How? (internal architecture)	Flag carriers, focus on quality – innovation	Budget airlines, focus on leanness & efficiency	'Full service' infrastructure	Call centres, Internet supported by full infrastructure

firmly called for a communications strategy that highlighted modern technical skills, modern aircraft, international experience, network size and Western pilots ... it was safe, conventional wisdom supported by substantial research data ... our team looked into the crystal ball and made a number of predictions. First, that all the national airlines of note would become increasingly homogeneous in terms of hardware benefits ... secondly, while reliability and modernity were important to customers, such attributes would eventually become basic "givens" and the distinctive differential would increasingly relate to what goes on during the flight – the on-board travel experience, the personal service and the service-related comforts.'[8] This sort of thinking both influenced and was consistent with the broad outlines of thinking at SIA: sustainable competitive differentiation would come from superior service, a well-known and potent brand icon, and constant innovation.

Another current example of strategic innovation is the trip to space that will be possible in the near future through Virgin Galactic, the first commercial 'spaceline' company, supported by Virgin. It currently costs US$200,000, but over the next few years Virgin aims to reduce the price point to levels that are affordable for more people, extending the potential market and making a trip to space an attractive option for celebrating special occasions or fulfilling one's personal dreams of space flight.

In the earlier section on capabilities, we discussed the mode of innovation relating to new products and services, as well as the dimension of developing a novel business model/organisational architecture. New products and services can either be incremental proliferations of existing offerings (for example, new flavours of ice cream or new varieties of washing liquid), or offer significant value added as perceived by the customer (for example, an MP3 player that is so successful that its name begins to stand for the product; an Internet search engine that seems to always find what you are looking for; an electronics company that periodically comes up with ground-breaking, market-driving products that create entirely new markets). If we combine the two dimensions of products/services (the 'what'), and the business model

Figure 8.2
A typology of strategic innovation

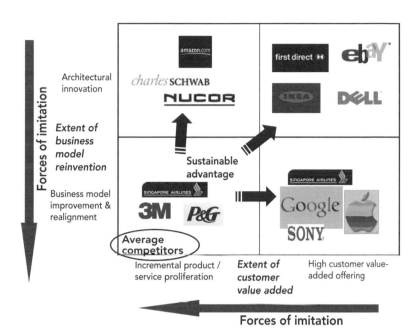

(the 'how'), we can derive the following typology of strategic innovation, shown in Figure 8.2.

Leading companies who are strategic innovators need to keep in touch with the market and sustain innovative efforts to move towards the top right-hand side of the diagram (as the arrows in the centre of the figure suggest). The forces of imitation continually pull companies towards the lower left point, however, where average competitors are located. Leading companies also need to worry about strategic alignment, striving to create unique internal configurations (processes, systems, cultural values) that cannot be copied by competitors easily, which operationalise their core competencies that in turn support their strategy. If all of this is in line with what the market wants either explicitly or latently, then a winning combination is created.

Fostering Strategic Innovation

How can a company extend its chances of being a strategic innovator, and what are some practices that foster innovation? To begin with, there are several structured frameworks for managing innovation, one of which is shown in Figure 8.3.

Such frameworks are useful, but they apply mostly to what happens after the new ideas arrive, and to intra-company processes rather than networks of innovation. A more vexing question is: how can organisations have higher chances of accessing and investing in novel, potentially valuable ideas before the bandwagon starts?

One way is engaging in 'idea brokering', identifying and using existing ideas in new ways; for example, Henry Ford used the idea of the assembly line in meat packing as an inspiration for the assembly line in car manufacturing, which was at the time an inefficient, craft-based production process which produced cars for the elite. A related way to foster innovation is drawing from inter-organisational networks and from strategic alliances to access ideas and resources for developing a complex new offering. One example is Apple's development of the iPod, which only took eight months from the start of the project to market entry. Apple only manages the brand and designs the user interface; everything else is supplied by a network of partners. The lion's share of the value, however, is captured by Apple, since it owns the iPod brand. A third way to foster innovation is to develop or discover novel ideas through a deep understanding of the customer. The iPod, for example, was introduced after similar products were already available on the market (the first movers) – some of which had more extensive features and excellent technology. However, it was Apple that could get under the skin of the teenage psyche with sleek design, evocative advertising and promotions, and careful management of product availability, creating a 'cool' aura around the iPod that swiftly rendered it the market leader. SIA's new offerings, in addition, are based on a careful understanding of customers' lifestyles, wants and needs as well as on extensive preparation and testing to ensure that their implementation is up to the usual high standards. A fourth consideration is the need

Figure 8.3
Managing innovation

Moving from an Idea to Cash

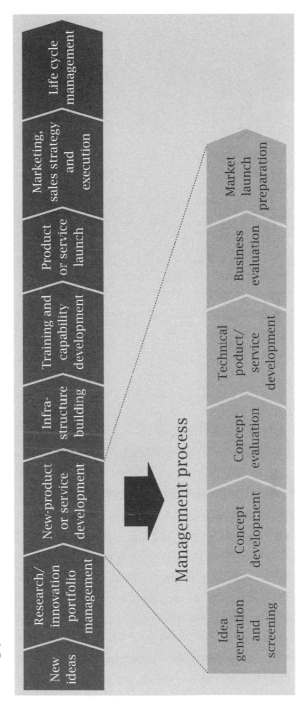

Source: Boston Consulting Group.

to create an internal culture and structure that support innovation, learning and change. There has to be a clear call from leadership about the importance of innovation; role modelling by the most senior levels of the organisation; reward and evaluation systems that monitor and reward innovation; dedicated roles for innovation-related activities such as idea brokering or network engagement; and dedicated spaces or events for idea exchange and cross-pollination. These have been pursued by SIA in different ways, as discussed in earlier chapters. The aim would ultimately be to create a learning organisation; an organisation with a flexible and adaptive culture and structure and open mindset, which encourages continuous change and development.

Managers therefore have to ask themselves: To what extent is my company a strategic innovator? Do we have a novel business model that cannot be copied easily? Do we continuously offer novel products and services to the market that really add value? Do we engage in process innovations that increase organisational efficiency or add value to customers? Do we engage in innovative behaviours and practices such as idea brokering and use of inter-organisational networks? Do we have the right culture, structure and processes in our company to foster innovation? If the answer to any of the above questions is not positive, alarm bells should sound.

Role of the Institutional Environment

Can a company succeed simply because it is located in the right place? Some argue that SIA could not have been a market leader if it was located elsewhere. The institutional environment certainly plays a role in company success, and in this section we use Porter's diamond model of national competitive advantage (see Figure 8.4) to understand how being located in Singapore has been advantageous for SIA.

If a company can be successful in an environment where rivalry is intense, and it follows robust strategies in that environment, then it has much higher chances of being successful elsewhere. SIA faces

Figure 8.4

How the institutional environment benefits SIA

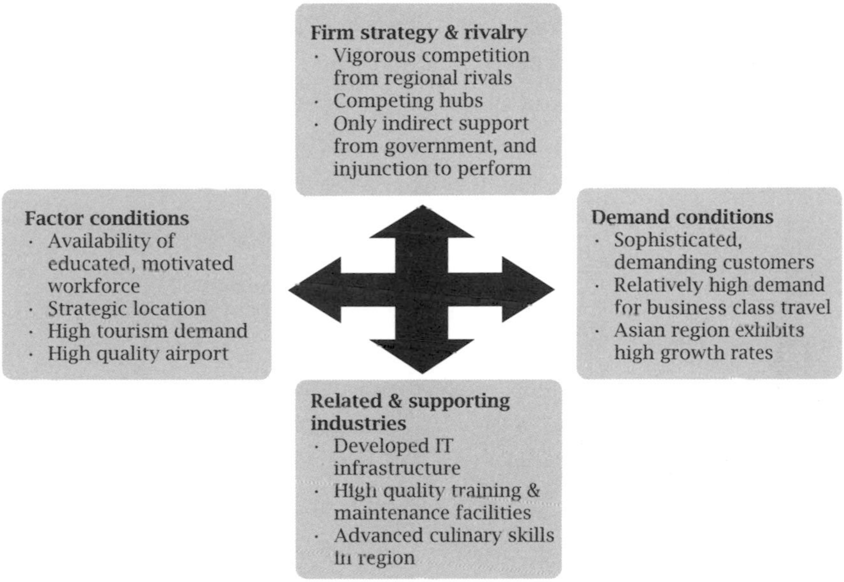

Firm strategy & rivalry
· Vigorous competition from regional rivals
· Competing hubs
· Only indirect support from government, and injunction to perform

Factor conditions
· Availability of educated, motivated workforce
· Strategic location
· High tourism demand
· High quality airport

Demand conditions
· Sophisticated, demanding customers
· Relatively high demand for business class travel
· Asian region exhibits high growth rates

Related & supporting industries
· Developed IT infrastructure
· High quality training & maintenance facilities
· Advanced culinary skills in region

vigorous competition from regional rivals, based in competing hubs (for example, Cathay Pacific in Hong Kong, Malaysian Airline System in Kuala Lumpur, Thai Airways in Bangkok). Without the benefit of a national market given the small size of Singapore, SIA was 'born global', thrown into regional and global competition from day one, and it has had to be successful without any direct state assistance. J. Y. Pillay comments,[9] 'One great advantage SIA enjoyed was that the authorities were scrupulous in observing a hands-off policy. They did what every far-sighted government should do, in the way of creating an efficient infrastructure, negotiating traffic rights, preserving labour peace, and so forth. But there was no interference with SIA, and no subsidies. SIA's guiding imperative was that nobody owed us a living. Call it confidence, pride, hubris, or whatever. We were determined to take on the competition entirely on our own.'

Secondly, if a company can satisfy very demanding and sophisticated customers, it means it has raised its quality and service quality to a level which can stand up to the most able competitors in global markets. SIA has had to please very demanding customers; service levels in Singapore are generally high, and there is a culture of expecting high quality when one buys from the market leader. In addition, the relatively high economic growth rates in the region aided SIA in achieving higher returns, which were in turn invested in improving the levels of service, for example, by renewing the fleet at a faster rate than competitors and by developing a longer and more holistic training programme for cabin crew than competitors.

Thirdly, there are several related and supporting industries in Singapore, whose high levels of quality and sophistication have benefited SIA. For example, Singapore is known as one of the most technologically advanced and wired nations in the world; this has a positive effect on SIA's use of technology, for example, in enabling the services offered via the Internet and mobile phones. In addition, the quality of education in Singapore is high, which is a positive factor promoting the high standard of development programmes for SIA employees. Furthermore, we suspect it is no surprise that SIA was the first airline to introduce airline cuisine which passengers actually looked forward to consuming, considering that Singapore is one of the acknowledged gourmet capitals of the world.

Fourthly, if a company can draw from ample and high quality factors of production, it stands a better chance of becoming an effective competitor. Again, Singapore has offered a lot in this regard: availability of a motivated and educated workforce, a strategic location, high tourist demand, and an airport that is acknowledged as one of the best in the world. Figure 8.4 summarises the above discussion.

The Role of Culture

We have briefly noted some of SIA's cultural values in the preceding chapters; we will now highlight some salient ones that we believe underlie a lot of the practices that make SIA a winner in the intensely competitive aviation industry. Porter's diamond framework does not capture the role of culture (which is to be expected since Porter is an economist), but in this case it is worth addressing an issue that gradually became obvious to us: that several of SIA's key cultural values are derived from the contextual, national culture.

For example, in SIA there is a strong *sense of collective destiny*. This developed from SIA's early days, when employees knew that if the airline did not do well it would not be subsidised but would be closed down by its main owner, the state. This sense of collective destiny is sustained by the company's reward and evaluation policies that use a company-wide formula and encourage peer pressure to perform. At a national level, the same sense of collective destiny has been cultivated over the years.

Secondly, there is a high level of *organisation and continuous drive for efficiency*, values that characterise both SIA and Singapore. As discussed in earlier chapters, SIA emphasises not only quality but efficiency and obsessive reduction of wastage, as well as seamless implementation. At the national level the scarcity of resources has meant historically that Singapore could only succeed by focusing on added value products and services (periodically shifting the focus to progressively higher value-added products and services), with high levels of efficiency.

Thirdly, both SIA as well as Singapore have a cultural value of *pragmatism*. Decisions are taken on a 'what-will-work' basis. No one is afraid of recognising that something may not be working and a new solution may be needed. Both at SIA as well as in Singapore, there is a clear understanding that the world is changing and that current ways of thinking and the way things are done need to be continuously re-examined.

A fourth common value is *continuous improvement* in a substantive way – not just incremental improvements or re-arrangements to give a surface impression of improvement, but a real effort to continuously look for ways to do things better and more efficiently. This is clear at both the national level, as well as with regard to SIA's internal policies and external offerings. Innovation occurs partly by inspiration, but mostly by an open search for ideas, a deep understanding of the customer, and sound internal development before a new service introduction. SIA has been very effective at producing innovations that customers actually use and that can provide competitive differentiation, and the company is not sentimental about challenging and letting go of any outdated practices. Batey comments, 'Once you become a global brand leader in both profits and reputation, there is a tendency to move to a defensive strategy, to protect your treasure, to look for safeguards, rather than retain the adventurous spirit that won you fame and fortune in the first place. In SIA's case, you can bet your bottom dollar that, while they have enjoyed amazing success, they will never waver in their tireless commitment to provide consumers with the best air travel experience in the world.'[10]

The cultural value of continuous improvement at SIA can be better understood by considering the cultural background of Singapore. The historical evolution of the city-state is remarkable, moving from a developing country status to being a world-class metropolis today. First Singapore leveraged its location to become a trading and trans-shipment hub for cargo ships on their way to other parts of Asia. Then investment was placed into manufacturing. Gradually it was realised that low-value-added manufacturing would move to cheaper locations, and the focus moved to high-value-added products and services – IT, chemicals, biotechnology and finance. Then the focus moved to creating a learning nation; and becoming a global schoolhouse, the place where anyone can go to receive high quality education.

There is therefore some truth to the suggestion that SIA's market leadership is aided by being based in Singapore. However this would be a very partial explanation of its success, which in no way devalues it, since national success is not achieved by chance either, but based on effective public policy decisions and investments. Some even believe that the beneficial effects were not mainly from the nation to the airline, but rather the other way round! According to

Batey, 'this is an unusual case of a national airline brand successfully helping to shape the global stature of its country, rather than the reverse!'[11]

What really matters at both the national and the organisational levels are robust strategies, seamless implementation and continuous vigilance and realignment when necessary. As J. Y. Pillay puts it, 'A credible and respected brand is the end-product of a long chain of strategies and initiatives, and disciplined execution, not the starting point ... SIA's goal from the outset was to offer superior service in every area, at a competitive price, while yielding a surplus to finance expansion and modernisation, and to provide a satisfactory return to shareholders. All this while keeping employees satisfied, happy and motivated.'[12]

We have argued in this chapter that there is a need to be clear about the company's generic strategy; that a combination of generic strategies is possible; that a company should nurture and invest in capabilities and core competencies that support its strategy; and lastly that a company should strive to foster strategic innovation. We also examined the enabling role of the institutional environment, as well as the pivotal role of culture, which should both be carefully considered when a company aims to develop sustainable advantage. Our study of SIA has shown that while the above are incredibly difficult to achieve, together with strategic alignment (discussed in Chapter 7), they are key ingredients of success. The organisations that can play at this level can create near-unassailable advantages and extraordinary performance.

END NOTES

1. See Porter, M. (1985) *Competitive Advantage: Creating and Sustaining Superior Performance*. New York: Free Press.
2. Porter (1985) p. 11.
3. Porter (1985) p. 15.
4. Porter (1985) p. 20.

5. See Wernerfelt, B. (1984) A Resource-Based View of the Firm. *Strategic Management Journal*, 5(2): 171–80.

6. Quoted from a speech by J. Y. Pillay, chairman of the Singapore Exchange Ltd, at the Right Angle seminar 'Rising Above the Crowd – Maintaining Your Presence in a Rough Marketplace', 15 March 2002.

7. Markides, C. (1997) Strategic Innovation, *MIT Sloan Management Review*, 38 (3), pp. 9–23.

8. Batey, I. (2002) *Asian Branding: A Great Way to Fly*. Singapore: Prentice Hall, pp. 117–8.

9. Quoted from a speech by J. Y. Pillay, chairman of the Singapore Exchange Ltd, at the Right Angle seminar 'Rising Above the Crowd – Maintaining Your Presence in a Rough Marketplace', 15 March 2002.

10. Batey, I. (2002) *Asian Branding: A Great Way to Fly*. Singapore: Prentice Hall, p. 137.

11. Batey, I. (2002) *Asian Branding: A Great Way to Fly*. Singapore: Prentice Hall, p. 124.

12. Quoted from a speech by J. Y. Pillay, chairman of the Singapore Exchange Ltd, at the Right Angle seminar 'Rising Above the Crowd – Maintaining Your Presence in a Rough Marketplace', 15 March 2002.

CASE STUDY: STRATEGY AND ORGANISATION AT SIA – CREATING A GLOBAL CHAMPION[1]

Even though the airline industry has enjoyed reasonable growth, it has also been plagued by over-capacity, commoditisation of offerings, cut-throat rivalry exacerbated by the entry of low cost carriers and price wars, and intermittent periods of disastrous under-performance.[2] Rising and uncertain oil prices have not helped, and neither have the SARS crisis, bird flu, the Asian tsunami, and rising terrorism concerns. In 2006, the global airline industry generated a net loss of US$500 million, or 0.1% of revenues, accumulating net losses of US$42 billion between 2001 and 2006.[3] In 2007, the airline industry made a modest net profit of US$5.6 billion on revenues of US$490 billion, equivalent to less than 2% margin.[4] The outlook for 2008 onwards remains bleak. Not surprisingly, the industry is regularly rated as one of the worst performing industries in the Fortune Global 500 rankings.

In this tough industry environment, Singapore Airlines (SIA) has consistently outperformed its competitors throughout its more than three-and-a-half decade long history, since its reincarnation from Malaysia-Singapore Airlines into SIA in 1972. SIA is the most awarded airline in the world, recognised innovation and service leader, and the only airline to be listed in *Fortune* magazine's global 50 most admired companies.[5] It not only regularly outperforms competitors in terms of financial performance, but it has never shown an annual loss since its inception as an independent airline. Figures 1 and 2 show SIA's performance for the period 2003–2008 (see also Appendices 1 and 2 for further financial and operating information).

Since strategy professor Michael Porter's influential suggestion that differentiation and cost leadership are mutually exclusive strategies,[6] and that an organisation must ultimately choose where its competitive advantage will lie, stick to that choice and make the right investments to implement and support it, there has been fierce debate about whether a combined cost leadership/differentiation strategy can be achieved and sustained over the longer term. For 'full service' airlines, as well as service organisations more broadly, delivering excellent service usually comes at a premium cost to the company. SIA, on the other hand, has managed to deliver premium service to some of the

Figure 1
Group profitability

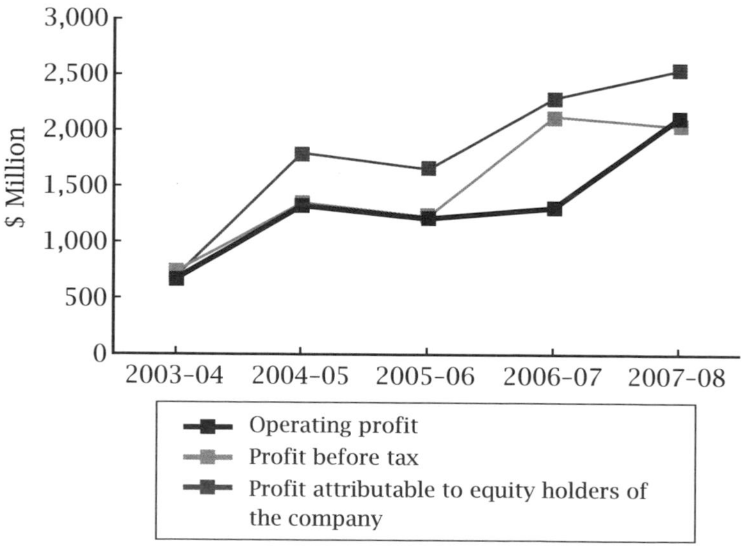

Source: Singapore Airlines Annual Report, 2007-2008.

216

Figure 2
Group profitability ratios

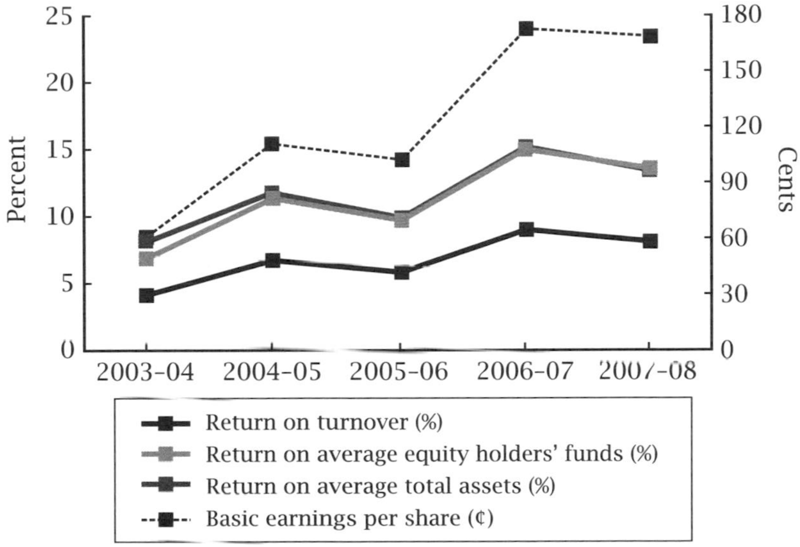

Source: *Singapore Airlines Annual Report, 2007-2008.*

most demanding airline customers, who have sky-high expectations, at a surprisingly efficient level of costs. A usual metric of airline costs is cents per available seat kilometre (ASK),[7] where flag carriers tend to have costs of US$0.09 to US$0.14, and budget carriers US$0.045 to US$0.075.[8] SIA's costs per ASK were US$0.058 in 2007-2008 and US$0.055 in 2006-2007.[9]

Similar to many other organisations with a reputation for providing excellent service, SIA displays characteristics such as top management commitment to excellence, customer-focused staff and systems, and a customer-oriented culture. Dr Cheong Choong Kong, former CEO, says, 'Our passengers ... are our raison d'être. If SIA is successful, it is largely because we have never allowed ourselves to forget that important fact.' The current SIA chairman, in his letter to shareholders, notes: 'I can assure you that our customers all over the world will see and experience a suite of products and services which will continue our leadership role at the premium end of the airline industry.'[10] Most companies make similar claims. What distinguishes SIA from them is that the values of cost-effective service excellence do not remain in the abstract; they are enshrined in a unique, self-reinforcing system of organisational processes and activities that makes the values real for all employees, who in turn enact them in their customer interactions and in their daily work. This same system also delivers efficiency of an order that SIA's competitors find it very hard, if not impossible, to match.

SIA's organisational activity system is based on five pillars that support and operationalise the core competency of cost-effective service excellence: the pillars are rigorous service design and development; total innovation (integrating continuous incremental improvements with discontinuous innovations); profit and cost consciousness ingrained in all employees; holistic staff development; and reaping of strategic synergies through related diversification and world-class infrastructure. Figure 3 below portrays these pillars.

Figure 3
The five pillars of SIA's organisational activity system

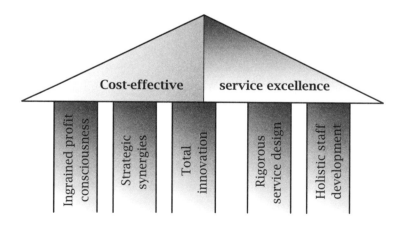

Rigorous Service Design and Development

Twenty-five years ago, marketing professor Lyn Shostack complained that service design and development were usually characterised by trial and error.[11] Unlike manufacturing organisations where R&D departments and product engineers would routinely be found, systematic development and testing of services, or service engineering, were not the norm. Things appear to have changed little since then. For SIA, however, product design and development have always been a serious, structured issue.

SIA has a service development department that hones and thoroughly tests any change before it is introduced. This department undertakes research, trials, time and motion studies, mock-ups, assessing customer reaction; indeed whatever is necessary to ensure that a service innovation is supported by the right procedures. Underpinning the continuous innovation and development is a corporate culture that accepts change as not just inevitable but as a way of life. A trial that fails or an implemented innovation that is removed after a few months is seen as acceptable. In some organisations, personal reputations can be at stake and so pilot tests 'have to work'. At SIA a failed pilot test damages no one's reputation.

In some organisations, service, and indeed product, innovations live beyond their useful years because of political pressure or lack of investment resources for continuous innovation and renewal. At SIA it is expected that any innovation will likely have a short shelf life. One recent example is the discontinuation of FAST (Fully Automated Seamless Travel), a check-in process involving biometric technology, where customers could get their seat on the plane and clear immigration within one to three minutes. This process was developed jointly by SIA and the Civil Aviation Authority of Singapore, and while it worked well, usage was lower than anticipated given that the regular channels at the airport were also highly efficient.

SIA recognises that to sustain its differentiation, it must maintain continuous improvement, and be able to terminate programmes or services that no longer provide competitive differentiation. Mr Yap Kim Wah, senior vice president of the Product and Service Department, says, 'It is getting more and more difficult to differentiate ourselves because every airline is doing the same thing ... the crucial fact is that we continue to say that we want to improve. That we have the will to do so. And that every time we reach a goal, we always say that we got to find a new mountain or hill to climb ... you must be able to give up what you love.'

These comments on the need to continually innovate raise the issue of sustainability of competitive advantage. SIA's sustained superior performance relative to its peers shows that it has achieved this, but what is it that makes it so difficult to imitate SIA? As discussed below, it is easier to imitate fragments of a business system rather than the whole system; if such a system is internally consistent and self-reinforcing, held together by robust, customer-focused processes and the glue of cultural values, it becomes almost impossible to imitate.

The stakes are raised for SIA, not only by its competitors but also by its customers. A company with a sky-high reputation attracts customers with sky-high expectations. SIA's research team has found that SIA attracts a disproportionately large number of very demanding customers, who expect the best. 'Customers adjust their expectations according to the brand image,' says Mr Sim Kay Wee, senior vice president of the Cabin Crew Department. 'When you fly on a good brand, like SIA, your expectations are already sky-high. And if SIA gives anything that is just OK, it is just not good enough.'

Combined with its extensive customer feedback mechanisms, SIA treats its customers' high expectations as a fundamental resource for innovation ideas. Weak signals are amplified. Not only written comments, but even verbal comments to the flight crew are taken seriously and reported back to the relevant sections of the airline. Ms Lim Suet Kwee, senior rank trainer, says, 'All feedback given by customers is taken very seriously because we have to look into why there was such a particular feedback and also if there are ways we can improve on that.' An additional source of intelligence is SIA's 'spy flights', where individuals travel with competitors and report detailed intelligence on competitive offerings.

220

Lastly, SIA recognises that its competition does not just come from within the industry. As a rule, SIA sets its sights high and instead of aiming to be the best airline, its intention is to be the best service organisation. To achieve that, SIA employs broad benchmarking not just against its main competitors, but against the best-in-class service companies. Mr Yap Kim Wah says, 'It is important to realise that [our customers] are not just comparing SIA with other airlines. They are comparing us against many industries, and on many factors. So when they pick up a phone and call up our reservations, for example, they are actually making a mental comparison, maybe subconsciously, to the last best experience they had. It could be with a hotel; it could be with a car rental company. If they had a very good experience with the hotel or car rental company and if the next call they make is to SIA, they will subconsciously make the comparison and say "How come you're not as good as them?" They do not say "You have the best telephone service system out of all the other airlines I've called". Our customers, albeit subconsciously, will benchmark us against the best in almost everything. The new ball game for SIA is not just to be the best of the best in the airline industry but to work at being the best service company.'

Total Innovation: Integrating Incremental Development with Unanticipated, Discontinuous Innovations

An airline has a multitude of sub-systems such as reservations, catering, maintenance, inflight services and entertainment system. SIA does not aim to be a lot better but just a bit better in every one of them than its competitors. This not only means constant innovation but also total innovation – innovation in everything, all of the time. Importantly, this also supports the notion of cost-effectiveness. Continuous incremental development comes at a low cost but delivers that necessary margin of value to the customer. Mr Yap Kim Wah elaborates, 'It is the totality that counts. This also means that it does not need to be too expensive. If you want to provide the best food you might decide to serve lobster on short-haul flights between Singapore and Bangkok, for example, however you might go bankrupt. The point is that, on that route, we just have to be better than our competitors in everything we do. Just a little bit better in everything. This allows us to make a small profit from the flight to enable us to innovate without pricing ourselves out of the market. We want to provide excellent and all round value for money. This makes it much harder for our competitors. Therefore, in SIA, it's about coming up with new things all the time. We want to be a little bit better all the time in everything we do.' Recently SIA built a US$1 million simulator that mimics the air pressure and humidity in the air, so that food can be tasted under these conditions which affect taste buds. One decision was to reduce the use of spices in its food. It also added Berlitz channels to its KrisFlyer entertainment system, which enable passengers to learn some of the local language of their destination.

Whilst cost-effective, incremental improvements are an important basis for its competitive advantage, SIA also implements frequent major initiatives that are firsts in its industry, both on the ground and in the air. One example is its Outstanding Service on the Ground programme. This initiative was led by the managing director and involved working with the many other parts of the organisation with an impact on customer service before and after the flight to ensure a seamless and efficient service. SIA's latest service excellence initiative, called Transforming Customer Service (TCS), involves staff in five key operational areas – cabin crew, engineering, ground services, flight operations and sales support. The development programme is about building team spirit among staff in the key operational areas, and is aimed at ensuring that the whole journey from the purchase of the ticket onwards is as pleasant and seamless as possible for customers, both internal and external. The most recent initiative is called SOAR, which stands for 'Service Above All the Rest', where all staff go through a one-day service-oriented training and dialogue with senior managers. Below are examples of internal posters that SIA uses to communicate such initiatives to staff and gain their commitment.

SIA employs a total innovation approach captured in their '40-30-30' rule, aiming for a holistic approach to service improvement. SIA focuses

Source: Courtesy of Singapore Airlines.

40% of the resources on training and invigorating its people, 30% on the review of process and procedures, and 30% on creating new product and service ideas. Total innovation is about cost-effective service excellence based on the totality rather than just one aspect of the customer experience.

In addition to continuous incremental innovations, SIA's reputation as a service innovator is also based on unanticipated, discontinuous service innovations. SIA strives to gain a deep understanding of trends in customer lifestyles, and debates their implications for the future of better service in the air. Mr Yap Kim Wah says, 'Most new changes that really secure the "wow" effect are those things that customers never expected ... we have a product innovation department that continuously looks at trends and why people behave in a certain manner, why they do certain things. And then we do a projection of three to five years of what is going to happen ... for the airline, it's not just about having a smoother flight from A to B. That will be taken for granted. It is really about what the customers' lifestyle needs are. Can we meet these lifestyle needs?'

Examples of innovations that have helped over the years to set SIA apart from its competitors include the KrisFlyer on-demand entertainment system for all classes of travel, Internet and phone check-in for all classes, and the full-sized Spacebed and on-board e-mail and Internet services for business and first class. In late 2006, SIA became the first airline to fly the A380 jet, and is currently working on developing the inflight offerings in that aircraft that will perpetuate its differentiated position as a leader in its industry.

SIA has made a clear strategic choice of being a leader and follower at the same time. It is a pioneer on innovations that have high impact on customer service (for example, inflight entertainment, the widest bed in business class, the world's longest non-stop flight from Singapore to Los Angeles, suites on the A380). However, it is at the same time a fast follower in areas that are less visible from the customer's point of view. In doing so, SIA relies on proven technology that can be implemented swiftly and cost-effectively. For example, SIA's revenue management and customer relationship management (CRM) systems used technology with which its providers/implementation partners had ample experience to ensure smooth, cost-effective implementation, rather than going for the latest technology available, which would not only be much more expensive, but also carry a higher implementation risk. Rather than trying to be a leader in everything, SIA strives to be a leader where it counts from the customer's perspective.

Profit Consciousness Ingrained in All Employees

Though SIA is totally focused on the customer and is constantly improving its service, managers and staff are well aware of the need for profit and cost-effectiveness. All staff from the top to the bottom are able to deal well with the potentially conflicting objectives of excellence and profit. This is firstly created by a cost and profit consciousness. 'It's drilled into us from the day we start working for SIA that if we don't make money, we'll be closed down,' says Mr Yap Kim Wah. 'Singapore doesn't need a national airline. Second, the company has made a very important visionary statement that "We don't want to be the largest company. We want to be the most profitable". That's very powerful.'

Any proposed innovation is analysed very carefully on the balance of expected customer benefits versus costs. Station managers and frontline staff constantly trade off passenger satisfaction versus cost-effectiveness – the customer has to be delighted, but in a cost-effective manner. During the development of the A380, there was careful consideration of how the cabin configuration would affect profitability. According to Mr Sim Kim Chui, vice president of the Product Development Department, who led the A380 project, the ideas arising from focus groups with frequent flyers were prioritised and the top ones chosen for inclusion, but their implementation was carried out with profitability in mind. He says, 'So it's important to look at all these ideas, and we shortlisted the better ones ... Of course at the end of the day the aircraft must make money. I was reminded time and again that this aircraft is not to win awards per se ... Don't go win the best design award and at the end of the day we don't make any money.'

Profitability does not just come by controlling costs, but also by the ability to charge a premium price, the true test of differentiation. With regard to the A380 project, even though according to the manufacturer the aeroplane could carry 555 passengers, the final seat count on SIA's A380s is 471 passengers. Mr Sim says, 'The safe approach is to cram it with as many seats as possible and then you know the risks are lower, but I think [keeping the final seat count low] is important for the positioning of Singapore Airlines as a premier carrier; we are not selling a commodity here. So this aircraft must be different from all the others; it must offer the best, fit customer expectations and then we can charge a premium.'

Further, in everyday operations, staff keep in mind the importance of reducing wastage without compromising customer service. Citing some examples, senior rank trainer Mr Patrick Seow says, 'On flights, we try to minimise the number of bottles of wine we need to open, by gauging the passengers' demand for it, rather than just automatically opening X bottles and at the end of the day throw the balance away. In that sense we do our best to save costs. Through feedback that was collected from the passengers in survey forms, we find that because of the late departure of the flight, 30% of passengers choose not to eat. So we feel that maybe we don't need to stock 100% meals for every passenger.'

According to Mr Sim Kim Chui, it is important to prioritise customer needs and spend only on the top ones, and to reduce wastage without affecting customer service. He says, 'Why is it so important that we prioritise passenger needs? If I have $100 to spend, I must spend it on what is important to the customer. No point giving me a shopping list and trying to do too many things. SIA would deliberately not spend on certain things that it thinks the customer deems as low priority; but whatever the customer ranks as high priority, it is where we'll put the money ... The second consideration is to reduce wastage, by taking away things that will not affect the customers in any way. So in SIA, prudent wastage reduction is what we do day in day out. You'll be surprised how much wastage we can reduce. Keep your costs down without affecting your service in any way.'

Finally, like many other service organisations, SIA has a reward system that pays bonuses according to the profitability of the company. However, for SIA the same percentage applies to everyone – the same formula is used throughout the company. As a result there is a lot of informal peer pressure from individuals within the organisation; staff and managers appear to be quite open in challenging many decisions and actions when they see resources being wasted or money being inappropriately spent.

SIA builds team spirit within its 6,600 crew members through its 'team concept', where small teams of 13 crew members are formed and they fly together as far as possible for at least two years. This leads to the development of team spirit and social bonds within the team that reinforces the culture of cost-effective service excellence and the peer pressure to deliver SIA's promise to customers.

Achieving Strategic Synergies through Related Diversification and World-Class Infrastructure

SIA utilises related diversification to reap cost synergies and at the same time control quality and enable the transfer of learning. Subsidiaries serve not only as the development ground for well-rounded management skills and a corporate rather than a divisional outlook through job rotation, but also as sources of learning.

In addition, related operations (such as catering, aircraft maintenance, airport management) have healthier profit margins than the airline business itself because competitive intensity is lower and industry structure is more favourable. SIA Engineering Company, for example, ensures that SIA does not have to pay expensive aircraft maintenance fees to other airlines; rather it sells such services to other airlines at healthy margins. SIA's fleet, one of the youngest in the world, enables lower maintenance costs, higher fuel efficiency and higher flight quality. Over the past 15 years though, SIA's average fleet age has fluctuated between 58 and 77 months (see Figure 4); it remains less than half of the industry average, with various estimates at 158 months or 177 months.[12,13]

SIA's inflight catering centre produces SIA's own inflight cuisine, ensuring high quality, reliability and responsiveness to customer feedback, as well as caters for other airlines at a healthy margin. SIA's Singapore Airport Terminal Services subsidiary provides several ground

Figure 4
SIA age and size of fleet

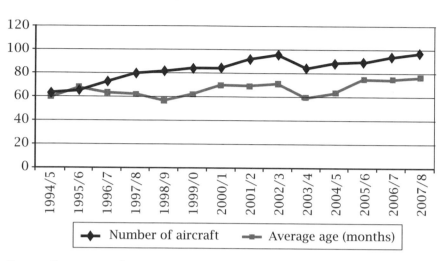

Source: Singapore Airlines Annual Reports.

services at Changi Airport, which is regularly voted as the best airport in the world. This excellent airport management and infrastructure entices passengers who are travelling on to Australia, New Zealand or other countries in the region to pass through Changi Airport and to choose SIA as their carrier. Changi Airport is also one of the most cost-efficient major airports, for example, landing charges for a 747 are US$2,000, as opposed to US$3,500 in Hong Kong and US$7,500 at Narita.[14]

SIA's subsidiaries operate under the same management philosophy and culture that emphasises cost-effective service excellence. Even though they are part of the group, they are quoted separately on the Singapore Stock Exchange and are subject to market discipline with very clear profit and loss expectations. In SIA, therefore, the conventional wisdom of outsourcing (outsource 'peripheral' activities and focus on what you do best) does not readily apply. External suppliers cannot offer the same value to SIA that its own subsidiaries can. This kind of related diversification of SIA leads to strategic synergy benefits in terms of reliability of key inputs, high quality, transfer of learning, and at the same time cost-effectiveness. SIA's operating costs are shown in Table 1.

Table 1
SIA's operating costs

	2007–08		2006–07		Change	
	$ million	%	$ million	%	$ million	%
Fuel costs	4,054.9	36.5	3,881.3	37.6	+173.6	+4.5
Staff costs	1,841.1	16.6	1,685.5	16.3	+155.6	+9.2
Depreciation	1,165.1	10.5	1,006.1	9.8	+159.0	+15.8
Handling charges	771.0	6.9	752.6	7.3	+18.4	+2.4
Sales costs	658.7	5.9	620.5	6.0	+38.2	+6.2
Inflight meals and other passenger costs	613.9	5.5	601.8	5.8	+12.1	+2.0
Aircraft maintenance and overhaul costs	538.8	4.9	433.9	4.2	+104.9	+24.2
Airport and overflying charges	536.1	4.8	515.4	5.0	+20.7	+4.0
Rentals on leased aircraft	304.2	2.7	313.8	3.0	-9.6	-3.1
Communication and information technology costs	104.6	0.9	110.1	1.1	-5.5	-5.0
Other costs	527.2	4.8	395.9	3.9	+131.3	+33.2
	11,115.6	100.0	10,316.9	100.0	798.7	+7.7

Source: Singapore Airlines Annual Report, 2007-2008.

Developing Staff Holistically[15]

Ms Lim Suet Kwee, senior rank trainer and senior flight stewardess at SIA, says, 'In Singapore, we always want to be the best in a lot of things. SIA is no different ... we have been taught many things from young, from our Asian heritage ... filial piety, care and concern and hospitality ... at SIA the most important part is to try and do whatever we can to please the customer. How do we do it? Sometimes, people do wonder how we manage to do it with the limited time and resources on a flight, yet we manage somehow. Call us magicians.'

In addition to Asian values, this attitude is aided by continuous training and development. Senior managers say that 'training in SIA is almost next to godliness'. Everyone, no matter how senior, has a training and development plan with clear goals. New cabin crew undergo training for four months, longer than any other airline. This includes not only functional skills, but also soft skills of personal interaction and poise, and the emotional skills of dealing with the consequences of serving very demanding passengers. Mr Patrick Seow, senior rank trainer at the SIA Training School, says, 'A large portion of cabin crew training is actually centred on soft skills. So you are correct in saying that SIA cabin crew look a certain way, act a certain way and have certain manners. We actually pay attention to how they should treat the passengers, how they should position themselves when they come into contact with the customers. For instance, you will see that in the aircraft environment, cabin crew always go down to the eye level of the customers.' SIA's training of the Singapore Girl is likened to that in a 'finishing school'. Mr Sim Kay Wee elaborates, 'The girls are transformed from the time they come in, and by the time they finish their training, they look totally different. Their deportment, the way they carry themselves ... There's a great transformation there.'

In addition to such training, SIA also encourages and supports activities that might on the surface be seen as having nothing to do with service in the air. Crew employees have created groups such as the Performing Arts Circle, which stages full-length plays and musicals, the Wine Appreciation Group and the Gourmet Circle. These activities help to develop camaraderie and team spirit, as well as personal knowledge of the finer things in life, which filters into the personalised and exceptional service that the crew delivers in the air.

Development is continuous. This is reflected in the type of training that the Singapore Girl receives as customers get more sophisticated and with higher expectations. Mr Yap Kim Wah comments, 'While our Singapore Girl is our icon, and we're very proud of her and her achievements, we continue to improve her skills; we continue to improve her ability to understand the appreciation of wines and cheeses, for example, or our Asian heritage ... the enhancement must be continuous.'[16]

Cabin crew can select the refresher courses they wish to attend; on average they attend three to four days of such courses in a year. Popular courses include those on basic and intermediate transactional analysis (a counselling-type course), leadership and European languages. The company is moving from a system of directing which courses cabin crew should attend, to one of self-directed learning, where staff take responsibility for their own development.

Even before development starts, there is substantial effort to ensure that the company hires the right staff. For example, entry qualifications for cabin crew applicants include both academic (at least a polytechnic diploma, meaning that they have spent 13 years in school) as well as physical attributes. The recruitment process is extensive, involving three rounds of interviews, a 'uniform test', a 'water confidence' test, psychometric tests, and a tea party. Over 16,000 applications are received every year, and the company hires around 500 to 600 new cabin crew to cover attrition rates of around 10%. This includes both voluntary and directed attrition. If, for example, a Singapore Girl becomes pregnant, she has to leave the airline. There is a scheme that allows these stewardesses to re-apply to join the airline. After the Singapore Girls start flying, they are carefully monitored for the first six months, through a monthly report by the inflight supervisor. At the end of the probationary period, 75% get confirmed, around 20% get an extension of the probation, and 5% leave.

SIA's Strategy

SIA is positioned as a premium carrier with a high level of innovation and an excellent level of service. It has made a strategic choice of giving priority to profitability over size. The internal organisational practices outlined above, such as continuous people development and rigorous service design, are key aspects of operationalising and sustaining this positioning and strategic choice.

At the corporate level, SIA follows a strategy of related diversification. The SIA group has 27 subsidiaries[17] spanning all aspects related to the operations of an airline, including Singapore Airport Terminal Services, SIA Engineering Company Limited and Singapore Airlines Cargo Pte Ltd. Its airline subsidiaries include 100% ownership of regional carrier Silk Air, budget carrier Tiger Airways (49%), and Virgin Atlantic (49%), and cover the key customer segments within the industry. CEO Chew Choon Seng says, 'We intend to play in all the segments – SIA at the high end, Silk Air on middle ground and Tiger Airways at the low end.'[18]

As part of its international strategy, SIA joined the Star Alliance, one of the three major airline alliances (the other two being Oneworld and SkyTeam) in April 2000. In the meantime various divisions of the SIA group have been quietly investing in China through strategic alliances with local organisations (cargo division, airport services and engineering services). As shown in Figure 5, East Asia is the predominant source of revenue for SIA in terms of where tickets are sold.

The use of information technology is an essential feature of SIA's strategy. SIA's website is one of the most advanced and user-friendly in the industry, where customers can check schedules, buy tickets, check in to a flight, manage their KrisFlyer account, find out about promotions, and even choose their meal for their next flight. Given that agents' commissions can be up to 7.5% of total operating costs (and reservations/ticketing a further 5.4%),[19] the effective use of IT can both significantly reduce costs and enhance service levels. One of Mr Chew Choon Seng's top priorities when he took over as CEO in mid-2003 was to cut non-fuel costs by 20% within three years, and outsourcing IT functions to IBM was an important part of that focus.

Figure 5
SIA's passenger revenue composition

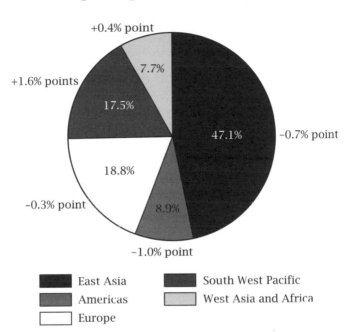

Source: Singapore Airlines Annual Report, 2007–2008.

SIA continues to focus on the customer experience through service excellence and innovation, as well as continuously striving for efficiency. Mr Chew Choon Seng says, 'The day we stop having visions or objectives to work to, then that is the day we atrophy. I can assure you we have no intention of doing that.'[20]

Turbulence on the Horizon?

Competitive conditions in the airline industry have not been getting any easier. Apart from wildly fluctuating fuel prices and security concerns, for example, another wild card for many airlines (and particularly SIA) is the risk of long-range aircraft by-passing their hubs. To cite an example, the Boeing 777-200LR launched in 2005 is capable of flying 17,500 km, almost halfway around the world and these planes are able to by-pass hubs like Singapore on flights from Europe to Australia. SIA has been seeking to get rights to fly from Australia to Europe and the US as a way of mitigating this risk.

Competitors are hot on SIA's heels, trying to close the gap in both service excellence and efficiency. This is not always easy to achieve; Malaysian Airlines' service quality is high, for example, but its efficiency is nowhere near SIA (available tonne-kms per employee is 355,000, around one third of SIA's).[21] Other competitors have embarked on aggressive growth while also competing on service quality. For example, Emirates has placed an order for 43 A380 aircraft, and prices tickets significantly lower than its main competitors.

The need to reduce employee numbers at SIA and introduce a variable component to wage packages based on company profitability after the 2003 SARS crisis has been stressful for its industrial relations climate. Minister Mentor Lee Kuan Yew became involved to resolve these issues, given the importance of SIA and the aviation sector to Singapore's economic prosperity. SIA has also taken steps to improve the industrial relations issues. The significant delays in delivery of the A380 have increased SIA's launch costs and delayed its capacity expansion plans. Lastly, higher-paying jobs elsewhere tempt SIA employees, many of whom decide to take up new challenges.

In 2006, the Singapore media expressed concerns regarding perceived service lapses at SIA.[22] Skytrax World Airline Awards had ranked SIA seventh in their 'Airline of the Year' rankings in 2006, down from fourth in 2005; and SIA's cabin staff in the same survey were ranked fifth in 2006, down from fourth in 2005. In the 2007 rankings, however, SIA made a comeback by topping the 'Airline of the Year' awards, with its cabin staff ranked second.

Meanwhile, critics and competitors complain that much of SIA's success is due to environmental factors and the role of the government rather than its own capabilities. Analysts note that one benefit of Temasek's 54.5% stake is perceived lower debt risk by lenders and therefore lower cost of borrowing (even though SIA does not need to borrow significantly, having a debt to equity ratio of just 0.11 times[23]). The industrial relations climate in Singapore is deemed to be less adversarial than elsewhere, enabling SIA to implement policies that could have caused friction in many other airlines. Critics also suggest that SIA's acquisitions have not fared that well. In 1999, SIA bought 49% of Virgin Atlantic, and wrote off 95% of the investment soon after 9/11. In July 2007, it emerged that SIA was considering selling its stake in Virgin. In 2000, SIA acquired a 25% stake in Air New Zealand, which was seriously impacted by the collapse of its debt-laden Australian arm, Ansett Airlines; this investment was also written off.

Many disagree with the suggestion that SIA's success is due to the state. Indeed, high levels of state aid to airlines that have supported many of SIA's competitors have never been awarded in Singapore,[24] where deregulation and encouragement of competition have been the norm. SIA's chairman says, 'We are unlike many of our competitors: we have never had government protection, or underwriting of our business in difficult times. We operate on a commercial basis and our people know that our customers have a choice of airlines.'[25]

Given these trends and critiques, how long can SIA sustain its competitive advantage and superior performance? What should it be doing to ensure that it remains a leader in this intensely competitive and unpredictable industry?

Discussion Questions

1. Why is it so difficult to make money in the airline industry?

2. What is SIA's strategy, and what core competencies support it?

3. How does SIA implement its strategy? What practices and activities are involved?

4. To what extent is there alignment among SIA's strategy, core competencies and organisational practices? Do you see any misalignments?

5. Imagine you are a strategy consultant; what would you recommend to SIA to sustain its competitive success in future?

6. What learning points can we take away from this case study?

APPENDIX 1: FINANCIAL STATISTICS

	2007–08	2006–07	% Change
Group			
Financial Results ($ million)			
Total revenue	15,972.5	14,494.4	+ 10.2 times
Total expenditure	13,848.0	13,180.0	+ 5.1
Operating profit	2,124.5	1,314.4	+ 61.6
Profit before taxation	2,547.2	2,284.6	+ 11.5
Profit attributable to equity holders of the Company	2,049.4	2,128.8	− 3.7
Financial Position ($ million)			
Share capital	1,682.0	1,494.9	+ 12.5
Treasury shares	(33.2)	–	n.m.
Capital reserve	95.6	44.9	+112.9
Foreign currency translation reserve	(130.7)	(59.5)	+119.7
Share-based compensation reserve	136.4	97.3	+ 40.2
Fair value reserve	443.4	(45.5)	n.m.
General reserve	12,931.7	13,567.9	− 4.7
Equity attributable to equity holders of the Company	15,125.2	15,100	+ 0.2
Return on equity holders' funds (%)	13.6	14.9	− 1.3 points
Total assets	26,515.2	25,992.0	+ 2.0
Total debt	1,656.7	1,879.4	− 11.8
Total debt equity ratio (times)	0.11	0.12	− 0.01 times
Value added	7,082.1	6,510.1	+ 8.8
Per Share Data			
Earnings before tax (cents)	209.5	185.2	+ 13.1
Earnings after tax (cents) – basic	168.5	172.6	− 2.4
Earnings after tax (cents) – diluted	166.1	170.8	− 2.8
Net asset value ($)	12.77	12.11	+ 5.5

Dividends

Interim dividend (cents per share)	20.0	15.0	+	5.0 cents
Proposed final dividend (cents per share)	80.0	35.0	+	45.0 cents
Special dividend (cents per share)	–	50.0	–	50.0 cents
Dividend cover (times)	1.7	1.7	–	

Company

Financial Results ($ million)

Total revenue	12,759.6	11,343.9	+	12.5
Total expenditure	11,115.6	10,316.9	+	7.7
Operating profit	1,644.0	1,027.0	+	60.1
Profit before taxation	2,077.6	2,291.1	–	9.3
Profit after taxation	1,758.8	2,213.2	–	20.5
Value added	5,183.5	5,107.2	+	1.5

Source: Singapore Airlines Annual Report, 2007–2008.

APPENDIX 2: OPERATING STATISTICS

	2007–08	2006–07	% Change
Singapore Airlines			
Passengers carried (thousand)	19,120	18,346	+ 4.2
Revenue passenger-km (million)	91,485.2	89,148.8	+ 2.6 times
Available seat-km (million)	113,919.1	112,543.8	+ 1.2
Passenger load factor (%)	80.3	79.2	+ 1.1 points
Passenger yield (cents/pkm)	12.1	10.9	+11.0
Passenger unit cost (cents/ask)	8.4	7.9	+ 6.3
Passenger breakeven load factor (%)	69.4	72.5	– 3.1 points
SIA Cargo			
Cargo and mail carried (million kg)	1,308.0	1,284.9	+ 1.8
Cargo load (million tonne-km)	7,959.2	7,995.6	– 0.5
Gross capacity (million tonne-km)	12,787.8	12,889.8	– 0.8
Cargo load factor (%)	62.2	62.0	+ 0.2 point
Cargo yield (cents/ltk)	38.7	38.4	+ 0.8
Cargo unit cost (cents/ctk)	23.4	24.5	– 4.5
Cargo breakeven load factor (%)	60.5	63.8	– 3.3 points
Singapore Airlines and SIA Cargo			
Overall load (million tonne-km)	16,659.2	16,486.8	+ 1.0
Overall capacity (million tonne-km)	24,052.1	24,009.7	+ 0.2
Overall load factor (%)	69.3	68.7	+ 0.6 point
Overall yield (cents/ltk)	85.0	77.5	+ 9.7
Overall unit cost (cents/ctk)	52.3	50.0	+ 4.6
Overall breakeven load factor (%)	61.5	64.5	– 3.0 points
Employee Productivity (Average) – Company			
Average number of employees	14,071	13,847	+ 1.6
Seat capacity per employee (seat-km)	8,096,020	8,127,667	– 0.4
Passenger load per employee (tonne-km)	618,295	613,211	+ 0.8
Revenue per employee ($)	906,801	819,232	+10.7
Value added per employee ($)	368,382	368,831	– 0.1
Employee Productivity (Average) – Group			
Average number of employees	30,088	29,125	+ 3.3
Revenue per employee ($)	530,859	497,662	+ 6.7
Value added per employee ($)	235,380	223,523	+ 5.3

Source: Singapore Airlines Annual Report, 2007–2008.

END NOTES

1. This case study is based on Heracleous, L., Wirtz, J. and Pangarkar, N. (2009) *Flying High in a Competitive Industry*, 1ˢᵗ edition, McGraw-Hill. Unless otherwise indicated, the sources of interview quotations are cited in this book.

2. See Costa, P., Harned, D. and Lundquist, J. (2002) Rethinking the Aviation Industry, *McKinsey Quarterly*, Special edition, Risk and Resilience: 89-100; and Doganis, R. (2006) *The Airline Business*, 2ⁿᵈ edition, Chapter 1.

3. IATA Annual Report, 2007.

4. IATA Annual Report, 2008.

5. http://money.cnn.com/magazines/fortune/globalmostadmired/2007/top50/index.html, SIA was listed at number 17 in 2007.

6. Porter, M. (1985) *Competitive Advantage*. New York: Free Press.

7. Available seats multiplied by distance flown.

8. Binggeli, U. and Pompeo, L. (2002) Hyped Hopes for Europe's Low-Cost Airlines, *McKinsey Quarterly*, 4, pp. 86-97; Doganis, R. (2006) *The Airline Business*, 2ⁿᵈ edition. Abingdon: Routledge.

9. Source: Singapore Airlines Annual Report, 2007-2008. Currency conversions conducted on 5 September 2008.

10. Mr Stephen Lee Ching Yen, chairman's letter to shareholders, Singapore Airlines Annual Report, 2005-2006.

11. Shostack, G. L. (1984) Designing Services that Deliver, *Harvard Business Review*, 62(1), January-February, pp. 133-139.

12. Singapore Airlines Annual Report, 2007-2008.

13. Emirates Annual Report, 2007-2008. Emirates average age of fleet during 2007-2008 was 67 months.

14. Doebele, J., 26 December 2005, The Engineer. *Forbes Asia*.

15. In addition to the named quotations, this section draws from in-depth interviews with Choo Poh Leong, senior manager, Crew Services Department, and Toh Giam Ming, senior manager, Crew Performance Department.

16. Chapter 6 presents a more detailed discussion of SIA's HRM policies.

17. See Singapore Airlines Annual Report, 2007–2008.

18. *Outlook*, November 2004, quoted in Doganis (2006) p. 263.

19. Doganis (2006) Chapter 7.

20. Doebele, J. (2005) The Engineer. *Forbes Asia*, 26 December.

21. Doganis (2006).

22. *The New Paper*, 18 June 2006, Slipping Up, SIA?

23. Singapore Airlines Annual Report, 2007–2008.

24. See Doganis (2006) Chapter 8.

25. Chairman's letter to shareholders, Singapore Airlines Annual Report, 2005–2006.

INDEX

Transforming Customer
Service (TCS), 96, 149, 222
Singapore Airport Terminal
Services (SATS), 90, 103, 159,
227, 232
Singapore Girl, 65-67, 87-88,
100-101, 143, 230-231
SkyTeam, 22-23, 90, 170, 232
South African Breweries, 179
Southwest Airlines, 9, 25, 56, 171
Space flights, 202
Spy flights, SIA, 95, 220
Star Alliance, 22-24, 44, 90, 170,
232
Strategic alignment, 169-188
Strategic imperatives, 51-59
    alliances, managing, 56-57
    commoditisation, avoiding,
    58-59
    cost control, 55-56
    creating differentiation,
    52-53
    herd instinct, avoiding,
    57-58
    technology, 54-55
Strategic innovation, 200-203
    in the airline industry, 201

frameworks for managing,
204-205
Strategic innovators, 203
Strategic misalignments, 178-185
Substitutes
    threat of, 43, 46, 48-49
Success factors, airline industry,
37-59

T

Terrorist attacks, 16, 74, 77-78
Transforming Customer Service
(TCS), SIA, 96, 149, 222
Turbo-prop engines, 2-3

U

United States, air travel, 29-30
US Federal Aviation
    Administration, 4

V

Virgin Atlantic, 6, 78-79, 90, 232,
235

W

Wal-Mart, 195
Wang Laboratories, 183